Why We Teach *Now*

Why We Teach *Now*

EDITED BY

Sonia Nieto

TEACHERS COLLEGE PRESS

TEACHERS COLLEGE | COLUMBIA UNIVERSITY

NEW YORK AND LONDON

Published by Teachers College Press, 1234 Amsterdam Avenue, New York, NY 10027

Library of Congress Cataloging-in-Publication Data

Why we teach now / Sonia Nieto, editor.
    pages cm
  Includes bibliographical references and index.
  ISBN 978-0-8077-5587-7 (pbk. : alk. paper)
  ISBN 978-0-8077-5624-9 (hardcover : alk. paper)
  ISBN 978-0-8077-7361-1 (ebook)
    1. Teaching—United States. 2. Teachers—United States—Conduct of life.
  I. Nieto, Sonia, editor of compilation.
  LB1775.2.W495   2015
  371.102—dc23   2014035643

ISBN 978-0-8077-5587-7 (paper)
ISBN 978-0-8077-5624-9 (hardcover)
ISBN 978-0-8077-7361-1 (ebook)

Printed on acid-free paper
Manufactured in the United States of America

*This book is dedicated
to all those teachers who know
why they teach*

Contents

Acknowledgments

Although my name appears as the editor of this book, many people have had a hand in bringing it to fruition. First and foremost, of course, are the 23 teachers who accepted my invitation to write an essay about why they teach *now* or, for those who have retired, why they remained in the classroom for over 30 years. These teachers, like so many others, bring their varied experiences, ideas, values, fears, hopes, and dreams to their work, all of which are richly documented in their essays. I am tremendously grateful to each of them.

To gather as wide a variety of teachers as possible geographically, as well as in terms of experience, ethnicity, grade level, and content area, I asked some of the most distinguished education scholars and teacher educators from around the nation to nominate teachers who they believed could write cogently and with conviction about why they teach now. My heartfelt thanks go to Wayne Au, David Bloome, Patty Bode, Christine Clark, Anaida Colón-Muñíz, Jeff Duncan-Andrade, Veronica Estrada, Kristen French, Sandy Grande, Tambra Jackson, Laurie Katz, Julia Lopez-Robertson, Ernest Morrell, Jodene Morrell, Enid Rosario-Ramos, Mariana Souto-Manning, and Joan Wink. In spite of their busy lives, they took the time to nominate outstanding teachers, most of whom graciously accepted my invitation. As you will see from the essays in this book, the teacher educators nominated exceptional teachers. In three cases, I asked teachers who had written essays for *Why We Teach* (2005) to write a new essay for this volume because two, Mary Ginley and Nina Tepper, had since retired and one, Mary Cowhey, is teaching something quite distinct from what she was teaching a decade ago. In another case, I asked Heather Brooke Robertson, a very impressive teacher I met at a national conference, to write an essay. Christina Puntel had been highly recommended for another project a few years ago but had a baby near the time I was going to interview her, so I asked her to write something for this book. Her lovely poem and reflection is the result. And, finally, I included Michael Silverstone, a teacher I have known for many years, as well as John Levasseur, a chemistry teacher who is also a graduate student and whom I met at the University of Massachusetts.

Writing and editing this book has been a challenge, not only because it has been disheartening to be reminded about the current context of public education as I've read policy statements and news reports in the media in the years since *Why We Teach* was published. The uncritical focus on accountability, and the blame game in which teachers, students, and families, particularly those who are most marginalized by the schools, are inevitably the losers, have also disillusioned me. At the same time, reading the teachers' essays has reinvigorated my sense of hope in the future of public education. With teachers such as these, our children are indeed in good hands.

I am always grateful to my editor, Brian Ellerbeck. I have been blessed to have Brian as the editor for the four books I've written for Teachers College Press. He is not only an outstanding editor, but also an astute observer of public education. He is, in addition, a constant source of motivation for me: I never have to worry about running out of ideas to write about because I know Brian will come up with enough projects to keep me writing to a ripe old age. Everyone else at Teachers College Press is also a pleasure to work with, from the Director, Carole Saltz, to other staff who have worked on this book, including publicist Emily Renwick, graphic designer Dave Strauss, production editor Karl Nyberg, Krithika Radhakrishnan and Noelle De La Paz, who assisted Brian in shepherding the manuscript to production.

I owe everything to my family, particularly my soulmate, Angel. I am indebted to my granddaughter/daughter Jazmyne, whom we have raised since the age of 2 and who lives with us. She continues to inspire us with her resilience and determination. I could not do this work without them or without the support and inspiration of my daughter Alicia, still a teacher after 20 years, and her husband Celso, who joined her in the profession a few years ago. My daughter Marisa, as well as her children and Alicia's children, my beautiful grandchildren, are a constant source of energy. If not for the children, why would we do this work?

Part I

INTRODUCTION: FROM *WHY WE TEACH* TO *WHY WE TEACH NOW*

"Teaching is a way to live in the world." Building on this simple but elegant idea, 1st-grade teacher Mary Cowhey, in a long spontaneous message she wrote to me over a dozen years ago, described the reasons she teaches. What started out as a long email to me was later published in my book *What Keeps Teachers Going?* (2003). The book generated a good deal of interest because it seemed to capture the hopes and dreams of teachers at a crossroads in public education. The school reform movement, initiated after the publication of *A Nation at Risk* in 1983 (National Commission on Excellence in Education), but not yet in full virulent bloom, was just beginning to be felt through new federal legislation in 2002 (No Child Left Behind, or NCLB). On another level, *What Keeps Teachers Going?* also made it clear that teachers' voices were conspicuously absent in most discussions of public education and school reform. This realization became the impetus for my subsequent book, *Why We Teach* (2005), a book of essays in which teachers spoke for themselves about why they teach.

WHY WE TEACH: THE FIRST ITERATION

Why We Teach (2005) is an edited book that includes essays or reflections written from the heart by 21 K–12 practicing teachers ranging from a first-year teacher to one who had taught for over 35 years. My intention in writing that book was to focus on teachers' perspectives about what makes teaching consequential. The core message of the book was one of hope for individual teachers, for the teaching profession, and for public education in general. At the time of its publication, some effects of the reform movement and federal policies were beginning to have a direct impact in schools. Calls for privatization through vouchers, charter schools, and others were becoming louder and more insistent, and some school systems and states were beginning to respond with draconian policy changes.

A number of the teachers featured in *Why We Teach* wrote about these changes, but they were in the minority. Most of the teachers wrote about what made teaching compelling, about their days in the classroom with children, about how difficult but rewarding it was, and about their motivations for entering and staying in the profession. Veteran teacher Bill Dunn, in contrast to most of the others, tackled the growing standardization head-on, and he was outspoken about what he saw and experienced as a vocational high school teacher of English and social studies in an impoverished urban area. Bill wrote eloquently about the injurious effects of high-stakes standardized tests on his mostly Puerto Rican working-class students and about the disdain with which his students, as well as teachers in urban schools, were being treated. This is a brief excerpt from his powerful essay:

> Over the past 10 years my state has very rigidly defined what it means to be an educated student in a Massachusetts public school. There are clear winners and clear losers. Unfortunately, even the kids who pass the test in my school are considered losers because it usually takes them three or four tries. . . . Schools throughout the state have been forced to goose-step to the beat of mandated exams, and the result is a continuous drill, and in urban schools that drill goes on for 3 to 4 years. Gone are the interesting ideas and intellectual curiosity that made it a pleasure to teach. They have been replaced with the stress of doing the same thing over and over again. It's a lousy deal all the way around for students, teachers, and schools. Eventually it will be evident that it's a lousy deal for society as well because uninterested kids on the street often cross the line from victimized to victimizer. . . .
>
> So why do I teach? I teach because someone has to tell my students that they are not the ones who are dumb. They need to know that only the blissfully ignorant and profoundly evil make up tests to prove that they and people like them are smart. I teach because my students need to know that poverty does not equal stupidity, and that surviving a bleak, dismal childhood makes you strong and tough and beautiful in ways that only survivors of

similar environments can appreciate and understand. I teach because my
students need to know that in their struggle to acquire a second language, they
participate in one of the most difficult of human feats. My students also need
to know that four days of reading in a second language under high-stakes
testing conditions would shut down even Einstein's brain. I teach because my
students need to know that right and wrong are relative to one's culture, and
that even these definitions become laughable over time. I teach because the
people who make up these tests don't know these things, or worse, they do.

—Bill Dunn, "Confessions of an Underperforming Teacher,"
in *Why We Teach* (Nieto, 2005), p. 180.

When Bill Dunn died suddenly in 2011 at the age of 59, he was
heralded in the local newspaper as "a zealot for social justice." He was
indeed that. In addition, he had a prescient sense of the disturbing changes
to take place in public education in the coming years. Now, a decade after
he wrote his essay, conditions in public schools have worsened even more
than Bill might have imagined.

We should have seen these changes coming. Whereas in previous
decades it was generally agreed upon that a good-quality public education
in our nation was a birthright for every child regardless of station or rank,
this noble ideal has lost currency in the current discourse that privileges
functionalism over creativity. Today, growing numbers of classrooms are
dreary places where tests have become the only arbiters of excellence, and
where teachers have become little more than technicians not trusted to use
their imagination, creativity, and education. It is rare these days to speak of
the joy of teaching and learning, and even more rare to speak of teachers
as intellectuals. Rather than *learning, joy,* and *imagination,* the most
common words in teaching today have become *test prep, scores, DIBELS,
data walls,* and *AYP.* From policy briefs to movies, the messages are clear:
public schools are failing, teachers are incompetent, teacher preparation
programs are inadequate, and teacher unions are to blame for everything.
Typical of the solutions offered are more charter schools and schemes to
train teachers quickly through alternative routes and instant preparation
programs such as Teach for America. The result is, in effect, the wholesale
abandonment of public education and of teaching as a valued profession,
with children of color and those living in poverty the greatest losers. How
on earth has this happened, and how can we get on the right road again?

WHY *NOW?* WHY A SEQUEL?

The "now" in this sequel to *Why We Teach* is the most significant word
in the title. The pertinent question is not so much *why* teach, but rather
why teach *now?* Given the extraordinary changes in public education and
the teaching profession over the past decade, potential teachers would be
foolish not to ask themselves this question before thinking about entering
the profession. And the general public would be wise to think about
the repercussions of the current policy climate for the future of public
education, a system that—although certainly not perfect—had done much
in our nation's past, particularly in the decades of the 1960s and 1970s,
when sincere attempts were made to at least try to live up to its promise of
an equal education. The same, unfortunately, is not true today.

Given everything that has taken place in public education in the past
decade, it is time for a sequel to *Why We Teach*. We need to hear teachers'
voices again, this time to hear what they have to say about the current
vexing conditions in which they teach, and about why they teach *now*
in spite of these conditions. For teachers and others who believe in the
promise of public education, an antidote to the numbing and negative
messages is needed.

It is no exaggeration to say that teachers' voices have been silent, and
even silenced, in public conversations, debates, and especially in decisions
affecting their daily lives. This is because most teachers do not have access
to public spaces outside their immediate schools and classrooms. The same
is true of students, who are even more invisible in these contexts. See any
news report or movie about teaching, or read any public policy document,
any slick commission report, any research study in an education journal,
or even any article about "what works in education," and you will be hard
pressed to see teachers' and students' perspectives.

For me, to help bring the voices of teachers to a more public space
is an immense honor and also, I believe, a serious responsibility of those
of us who have greater access to the media and to decisionmakers than
do most teachers. It is not only because teachers know their students
better than anyone except their families, or because they know what our
classrooms and schools are (and should be), or because they live the day-
to-day messiness of teaching, but especially because, due to all these things,
they just have good ideas about teaching and learning. How could it be

otherwise? Yet in spite of their expertise and experience, it is rare to find schools where, for example, teachers are asked to consult with architects to help design or remodel school buildings, or with testing companies to help create meaningful assessments, or even, in some school districts, to develop curriculum. Too often, teachers receive architectural plans that have little to do with how schools should be planned, assessments created by big for-profit testing companies, and curricula designed by publishing conglomerates. It is time for teachers' voices to be heard.

This is not to claim that all teachers are excellent, caring, and committed; we all know teachers who should not be in the profession and even some who do more harm than good to the students they teach. But nobody enters the profession to harm those they seek to serve. Instead, they go into teaching with good intentions, great hopes, and an understanding that teaching, although difficult, can also be one of the most rewarding professions there is. Perhaps some of these people have not had the stamina or the conviction needed to persevere. But as I've seen much too often, many who might with time and support have become excellent teachers end up burned out and disenchanted with the lack of professionalism with which they're treated and with the conditions in public schools that make it hard to sustain the energy needed to do their best. It is to our detriment as a nation that these conditions still define teaching for too many of our educators.

Through my research, writing, and speaking for the past 40 years, I have attempted to give teachers and students a platform to express their ideas, values, and practices. In this book, I concentrate on teachers. *Why We Teach Now* challenges current notions of what it means to be a "highly qualified teacher" á la No Child Left Behind legislation, while it also challenges what counts as good pedagogy and what makes for a well-educated student. The official discourse on education embodied in NCLB language includes a focus on accountability, standards, credentials, and testing, accompanied by punitive measures for failing to live up to these. *Why We Teach Now*, in contrast, is based on what I call the "discourse of possibility," that is, a way of thinking critically but hopefully about teaching and learning, a stance embraced largely by teachers and others who view public education, on the whole, as an unfulfilled but nonetheless consequential ideal in the quest for equality and social justice. This "unofficial" discourse can be seen in teachers' attempts to control their professional lives through study and involvement in professional associations and unions, as well as in books, articles, and magazines that champion teachers and question the current damaging climate in education. It is my hope that *Why We Teach Now* will add to the growing calls to reject simplistic "fixes" for the complex problems of teaching and learning.

My intention in this book is to provide, through the voices of teachers, more hopeful answers to the question of why teachers persist in the profession despite the current context. Their hope, although boundless, is tempered by the difficult conditions in which teachers work. Mary Ginley, an outstanding teacher who was in the classroom for 42 years and who, in her essay in this book, "Kids Are Far More Than Test Scores" (Chapter 2), laments, "Why would anyone with any brains and imagination *ever* want to be a teacher?" And although she was frustrated and disillusioned in the last years of her career because of how the profession she had entered 42 years earlier had changed so drastically, she nevertheless concludes in her essay that, "It's because . . . in spite of everything, there are kids out there who need good teachers." Unfortunately, not all teachers have the stamina, the support, or the hope to stay in the classroom. Although some teachers may not have been cut out for teaching in the first place, most teachers enter the profession with a profound sense of service and the expectation that they could make a difference. We all lose when such teachers leave the profession.

For teachers who are becoming disheartened by the current state of affairs, for those just beginning their journey as teachers, and for those contemplating a life of teaching, I am hopeful that *Why We Teach Now* will give them the inspiration and energy to understand that their role as advocates is vital, not only for the well-being of their students but also for the future of the profession and our nation.

CONTRIBUTORS

The teachers whose essays you will read work in a variety of settings (urban, rural, and suburban) and range from relatively novice to very seasoned. They teach subject areas and grades from preschool to high school. They teach students of diverse ethnic, racial, linguistic, and social class backgrounds, and their own backgrounds are equally diverse. Some are award-winning teachers (for example, Mary Cowhey, Mary Ginley, Matt Hicks and Mary Jade Haney, among others); others are published authors (Mary Cowhey, Greg Michie, Michael Silverstone, Jesse Hagopian, and Jorge López). Most, however, are not known widely outside their schools, yet need to be as celebrated as those who have won awards or have had their work published because they are fiercely committed teachers who care about their students and about the future of public education.

What is clear is that all of these teachers share a passion for teaching, a deep-seated commitment to their role in the profession, and an insatiable curiosity about the world. Whether they have been teaching for 5 years or 30, they believe in the significance of public education in sustaining a democratic society and the power of teaching and learning to change lives.

ORGANIZATION

Why We Teach Now is organized in seven Parts. To frame the major issues addressed in the book, I wrote the first and final chapters, while the contributing teachers are the authors of all the other chapters. Each Part begins with a brief description of the overarching theme that is the subject of the section, and a brief description of the chapter in that section. Chapter 1 in Part I provides an analysis of the context of public education in the United States today, with particular focus on how the work of teachers is influenced by that context. In this chapter, I present both current obstacles to teaching, as well as what makes teaching a substantial endeavor nevertheless.

Part II includes essays by three former teachers who reflect on their careers in education, what they were able to accomplish, and their thoughts on the current situation in schools. The three essays in Part III focus on four teachers (one of the chapters is coauthored by teacher-sisters) and how teachers' identities can be defined by their role in society, whether it's through their families, their cultural identities, the geography in which they teach, or the reasons they chose the profession. An essential component of education is hope, and this is the theme of Part IV. Here, four teachers write about how they sustain hope in spite of pressures to rob them, their students, and the profession of this precious commodity. The four essays in Part V explain how teaching helps to heal both teachers and students. Teaching and fighting back are the major themes in Part VI, and the five teachers in this section write passionately about their activism and advocacy, from the classroom to the streets. And Part VII presents three teachers who look back in order to look forward, one to help define the person she is today, another to celebrate the fact that she continues to be inspired by her students and the profession at the age of 65, and a third to fuel his passion for social justice by deciding to teach in a different context.

Finally, Chapter 24 tackles the question of *Why teach **now**?* by suggesting some of the lessons to be learned from the teachers who have graced this book with their insights, hopes, and dreams for themselves, their students, and the future of public education in our nation.

CHAPTER 1

Public Schools and the Work of Teachers

Sonia Nieto

The old adage "Those who can, do; those who can't, teach"—a line from George Bernard Shaw's *Man and Superman* (2001)—couldn't have gotten it more wrong. These words were obviously uttered by someone who had never taught. In reality, just the opposite is true: *Those who can, teach.* Teaching *is* doing: It takes reflection, planning, nurturing, dreaming, scheming, imagining, effecting, judging, succeeding, failing, improving, and then figuring it out all over again. It takes imagination, perseverance, and lots of courage. Teaching is not for the faint of heart. It is not easy; it never has been.

Ask any teacher and she or he will tell you why teaching is impossibly difficult: It is hard to learn everything you need to know about your subject matter and, in the case of elementary school teachers, to learn enough about every subject well enough to teach it competently; it is challenging to try to reach students of vastly different experiences, backgrounds, and ability levels; it is tricky to come up with interesting and engaging lessons 6 hours a day, 5 days a week; it is demanding to keep up with the latest research and innovations—good, bad, and faddish—in the field; it is difficult to learn everything you need to know about your students and then figure out how to use what you know in your pedagogy and curriculum. Even that age-old question, "What shall I do on Monday morning?" is far more complicated than it sounds. It is not simply a question about a specific lesson for a particular day, but rather an existential question about teaching itself. "What shall I do on Monday morning?" can translate into everything from "What's the best way to teach long division?" to "How can I hook my students on reading?" to "How can I possibly reach Sabina today?" to the question many teachers ask as the school week is about to begin, "Why is it so hard to sleep on Sunday nights?"

In spite of all these challenges, people continue to enter the profession, excited by the opportunity to get to know and teach young people, and enthralled by what one can accomplish as a teacher. Certainly it is not money, fame, or luxury that brings teachers to the profession, or that keeps them there. It is instead an intangible *something* that makes teaching a compelling vocation, even a passion. But those who have not taught, who have not experienced the sheer joy of sharing knowledge, of having students "get it," or sparking a heretefore undiscovered passion for a particular topic; as well as those who have never experienced the terror of getting something wrong, or uttering a careless statement that may unintentionally hurt a student for years to come: These people cannot know what it means to teach. They are the ones who will continue to say, mindlessly, "Those who can, do; those who can't, teach."

Putting aside the panic and the fear, and in spite of the passion, commitment, joy, and excitement of teaching, it is hard to be a teacher today. The pertinent question addressed in this book is why teach *now*, especially in public schools. Given the current context of "education reform" that favors bureaucracy over creativity and rigidity over spontaneity, this is a significant question to ask. In the present situation, it is no surprise that teachers are leaving the profession in droves. According to Richard Ingersoll (2012), one of the nation's top researchers in teacher attrition, between 40 and 50% of teachers leave after just 5 years in the profession. Ingersoll, who had himself been a teacher, explained why he left: "One of the big reasons I quit was sort of intangible. But it's very real: it's just a lack of respect" (Riggs, 2013, p. 4).

Numerous studies have spelled out the lack of respect for teachers in more concrete terms. For example, a study of New York City teachers found that although the attrition of teachers in the city's schools had slowed during the recession that began in 2008, it again started climbing in 2012. A report reprinted from the *New York Times* (McAdoo, 2013) by the United Federation of Teachers (UFT) reported that of the more than 5,000 teachers hired from 2008–2009 in New York City, over one-third had left the schools by 2013. The main culprit for the high attrition rate? Disaffection with the job, including poor administrative support, lack of influence over school policies, student discipline, large classes, and inadequate time for planning (McAdoo, 2013).

What is especially troubling is that some of the very best teachers are leaving the field. According to a study by The New Teacher Project (TNTP), the 50 largest school districts in the nation lose approximately 10,000 "irreplaceable teachers" each year (TNTP, 2012). Who are irreplaceable teachers? In their study of four urban school districts serving more than 1.4 million students, TNTP identified irreplaceable teachers, who comprise approximately 20% of the teaching population, as those who each year help their students learn 2 to 3 additional months' worth of math and reading compared with the average teacher, and 5 to 6 months' more compared to low-performing teachers. Although irreplaceable teachers do not fit any particular mold and are, in fact, like their peers in many respects—they work in various demographic settings, teach similarly sized classes, and are as likely to teach in impoverished schools as are less-effective teachers—they differ from them in some key respects: They are, for example, keenly aware of their own effectiveness, and they tend to believe they can make a difference for their students in spite of out-of-school factors beyond their control.

Irreplaceability is not just about test scores in math and reading because test scores are only one indication of students' progress. TNTP (2012) also found that irreplaceable teachers are excellent pedagogues, creating more engaging learning experiences for their students. Even more significant, irreplaceable teachers make more of an impact in low-performing schools. The report found that when an irreplaceable teacher leaves a low-performing school, it can take up to 11 hires to find a teacher of comparable quality, compared to 6 hires in an average school. In addition, TNTP estimated that students who make these kinds of gains are also much more likely to attend college and earn higher salaries as adults, and are less likely to become teenage parents. TNTP calls the "pervasive neglect of the nation's best teachers" a disgrace (2012, p. 8).

A more personal example of a disheartened teacher who felt the need to leave the profession was documented in a *Washington Post* online article (Strauss, 2014). Explaining her decision to quit in a resignation letter, 25-year veteran teacher of kindergarten and preschool children Susan Sluyter wrote,

> I have watched as my job requirements swung away from a focus on the children, their individual learning styles, emotional needs, and their individual families, interests and strengths to a focus on testing, assessing, and scoring young children, thereby ramping up the academic demands and pressures on them. . . . I reached the place last year where I began to feel I was part of a broken system that was causing damage to those very children I was there to serve. (Strauss, 2014)

Her conclusion, she said, was to quit "with deep love and a broken heart."

Why this situation has worsened over the past decade, and teachers' responses to the changing context of teaching, are considered in this chapter. Conditions both in and out of school have created this context.

THE EDUCATIONAL REFORM (DEFORM?) MOVEMENT

The school reform movement prompted by *A Nation at Risk* (National Commission on Excellence in Education, 1983) began slowly, building up steam with increasing fervor in the years since. Although educational reform had traditionally meant such things as smaller class sizes, more and better professional development, an enriched curriculum, and increased access to high-quality education for a greater number of students, in more recent years "reform" has come to mean standardization; high-stakes testing; the chartering of public schools; privatization; rigid accountability for teachers, students, and administrators; and other damaging policies that have done little to promote student learning or engage teachers. It is no wonder that teaching has become a less appealing profession.

When the original *Why We Teach* was first published in 2005, the No Child Left Behind Act (NCLB) of 2001 had not yet had the significant impact on students, teachers, and schools that it has since had. Race to the Top (RttT; S844-112th Congress, 2011), a competitive federal policy that pits states against one another for funding, came later, and it continued the steady drumbeat of competition, with clear winners and losers. More recently, the Common Core State Standards (National Governors Association Center for Best Practices & Council of Chief State School Officers, 2010), although lauded by many policymakers and some teachers, has already led to widespread fears that the testing to accompany these new mandates will result in yet more restrictions as well as punitive policies directed at students and teachers.

Privatization and the ongoing marketization of public education have also been flourishing. Using the catchword "choice" to define competitive marketing principles—as if schools were a business—most of the new "reform" policies nevertheless have not made a noticeable difference in student learning or school efficiency. Charter schools, for instance, have become the buzzword in some cities. Besides sometimes having restrictive admission policies, they often do not have the resources to teach English language learners or students with special needs, generally the two categories of students needing the most support. In addition, although publicly financed, charter schools are often run as quasi-private businesses, are usually not unionized, and drain money from neighborhood schools. There are now more charter schools and voucher programs—some even supporting religious schools—than at any time in U.S. history (Miner, 2013).

The transformation of neighborhood schools to charter schools goes something like this: A school is deemed "underperforming" based on students' scores on high-stakes standardized tests; teachers are fired; the school is closed; and a charter is given to a particular group to take over. In many cities, charters are proliferating at an unprecedented rate—with cities such as Chicago, New Orleans, and Philadelphia leading the way—even though results have been largely unspectacular. In Chicago, for instance, there is no discernible evidence that charters are better than the many neighborhood schools they have replaced. According to a recent report, charter schools such as those run by Kipp and Urban Prep have resulted in closing neighborhood schools and in renovation costs to the tune of over $18 million, and yet they have not generally yielded better learning outcomes. One example: Chicago charter schools where at least 90% of students are eligible for free and reduced lunch perform, on average, significantly *worse* than neighborhood schools with similar demographics (Caref, Hainds, Hilgendorf, Jankov, & Russell, 2012).

Comparable results have been found nationwide. David Berliner and Gene Glass have written an exhaustively documented book about the "myths and lies" surrounding public education, including those about charter schools (Berliner & Glass, 2014). They cite, for example, the first national assessment of charter schools released by the Center for Research on Education Outcomes (CREDO) in 2009. That report found that 80% of charter schools are no better or worse than traditional public schools in terms of math and reading gains. Ironically, some of the states most active in turning traditional schools into charter schools—Arizona, Florida, Ohio, and Texas—are also among the states where students in traditional public schools outperform students in charter schools (Berliner & Glass, 2014).

The Common Core State Standards (CCSS), the latest in a string of mandated standards, has both its supporters and its detractors, but even those who support the attempt to promote more rigorous and authentic learning among the nation's students worry about how the CCSS was developed and paid for, and how it will be implemented. Among its most fervent critics is Diane Ravitch, who has written repeatedly on her blog about the problems associated with the CCSS (see http://dianeravitch.net/). Alarmed with the growing testing to be shepherded in by the new standards, the Network for Public Education, an education advocacy group, announced a call for congressional hearings to "investigate the over-emphasis, misapplication, costs, and poor implementation of high-stakes standardized testing in the nation's K–12 public schools" (Network for Public Education [NPE], 2014).

The NPE was particularly concerned with the quality of the tests; whether it was legal for the government to have funded two testing consortia for the CCSS; whether the new standards really promote the kinds of skills needed in the 21st century; whether the tests will be culturally biased; the effect of increased testing on teaching quality; and a host of other concerns.

Anthony Cody, an award-winning former teacher, has written a detailed critique of the CCSS, focusing on what he calls its "ten colossal errors" (Cody, 2013). These include the undemocratic way in which the CCSS was developed and adopted by a self-selected group of testing company representatives and paid for by the Gates Foundation; the fact that teachers, parents, and students were excluded from its development; that it violates what the research says about how children learn; that it is inspired by a market-driven vision of education; and that it leads to tightly controlled curriculum and pedagogy, among other problems. Another criticism of the CCSS: Although it included standards for early childhood education, its development excluded any early childhood professionals. The fear is that it will lead to long hours of direct instruction in literacy and math and crowd out more important activities that should be part of early childhood education (Miller & Carrlson-Paige, 2014).

The critiques of the CCSS have echoed a chorus of previous critiques of standardization movements, including NCLB, RttT, and others. Although focused on education, these efforts are part of a larger sociopolitical context that affects schools, teachers, students, and even democracy itself.

THE BROADER CONTEXT

Because public schools do not exist in a vacuum, a school's success or failure is largely dependent on conditions outside the four walls of the school building. Jean Anyon hit the nail on the head when she wrote that "macroeconomic policies like those regulating the minimum wage, job availability, tax rates, federal transportation, and affordable housing create conditions in cities that no existing educational policy or urban school reform can transcend" (Anyon, 2005, p. 2). As a result, a school's policies and practices, or the effectiveness of teachers in any particular school, although immensely important, do not by themselves explain the longstanding problems of educational inequality. Poverty and its attendant ills—inadequate housing, lack of proper nutrition and medical care, parents' joblessness, and a pervasive sense of hopelessness, not to mention persistent racism and neglect—are part of the larger context in which schools exist. Educator Stephen Krashen has written often and persuasively on this issue. He argues that the perception that U.S. schools are failing is based largely on American students' international test scores. In a letter to *The New York Times,* he wrote:

> Rarely mentioned is the finding that middle-class American students in well-funded schools score at the top of the world on these tests; *our overall scores are unspectacular because we have the highest percentage of children living in poverty among all industrialized countries.* The problem is thus not teacher quality. The problem is poverty, which means poor diet, poor health care, and little access to books. Quality teaching has little effect when students are hungry, sick, and have nothing to read. (Krashen, 2012, emphasis added)

Poverty and Inequality

The bedrock of any democratic society is its public education system. At the very least, the semblance of equal opportunity, is essential for democracy to exist. Yet, in the United States, a disturbing trend in the past several decades has been a dramatically growing inequality. This situation is troubling not just for public education but also for our society as a whole. Nothing less than the future of our democracy is at stake.

Poverty in the nation has grown steadily since 2007, increasing from 12.5 to 15% (Stanford Center on Poverty and Inequality, 2014) According to the 2010 U.S. Census Bureau, 46 million Americans, or one in six, were living below the federal poverty rate, the highest number in our history (DeNavas-Walt, Proctor, & Smith, 2011). The situation is even worse for children. In its most recent annual review, the Children's Defense Fund (CDF) reported that one in five children lives in poverty, with 40% of those living in extreme poverty. The CDF also found that children under 5 are the *poorest* age group in the nation, with 60% more likely to be poor than adults aged 18 to 65. Moreover, child poverty increased 36% from 2000 to 2010, primarily as a result of the Great Recession. Even after the official "end" of the recession, however, child poverty has remained at record levels (CDF, 2014). The fact that the proportion of 25- to 54-year-olds without gainful employment is at an all-time high, even after the official end of the recession, also contributes to the growing inequality (Stanford Center on Poverty and Inequality, 2014). But poverty affects not only the unemployed. The CDF reported that poverty is possible even when families are employed. For instance, in 2012, more than two-thirds of children living in poverty lived in families with at least one employed family member (CDF, 2014).

The lack of affordable housing in middle-class neighborhoods is another factor in the growing inequality. In an analysis of the connection between national and metropolitan data on public school populations and state standardized test scores, Jonathan Rothwell discovered that in the 100 largest metropolitan areas, housing costs an average 2.4 times as much, or nearly $11,000 more per year, near a high-scoring public school than near a low-scoring one. Put another way, the average low-income student attends a school that scores at the 42nd percentile on state exams, whereas the average middle- to high-income student attends a school that scores at the 61st percentile on state exams. Rothwell concludes, "Limiting the development of inexpensive housing in affluent neighborhoods and jurisdictions fuels economic and racial segregation and contributes to significant differences in school performance across the metropolitan landscape" (Rothwell, 2012, p. 1). Zip codes make a difference, a truth that has never been more obvious.

Inequality also affects children's health, and consequently their ability to learn. Melissa Bright and her colleagues at the University of Florida Institute of Child Health Policy found that when children experience three or more stressful events, they are six times more likely to suffer from a mental, physical, or learning disorder than children who haven't faced such traumatic experiences. The adverse conditions she and her team reviewed included economic hardship, exposure to domestic and neighborhood violence, poor caregiver mental health, exposure to drug abuse, parental divorce, and having a parent in jail, all conditions more likely to have an impact on children living in poverty than on those living in more economically stable conditions (University of Florida, 2014). Life expectancy is also affected by poor health. In a story by Zöe Carpenter in *The Nation,* Steve Woolf, director of the Center on Society and Health at Virginia Commonwealth University, found that people in the top 5% of the income gradient live approximately 9 years longer than those in the bottom 10%. Americans living in poverty are also at greater risk for nearly every major disease and cause of death, including cancer, heart disease, and diabetes (Carpenter, 2014).

The Changing Face of Public Schools in the United States

Given the negative statistics just detailed, an equal and high-quality education is out of reach for many of the nation's children, who are increasingly Latino/a, African American, Asian American, and American Indian. In addition, the nation's changing demographics complicate the issue of inequality. Currently, children of color constitute the majority of 1- and 2-year-olds in the United States, signaling an enormous change in U.S. school enrollment in the coming years, and by 2019, children of color will be the majority of all children in the nation (CDF, 2014). Nearly one in three children of color is disproportionately poor, some living in unspeakably harsh conditions, with grave implications for the future of public education and for national stability. The parents of these children are more often unemployed than the parents of their White middle-class peers, and they tend to have inadequate health care, poorer nutrition, and worse housing than the general population.

As of 2012, about 63% of the general population was White, and Latinos, at 17%, made up the largest percentage of non-Whites (U.S. Bureau of the Census, 2014). By 2050, people of color will outnumber Whites by 53 to 47%, an unprecedented change in U.S. population (Taylor & Cohn, 2012). In California, the shift has already taken place: in 2014, Latinos surpassed Whites as the largest racial/ethnic group; New Mexico, where 47% of the population is Hispanic, has had a large Hispanic population for many generations (Lopez, 2014).

These changing demographics are largely due to increasing immigration, aided by more births among people of color and fewer among Whites. According to the Center for Immigration Studies, the number of immigrants, both legal and undocumented, reached a record of 40 million in 2010, an increase of 28% since 2000. Although the largest overall numbers continue to be from Mexico, immigrants from countries with the largest percentage increase are from various countries in Central and South America, as well as from China (Camarota, 2012).

Although our diversity should be cause for celebration and affirmation, the fact that so many children of diverse backgrounds live in poverty is a serious concern. In many cases, they also attend poorly resourced schools. According to *The Condition of Education,* the annual report to Congress from the National Center for Education Statistics (Kena et al., 2014), in the 10-year period from 2001–2011, the number and percentage of students who attended poor schools rose from 12 to 19%, whereas the number who attended a low-poverty (that is, a middle-class or above) school decreased from 45 to 28%. This means that many children, both White children and children of color, attend schools with far fewer resources (including fewer high-level courses, and less access to technology and to experienced teachers) than schools in middle-class neighborhoods. Clearly, our schools are getting poorer, as are many of the children who attend them. At the same time, these are the children who experience larger classes, dramatically less participation in preschool education, and more suspensions and expulsions—even in the early grades—than their middle-class counterparts (U.S. Department of Education Office for Civil Rights, 2014).

Public schools inevitably reflect the changing demographics of the nation as a whole. In most urban areas—and increasingly in urbanized suburbs, rural areas, and suburbs as well—children of color make up the majority of public school enrollments; in many cities, they are an overwhelming majority, sometimes comprising 80%, 90%, or even a higher percentage of the total school enrollment. Although general public school enrollment increased from 47.7 to 49.5 million from 2000–2010, the increase was uneven in terms of racial and ethnic representation. For example, the number of White students enrolled in pre-K through 12th grade actually decreased, from 28.7 to 25.6 million, reducing their proportion of school enrollment from 60 to 52%. In the same time period, the enrollment of Black students increased by 1 percentage point, whereas enrollment of Hispanic students—the fastest-growing population—increased from 17 to 24% of total school enrollment. In terms of linguistic diversity, one in four children in the United States speaks a language other than English at home, and over 9% of all children in U.S. classrooms are emergent bilinguals (Kena et al., 2014).

The shifting demographics of the United States should give us pause about where the country is headed, how our public education system needs to change to accommodate the new reality, and how our children can be prepared for a nation that looks exceedingly different from what their parents experienced. Rather than fear the growing diversity, we should welcome it as an opportunity to once again invest in our public schools as the greatest potential leveling agent for all students and all families. The 2014 Children's Defense Fund report put it best:

> The greatest threat to America's economic, military, and national security comes from no enemy without but from our failure, unique among high income nations, to invest adequately and fairly in the health, education and sound development of all of our young. (Children's Defense Fund, 2014, p. 2)

NOW, MORE THAN EVER, WE NEED GOOD TEACHERS IN THE PROFESSION

Some of the preceding can be called the "bad news" in public education. It includes rapidly growing privatization, the national obsession with standardized testing, the unprecedented marketization of schooling, and escalating inequality. On the other hand, the fact that our nation is growing more diverse gives us a tremendous opportunity for growth and development. It is diversity that largely fuels the American Dream, as people from all corners of the globe bring their hopes for a better life to these shores, working tirelessly and creatively to make those hopes a reality. Unfortunately, given the grave conditions described previously, such dreams are now more elusive than ever.

That being the case, what can be done? This is a particularly crucial question for the nation's educators and those who may be contemplating a career in education. They need to consider such questions as whether they should remain in education, or if they should even begin.

Although this is a gloomy time for public education in many ways, I would argue that it is *precisely* the right time for enthusiastic and courageous young people to commit to the profession, and for excellent teachers already in the profession to remain. This is not to imply that teachers alone can turn the situation around; after all, it was not teachers who got us into this situation in the first place, and teachers by themselves do not have the power to get us out of it. On the contrary, the current dismantling of public education is due primarily to those individuals and organizations with pecuniary, conservative, and neoliberal ideological interests behind the "education reform" agenda of the past three decades. As in all such cases, "follow the money" is the best advice (see, for example, Apple, 2006; Berliner & Glass, 2014; Miner, 2012). In the meantime, the responsibility for restoring public education to its more noble goals rests with all of us. Teachers have been in the forefront of efforts to do so, and as you will see in the subsequent chapters, they continue to have an enormous impact. They know that teachers *can* and *do* make a difference in the lives of their students, in their schools, in the profession, and in the nation as a whole.

Although teachers rarely make headlines (except in the case of "failing schools" or in other disparaging media accounts), they are the true heroes of U.S. public education. I am not just referring here to award-winning teachers, but to the general population of teachers who, in the majority, enter the profession with high ideals and great hopes. There are, of course, always exceptions to the rule, but in general, teachers give selflessly of their time, energy, and, often, their own money to educate their students. They spend countless hours researching and preparing their lessons, scavenging wherever they can to create engaging and powerful learning environments. They take courses, attend conferences, and try to keep abreast of the latest innovations and resources in the profession, often at their own expense. They consult with colleagues and families to provide their students with the best education they can. Their efforts are uneven, sometimes spectacular, sometimes not so much. But they continue to teach because they care about young people, are passionate about what they teach, and are inspired by the possibilities of their work.

In the pages that follow, you will meet 23 teachers who epitomize what it means to be committed and caring teachers at a time when being in the profession is so hard. They work in settings as different as a small rural one-room schoolhouse to an urban school with many hundreds of students, and in classrooms where only English is spoken to those in which students from around the globe speak many different languages. They are activists, quietly or loudly, whether in their own classrooms advocating for their students or their students' families for needed services, in unions and teacher organizations, or in the streets and on picket lines. By working for, and on behalf of, their students and the ideals of an equal and high-quality education for all our children, they define what it means to be a teacher in the second decade of the 21st century.

LOOKING BACK

Although teaching has always been difficult, today it is far different, in many ways more stressful and complicated, than it has ever been. Teachers who began teaching after No Child Left Behind (NCLB) was passed into law in 2001, and after the enormous policy changes that followed, may think that teaching was always this way. Veteran teachers, those who have spent many years in the classroom, have felt these changes most directly because they know it could be different.

Part II, "Looking Back," presents the essays of three recently retired teachers, one who taught for 42 years, another for 35, and the third for 33. Mary Ginley, one of three teachers in this book who wrote an essay for the first volume of *Why We Teach* in 2003 (a second is Nina Tepper, whose essay follows Mary's; the other is Mary Cowhey, whose essay appears in Part VI), reflects on some of the many challenges she faced when, after retiring as a teacher in Massachusetts, she moved to Florida and taught for another 6 years. Her poignant question addressed earlier, "Why would anyone with any brains and imagination *ever* want to be a teacher?", is the subject of her chapter. An exceptional, caring, and award-winning teacher, Mary finds it hard to believe what has happened to public education since she first began teaching. And although discouraged by the current situation, she is ever hopeful that people "with brains and imagination" will indeed choose to be teachers and, in the process, help change the discourse in public education.

In Chapter 3, we hear from Nina Tepper, a teacher who worked first in Boston, then in Holyoke and later in Springfield, before moving to Cape Cod, all in Massachusetts, to teach for the final years of her career in a high school in nearby Plymouth. Nina had always thought of herself as, first, an advocate for social justice and, second, as a literacy specialist.

Having evolved from a teacher of English as a Second Language (ESL) to a consultant teacher of literacy (reading & writing) across the curriculum, was her way to empower all students regardless of age, race, social class or family situation to develop the literacy skills to overcome obstacles in life, thereby contributing to make a small difference in the world. Ever ready to support her students, Nina's reflections help explain why some of the most committed and persistent teachers remain in the classroom in spite of the many changes going on around them, some of which were discussed in Chapter 1.

In her essay, Berta Berriz, a recently retired bilingual and ESL teacher, is joined by some of her colleagues from the Boston Teachers' Union (BTU) School, where she taught for the final years of her career. Although Berta and her colleagues contend with some of the same issues as teachers in any other urban public school, the BTU School offers a radical departure from most by providing teachers with the freedom to collaborate, create curriculum, and work closely with families. At the end of the essay, Berta describes a project on portraiture that epitomizes this freedom, including the work of some of her students.

The three essays together point to the highs and lows of teaching, but they also provide an antidote to the despair and disillusionment currently characterizing much of public education. In spite of the difficulties, the obstacles, and the heartache they experienced, all three teachers would do it all over again, a testament not only to their resilience and commitment, but also to the rewards of this complicated profession of teaching.

Kids Are Far More Than Test Scores *or* Why I Continued to Teach in Spite of It All

Mary Ginley

In 2011, I finally retired from teaching. I had been in the classroom for 42 years. "How did you ever last so long?" a young teacher recently asked me.

"God only knows," I answered. "It seemed like a good idea at the time."

"I don't think I can make it 10 years," she said honestly. "It gets harder and harder every year."

"I know," said I. "I know."

About 15 years ago, I spoke at an Honor Society induction in Longmeadow, Massachusetts. I don't remember everything I said to those kids, but I clearly remember asking them to consider becoming teachers.

"You can be anything," I told them. "Think about being a teacher. You will be in a profession that demands your energy and imagination, your heart and soul. It will be enormously demanding but more fulfilling and rewarding than you can begin to imagine. Think about it. It's not a bad way to spend a life."

Would I give that same speech now? There are days when I am certain I would *never* give that speech again and others when I'm not so sure.

So, what happened in 15 years to move me from "Being a teacher is one of the best things you can do with your life" to "Why would anyone really encourage young people to go into teaching?" Much as it breaks my heart because I want my grandchildren taught by the best and the brightest, there are days when I just can't see why creative, competent, imaginative, smart young people would choose a profession where they aren't allowed to make any decisions and have to follow scripted curriculums. Why would anyone with any brains and imagination *ever* want to be a teacher?

In 2005, I retired from teaching in Massachusetts and my husband, Jerry, and I headed for Florida. It was time to head for the beach, to walk that beach early in the morning and again at sunset. It was time to be someplace warm.

But it wasn't time to stop teaching. I loved teaching. I loved spending my days with children. I loved sharing beloved books, challenging them to think again about things they took for granted. I loved watching that "aha" moment when they got it. I loved watching kids grow and change and learn. I wasn't ready to give all that up.

I knew Florida would be different. I knew my new school would be different from the child-centered, imaginative place I was leaving in Massachusetts. I just didn't know how different.

Much as I loved being a public school teacher, I knew teaching was changing. I knew that in an effort to raise educational standards across the country, schools were changing. And I knew that Florida was probably one of the leaders of the pack in designing test-driven education. I knew all that and yet the classroom of 2005 in Florida was so unlike the classrooms I had taught in the first 30 years of my teaching career, it took my breath away.

Yes, I had planned to teach in Florida. What I didn't plan was to find myself in a world where I had little power over what happened in my classroom day after day. What I didn't plan was to teach in a place where the most important decisions about my students—what I taught, when I taught it, how I taught it, how many minutes I taught it, and how I checked to see if they "got it"—would all be made by people who didn't know them or me. What I didn't plan was to have a principal who believed that the *only* thing that mattered was good test scores and that the *only* way to get them was to follow the district plan exactly ("Why are you on page 42 today when the district calendar says you should be on page 58?") What I didn't plan was to be in a school where the *only* way to teach reading was through the reading book and worksheets. What I didn't plan was to be told that there was no time in the schedule for writing because that was tested last year or for social studies because that isn't tested at all. What I didn't plan was to be in a school where the kids were allowed to have recess only on days they did not have physical education (PE). What I didn't plan was that the schedule would be so tight that there would be no time for building community, for morning meeting, for reading favorite novels to the kids, for class meetings or discussions based on what was going on in the classroom, in the town, in the state, in the country, in the world.

In a matter of weeks, I had gone from "I want to keep teaching because I love it" to "I need to keep teaching to pay the mortgage." It wasn't good, not for me, not for the kids. And I knew that if I really needed to stay to pay the mortgage, I needed to find a way to do my job and not get fired while at the same time, somehow, in some way do the right thing for the kids who came to me every day.

In general, I decided it was far better to ask forgiveness than to ask permission. So we *did* read novels and discuss them. We *did* carve out time for social studies. We *did* stop and talk when issues presented themselves. We *did* stay on page 46 in math (even if we were supposed to be on page 55) and we did that exploration with manipulatives and fractions so kids would begin to see what a fraction actually was. And when administration came in and frowned and asked questions, I would apologize and tell them I'd try harder to stick to the curriculum in the days to come.

One of the biggest problems was one of time. How could I even get to know these kids with a schedule as tight as the one I was expected to keep? There was an easy solution to that. I opened the classroom 30 minutes early each day.

Originally, I told kids they could come in early if they needed help with work they didn't understand or if they wanted a quiet place to do their homework or wanted to use the computer. The kids had other reasons for showing up early. They brought their friends and sat and talked and laughed. They complained about little brothers, told me about scary people in their neighborhood or the cute new boy who moved in across the street. They played games on the computer and cheered each other on. And some did sit quietly and do homework or asked me to explain, one more time, how to reduce fractions to their lowest terms.

One morning Shary arrived even earlier than the regulars. She sat down at the table and sighed. I glanced over from across the room where I was getting out material for the day's work.

"Hi, Shary. Want help with last night's math?"
"No, I'm good," she answered still sitting there looking at me.
"Any homework to finish?"
"Yeah, I'll get to it." She sighed again.

I got up slowly and moved over to the table to sit across from her.

"Everything okay?"
"Well," she said, "want to know why I couldn't do my homework last
    night?"

"Tell, me. Why couldn't you do your homework last night?" (Shary *never* did her homework.)

"You know that girl, Jillian, at the middle school, the one who hanged herself last week?"

"I've heard about that, Shary. It was terrible."

"Well, she was one of my sister's best friends."

"Oh Shary, I'm so sorry. How's your sister doing?"

"Well, ever since Jillian did it, my sister's been saying that she was going to do it too."

"Hang herself?"

"Yeah. And my mom has been saying, 'Shut up. Stop saying that.'"

"Anyway, she said it at school and some kid told on her and then she had to go to the counselor and then people came to the house last night and they 'Baker Acted' her and said they were taking her to the crazy ward in some hospital. And my mom was crying, saying that Marisa was just talking, she didn't mean it and she just wants attention and Marisa was yelling at my mom that she *did* mean it, that my mom was a lousy mom and if she just paid attention for a minute she'd *know* that she meant it and as soon as she got out of that stupid hospital she was going to end it all because she was sick of her and sick of school and sick of everything. And then she left with the cops and my mom got drunk and yelled at me to mind my own business and go to bed. So I did."

I was silent for a minute. Shary had recited all this while staring at the table.

"Shary," I said hesitantly.

"Yeah?" She looked up hopefully.

"You've been through a lot. Sometimes when terrible things happen, it's good to talk about them. Would you like me to make an appointment for you to see the counselor today?"

"No thanks."

"Shary," I said patiently, "you shouldn't have to go through this alone. You need to talk to someone."

She looked straight at me. "So what do you think I'm doing right now?"

I moved around the table and put my arm around her. She started to cry.

So, why teach, in spite of it all? Because Shary is going to walk in and need someone to talk to and you're going to be the only one she trusts.

I think the thing that helped me as I muddled through my last 6 years of teaching was something my sister, Paula, told me years ago. She said that the teachers she remembered weren't the ones who showed her amazing things about the world or about literature or history or mathematics or science. They were the ones who saw something amazing in *her* and helped her see it too. I knew I needed to teach these kids to read well and do 5th-grade math, but my main job was to show them something amazing about themselves. Sometimes that was harder than showing them how to eliminate answers on a multiple-choice test, but it is so important.

I think about David as I write this. David was a sweet kid who always looked a little sad. He told me he wasn't that smart. He talked about a stepbrother who beat him up on a regular basis because he wasn't tough enough. He said that he wasn't afraid of the bad guys in the neighborhood because his stepdad had a gun under his bed and would blow a guy away if he tried to rob them.

David was bright but disorganized. I know he did his homework but he could never find it. His mom never showed up for conferences. She finally came to see me in December, a very heavy woman with a pretty face and jet black hair. David was one of five kids in the house (some hers from two previous marriages and one little one belonging to both of them). David was the product of her second marriage to a brutal man who terrorized her and then left her pregnant with David.

> "When I found out I was pregnant, I wanted to get an abortion," she told me. "I never wanted to have him. I hated his father but I couldn't have an abortion. I'm Catholic and I didn't want to go to hell."
>
> "I used to be beautiful," she sighed. "But then I got pregnant with David, and gained so much weight. I never lost that weight. Just look at me."
>
> "He looks just like his father. I can't even look at him. I hated that man so much."

And then she started to cry.

"I know it's not his fault I can't lose weight. And it isn't his fault he looks like his father. But I can't love him. I just can't. He tries so hard to get me to love him. He cleans up the kitchen without being asked, helps with the little kids, mows the lawn. None of the other kids do anything but I can't look at him."

We talked about therapy. I suggested Big Brothers Big Sisters. We talked about Weight Watchers. I talked to the counselor and got David someone to talk to once a week. And I went on loving David and knowing that I had one year to somehow convince him that he was smart, that he was valuable, and that no matter the messages he was getting at home, he was most loveable.

Why teach, in spite of it all? Because there's a David in every class and maybe, just maybe, I can help that kid. Maybe I can even help his mom.

I began teaching in September of 1969. I can still see those little 2nd-graders in Holyoke, Massachusetts. I said goodbye to my last class in June 2011. I do not hesitate when people ask if I would do it all over again. Of course I would. I haven't loved every minute of it. Some minutes have been tedious, some frustrating, some sad, and some downright painful. I've grumbled as I spent Sunday afternoons working on lesson plans and evenings grading papers that in my next life I'm getting a job that doesn't demand that I work nights and weekends.

But I have loved more of those minutes, hours, days, months, and years of teaching than not, laughed far more than I've cried, and gotten out of bed nearly every school day for 42 years looking forward to my day. Yes, of course, I'd do it again.

But would I do it *now*? Would I choose a profession where competence will be based solely on test scores? Would I choose a career where even *looking* outside the box might be problematic? Why would someone who is capable of complex problem solving choose a job where following the rules is the most important thing? Why would someone who loves to read and wants to put good books in the hands of children and watch those authors hook those kids put herself in a place where there's no time to read anything except the basal reader and no purpose for reading except to learn the strategy and skill of the week?

But Mary, a friend might say, not *all* schools are that rigid. Some schools still trust their teachers and run exciting, engaging programs. And I know that's true. I just listened to an interview on National Public Radio (NPR) with a 4th-grade teacher who is doing amazing things. Someone called in and asked how he could do the things he did, given the way schools are today. He said that he was most fortunate: He had a principal and a superintendent who made it clear to their staff that they had hired them, that they knew them and trusted them to do what was right for the group of children entrusted to them each year. They trusted their staff to provide a challenging, imaginative curriculum that would provide kids with the knowledge, skills, and attitudes they need.

And if young teachers are fortunate, they may end up in a district and school like that. But they shouldn't count on it.

It's been my experience that, in terms of how test-driven a school can be, they all fall along a continuum. In general, the more vulnerable the kids are, the more rigid the school will be. This is not always so but it's what I've seen time and time again. This means that our most vulnerable kids, our high-risk kids, our low-income kids, our children of color—these kids were the first to feel the pressure on teachers of "teaching to the test." Long before the suburbs started cutting programs to fund test-prep materials, inner-city kids were getting less music and art so they could have more reading and math, less real literature so they could have more workbook multiple-choice questions, less time with concrete materials in math so they could move faster through the curriculum. This means that making a difference in these schools is going to take more work, more imagination, more "tight rope walking" than if a teacher were to work in a suburban school. Still, who is going to do it if we don't do it?

"Why do you keep talking to me about college?" Jack complained one day. "I'm going to get out of school and get a job at Dollar General. Besides, my grandma says I'm just gonna end up in prison. You're wasting your time on me." Jack drove me nuts but Jack was bright. I suggested he think about law school. He'd make a great personal injury lawyer.

And he may end up at Dollar General or in prison, but not before I gave him my best shot.

There was no time in the schedule to read "real" books but I made time. We were reading *The Young Man and the Sea* by Rodman Philbrick one year. I chose it because it seems that quite a few of my kids were raising themselves and taking care of younger brothers and sisters. We had had some interesting discussions about the book and how kids survive when parents don't take care of them. We talked about how they survive but we also looked to the future and thought about what kind of parents *they* want to be, how they'll treat spouses, how they can grow up to be good men and women, people others can trust and kids look up to. (Am I dreaming?)

Matt was so tough and so fragile. His "IQ" was "low normal," which (can you believe it?) meant that he was *not* eligible for the resource room because he wasn't learning disabled, but he was *not* low enough for an ESE (special needs) classroom. He had emotional and behavioral issues, could barely read, found math incomprehensible, and, in general, wore me out. He called the police the year before because he was scared his dad would kill his mom. They came and his dad was arrested. Now that his dad is out of jail, he sees him every other weekend. His dad never hits him but he tells him he's stupid and clumsy and not worth anything. And that he will never forgive him for calling the cops on him a couple of years ago. (How do the courts *allow* this man access to this damaged child?)

One day as we walked to the playground, Matt said to me, "Do you think I'll be a good dad because you were my 5th-grade teacher?"

"What do you mean, Matt?"
"Well, I've been thinking about some of the stuff you say and I think
    I'm going to be a good dad because of what we talk about."

That's why I continued to teach even after the test became the *only* thing that mattered, because some little boy just might be a good dad because he had me in 5th grade.

I also continued to teach because, just maybe, I could help them become less self-centered, less bigoted, less apt to solve their problems with violence, less quick to judge. I continued to teach because I might be able to lead them to think critically, question the status quo, look for solutions to problems in ways that require compassion and imagination rather than force and anger. I continued to teach because I might be able to give them another way to look at history, at current events, at the things that happened every day on the playground and in their neighborhood. And I noticed that as I worked with kids on these things, it was very clear that I needed to practice what I preached. Kids are too smart to fall for "Do as I say, not as I do." The longer I taught, the less self-centered, less bigoted, less quick to judge I became. The longer I worked with kids, the better I became at thinking critically, questioning the status quo, and looking for compassionate, imaginative solutions to problems.

One Columbus Day, Serena came in and asked, "Mrs. Ginley, how come we don't have the day off?"

> "Because," said I, "it's a federal holiday and states can decide what stays open and what closes. Florida decided to keep schools open."
>
> "Is it because Columbus was a bad man?" she asked. "You said he was mean."
>
> "Well," I said, "that's not the reason Florida isn't closing the schools but, yes, I do think he was a bad guy. He was a very brave man and a brilliant navigator even if he was completely wrong about where he was when he came to the New World. But he wasn't a *good* man. Think about how he treated the people he met when he arrived."
>
> "What people?" Serena asked. "I thought there were only wild savages here when he came."
>
> "Savages? So were they people?" I asked.
>
> "Oh," said Serena. "I suppose."
>
> "I wonder what was meant by *wild savages*," I mused.
>
> "Well, they didn't wear any clothes, right?" she said.
>
> "Probably not," I acknowledged, "So people who wear clothes are civilized and people who don't aren't? And if you wear a *lot* of clothes, does that mean you're more civilized than if you only wear a little?"

Was Columbus good or bad? Did Europeans have a right to just take land and move Native Peoples out? Are people less civilized because they don't fit our idea of how they should live or dress? I continued to teach because someone had to raise these questions with kids.

I had a poster of Norman Rockwell's Ruby Bridges up in the classroom. I never said anything about it. I just left it there until someone asked about it.

"Hey," someone would always say a few weeks into the school year, "what's with that kid?"

"What kid?" I'd say.

"The little Black kid in the white dress with the cops."

"Hmmm . . . What do you think is happening here?"

Silence.

I taught 5th grade in Florida. The idea that I would have a class where *no one* knew the story of school integration blew me away.

"Somebody, take a guess. Look carefully."

And one by one, the guesses would come.

"She's being arrested because she skipped school."

"She's in trouble because she didn't do her homework."

"The cops came to bring her to a new foster home because her dad was hurting her."

"Look carefully at the picture," I'd say. "What else do you see?"

"Rotten tomatoes? Whoa . . . What's that all about?"

"Oooo, Mrs. Ginley, there's a swear on the wall."

"So, what's really happening?" someone would demand.

"I'll tell you tomorrow," I'd say.

"Whaaat? Why not now?"

"Because we have other things to deal with and I'd like you to think about it. But if you really want to know, Google it tonight. Her name is Ruby Bridges."

There was grumbling and a few kids would write her name down and the next day someone would know who she was. And I would tell the story of that little 6-year-old who first integrated the school in Louisiana.

An interesting discussion would follow every year. The kids were stunned. They were in a school where African American kids, Latino kids, Ukrainian and Russian kids, Asian kids all seemed to get along peacefully. They knew nothing of school segregation. They had heard about the bus boycott every year on Martin Luther King Day, but they knew nothing else about the civil rights movement.

So they would learn about *Brown vs. Board of Education*. And I would start asking questions: Would you go to this school if you were going to be the only Black kid, the first one to integrate the school? Would you send your child if she were going to be the only Black kid? What was good was that it was inconceivable to all of them how someone would object to integrated schools. However, I needed to take it a step further.

That was the 1960s. Now we're in the 21st century. "Segregation is against the law now," I'd say. "Does that mean discrimination and racism don't exist anymore?"

Most kids would nod their heads enthusiastically. There isn't any more racism. Not now. Martin Luther King and *Brown vs. Board of Education* changed all that, they said grinning.

But the African American kids in the class would look at each other and then at me. Usually one of them would slowly shake his or her head.

Rosa?

"Well, *I* think there's still racism," she said. "Like when I go in a store with
Liz [who's White] and we split up they follow me around and not her."
"Yeah," mumbled Eric, "people *look* at us different."

The White kids in the class are stunned. It never even occurred to them they might be living a life of privilege.

"I told my teacher last year that I wanted to go to Harvard," said Julie. "My teacher said it would be hard to get into Harvard and I might want to think about something else. Sarah said *she* wanted to go to Harvard and she told her she could make it if she tried. I wonder if it was because Sarah was White. Or maybe," she sighed, "Sarah is smarter than me."

Or maybe someone thought a child of color from Haiti who had an accent could never make it into Harvard.

And this is why I continued to teach . . . because someone has to make sure White kids realize that everyone isn't living happily ever after in a racism-free world and smart Black girls with accents know that they *can* go to Harvard if they set their minds to it.

I remember when high-stakes testing began to take on a life of its own back in the late 1990s. Most people weren't worried. We don't need to spend hours teaching kids the tricks to answering multiple-choice questions. We don't need to analyze past tests and spend big money on test-prep books and test-prep programs for the computer. If we just continue to teach well, kids will learn and the tests will take care of themselves.

However, as soon as the tests became the *only* way to measure success, then it was clear that the entire focus of education became *the test*. And many (but not all) superintendents and principals began to trust test-prep publishers far more than they trusted their own teachers. As the test became more and more important, anything that did not guarantee higher test scores became less important or unnecessary. In my school, we were required to use the reading book that was carefully aligned with the standards that would be tested (and even more insidious, it was formatted the way the questions on the test were asked). Each week, the kids were given a story, usually a chapter from a novel or an article from a longer piece. The publishers had found a story that would work well for teaching a skill (e.g., using prefixes and suffixes, using context clues, recognizing structures such as cause and effect) and elements of fiction and nonfiction (e.g., main idea, setting, character traits). The lessons for each day were in the teacher's manual. One day was devoted to reading the piece in the reading book, the rest to worksheets on the skill and theme that were carefully formatted to mirror the way test questions appeared on the state tests.

The problem was that the kids couldn't understand the story in the reading book unless they had some knowledge of what had happened in the story *before* this particular chapter, as well as some general background knowledge if the setting, vocabulary, and culture were not in their range of experience.

If I were going to use the piece in the reading book (which I tried really hard to do) there was no way I would have kids read something they absolutely couldn't understand. So I would spend a lot of time on Monday building background. For example, one story presumed that the kids knew about the Old West, stagecoach stations, smallpox, and Chinese acrobats (interesting combination, huh?). It's a great story if you read the entire book (a short novel by Lawrence Yep), but *unless* you read the beginning of the book *and* know something about the other things I mentioned, you cannot possibly understand the story.

So I spent Monday reading the first chapters to the kids, talking about where and when this took place. We googled smallpox ("Ewww!," said the kids) and talked about why a kid who had been the leader of the pack in her town would become a whiny recluse afraid to show her face after contracting smallpox. We talked about how the Chinese were treated when they came to build the transcontinental railroad. We saw a short video clip about Chinese acrobats.

By the time we read the section in the reading book the kids were ready—for the story, for the subtleties of language, and for the girl's growth. They could visualize what was happening and discuss it on many levels. Other 5th-grade teachers had done the same. The week before we had talked about the story and how we could teach it. It was a thoroughly satisfying week for all of us.

Unfortunately, we had had some observers (the reading director and assistant from the central office) pop in that Monday. They were not impressed. In fact, they were horrified. They sat down with us the following week to tell us that we were spending way too much time on background information and not enough time on the "skills."

I tried to keep quiet by just sitting there and taking volumes of notes (my way of keeping my temper in check when Lamaze breathing doesn't work) but of course at one point I couldn't stand it. I explained that the stories were plucked from the middle of books and made no sense unless the kids had some background. The supervisor did not skip a beat. She explained, very patiently, that *it really wasn't important that the kids understood the story*. The story was just a vehicle for teaching the skill of the week. I took a deep breath, gulped, and went back to taking notes, writing down very carefully in my book, "Understanding the story is not necessary if they have learned the skill of the week."

So I continue to teach because someone has to make sure kids understand the story and realize there is more to reading than getting the skill of the week. There is more to life than good scores on statewide tests, too. At a time when *everyone*—politicians, school officials, and maybe even mom and dad—are telling kids their worth can be summed up in a test score number, we need to be there to tell them they are far more than that test score.

More than 10 years ago, I wrote an open letter to kids that ended up in several newspapers across the state of Massachusetts.

Open letter to kids receiving MCAS scores this week.
Dear Students:

For all of you who took the MCAS tests in May, please remember that strangers gave you these scores. And that there are many ways of being smart.

These strangers do not know that you can speak two languages. They do not know that you can play the violin or dance or paint a picture. They do not know that you take care of your little brother after school, that your friends can count on you to be there for them, that your laughter can brighten the dreariest day.

They do not know that you write poetry, wonder about black holes, know exactly how much change you should get when you go to the market.

They do not know that you are trustworthy, that you are kind, that you are thoughtful. They do not know that you spent your summer with a 700-page Harry Potter book.

They do not know you. But we who know you—your moms and dads, your grandparents and teachers, your neighbors and friends—are proud of all you are and all you will be. MCAS scores will tell you something, but they will not tell you everything. There are many ways of being smart.

We still teach to let kids know that there are many ways of being smart. We teach because someone has to help them see that others, too, have their own ways of being smart. And we teach to let them know that, in spite of everything, they have some power over the course of their lives.

Why do we teach *now*? It was our choice. We chose it and for one reason: We chose it for the kids. We chose it because there are children in every city, every town, every village, everywhere who are waiting for us to show them they are far more than they ever thought they were and they can grow up happy if they choose to. And, hopefully, young people will continue to choose to spend their lives among schoolchildren. It's not a bad way to spend your life.

So I keep coming back to the same question: Why on earth would you choose a profession in which you are powerless? I can't answer that. Perhaps you get into it for the same reason that I stayed even after it was obvious that I clearly was in a totally different job than when I had started out. It's because somehow, even today, even with all the insanity, all the rules, all the poorly designed textbooks, all the directives not to bother teaching anything that is not tested, in spite of everything, there are kids out there who need good teachers. They need teachers who are willing to meet them where they are and help them become what they never dreamed was possible, teachers who are willing to ask the important questions, listen carefully to the answers, and ask more questions. They need teachers who demand that kids think, challenge the status quo, ask questions, and, in the words of Ms. Frizzle, the teacher in the wonderful Magic School Bus books, get messy.

That's our job and I think we can still do it in spite of everything. I think we can find ways to help kids discover their own giftedness, the enormous potential within themselves. My dear friend, Dorothy Cresswell, wrote a song that contains this line, "Thank God we're more than we thought we were." That's what teachers do. They help kids discover that they're more than they thought they were and that their classmates are more than they thought *they* were too.

My teaching career has come to an end. I look at the little ones who are at the bus stop near my home every morning and hope and pray they are going into classrooms taught by bright, imaginative young people who went into the profession with their eyes wide open. Teaching has never been easy but it is still a good way to spend your life. I chose it in the 1960s and have no regrets. Would I choose it now? Despite the misgivings I shared at the beginning of this essay, yes, I would absolutely still choose it. I am a teacher and can't imagine being anything else. Whatever I have done to enrich the lives of others, they have done far more to enrich my life. Whatever I've done to help them grow, they have done far more to help me grow. I would choose it again (and again and again) partly because those kids needed someone like me but even more, because I needed them. Together we discovered who we were and what we were meant to be.

CHAPTER 3

Staying True to Why I Teach

Nina Tepper

I never have a ready reply when people ask how I feel about my retirement from more than 30 years of public school teaching. What I feel most is reflective. I find myself reflecting on why I went into teaching in the first place, and how I survived the turbulence of perennial education reform. I ask myself, "Have I achieved my goals?"

As a peace and justice activist in the 1960s and 1970s, I thought, "If I could make a difference in the world, it would be as a teacher." I wondered then if I really could make a difference. I only have to go as far back as 2 weeks prior to my retirement date to find my answer.

THE POWER OF STUDENTS' STORIES

It was the final authors' party of my career, where every student in my Literacy Enrichment Classes stands up in front of an audience to read a story or poem about an important lesson they learned in their lives. There wasn't a dry eye in the room as both audience and students experienced the power of their voices in writing and the self-discovery that makes each one stronger.

Marcus opened the readings with a story about finding courage after being literally abandoned and emotionally neglected by his mother, who chose an abusive stepfather over her own son. Unable to handle the stress at home, his mother turned him over to a support agency that is now looking for a foster family to take him in. Marcus's writing helped him come to grips with all that he had been struggling with that school year. During classroom rehearsals, I noticed Marcus pause when he wondered in his text, " . . . if she still thinks of her son," but he always continued with the conviction that he wanted his story told. Again, at that point, Marcus paused, but when I looked over, his tears streamed down like rain. Standing next to him, I softly put my hand on his shoulder; he took a deep breath and continued. Looking out into the audience, I noticed my students spellbound, girls reaching to hold each others' hands and boys rapt with attention and respect.

Sandra came forward next, wiping tears from her eyes. When I asked if she was ready to read, she nodded that she was fine. Sandra read about feeling abandoned by her father, a drug addict, who left the family and never calls. It has made it difficult for Sandra to trust anyone because she doesn't know if they too might leave. By telling her story, Sandra found strength and support from her mother who, "never knew that was how Sandra felt." Her story has the power to heal her relationship with her mother and siblings as she acknowledged how important they all are in her life.

To lighten the mood, I invited Maria to read her funny story about jumping into her backyard pool during a winter snowstorm with her brothers and sisters. The whirlpool they created collapsed the pool sides, spilling her and her siblings over the frozen grass. Her words painted a hysterical picture of young children covered in mud and bits of grass shivering like "tiny mud monsters." Then Tina, who had only planned to read her poem, asked to read her story as well. The moment was one she didn't want to miss as she later confided, "I was afraid the kids in the other classes would not listen," but the mood in the room was clearly supportive and open. She read her story about how the "cops and DSS [Department of Social Services]" came to her house, putting her brothers in one car and sisters in another. As they drove away, she saw her parents being held back as they rushed toward her car. Clearly content with her decision to read, Tina confessed that she would have regretted not reading and was pleasantly surprised at how respectfully everyone reacted.

There were many stories of overcoming obstacles in school, sports, and home, with a sprinkling of funny, loving memories. Each story is unique and each story tells of the complicated lives with which our students come to us. Without searching for their stories, I would never have known, and what assumptions might I have made? When I thought I met all that a child could bear, I would meet another with even more to overcome. Each year teaching, I had grown to believe "I have seen it all," only to confront new challenges or stories I had to share with counselors to ensure my students got the support they needed.

Later I found little notes of thanks on my desk. One letter, written by Marcus, moved me deeply and sums up why I teach. In part, it reads,

> You have changed my life . . . YOU GOT ME TO WRITE!!! Another thing you have taught me was hope and now I have hope no matter how many obstacles there are . . . I am now strong and proud to be who I am.

Marcus had come to me alienated, angry, abandoned, and alone. This letter was a gift greater than any I had ever received from a student. Marcus validated the risks I took as a teacher to reveal the whole person first, by adapting curriculum to meet the individual needs and interests of my students, rather than focusing exclusively on teaching to a test. Designing authentic, relevant assignments prepared my students to write for other academic purposes by giving them the confidence they could express themselves in writing and confirming that they had something important to say. Writing workshop and journal reflections were also how I built trust and community, another condition for learning (Cambourne & Turbill, 1987).

A LIFE OF TEACHING

I have spent the majority of my career teaching in inner-city public elementary schools with large populations of second-language learners. I was later recruited as a member of a team of teachers to plan and open a public magnet middle school for the arts. That was as close as I came to fulfilling a dream I always had of opening my own school. Then later in my career, I became a high school literacy specialist, mentor, and coach. I have worked with many wonderful administrators and some who were unsupportive. I have survived the pressures of standardized curriculum and testing and ballooning class sizes, among other obstacles. As I faced the increasing demands of district- and state-mandated standardized testing and the precarious role of assessment in teacher evaluations, my challenge became staying true to why I teach while keeping my job.

One time, I was disciplined and suspended without pay for 5 days for brainstorming topics of interest to teens, in preparation for a bilingual TV talk show project, that were deemed inappropriate by one parent who complained to the principal. After a lengthy appeal and arbitration process, my teaching partner and I were totally vindicated. It was determined that we had acted responsibly when handling the sensitive content of the teen discussions, that brainstorming was a legitimate teaching technique, and that

the school system did not have any written curriculum or documents speci-
fying what content we could or could not cover with students. The story,
documented in *Why We Teach* (2005), highlights a time in my career when I
wasn't sure I could carry on. Through it all, I kept reminding myself of why
I went into teaching in the first place.

Now I find myself reflecting on how I remained a teacher with all that
could have chased me away years ago. Standardized education did not
address the needs of the majority of my students, who had always been at
risk both academically and socially. Many did not come to school, to use
the current jargon, "ready to learn." Every morning Dakota stopped by for
a handful of animal crackers because she never got up early enough for
breakfast. Saul stayed up until 4:00 in the morning playing video games and
came to school with only 2 hours of sleep. Joey had too many absences to
be promoted because his mother threw him out of the house many nights
to sleep in the car. He was thinking of dropping out. Nickie, like many of
her friends, showed little motivation to learn and did not have the guidance
at home with guardians who were barely there, or who were just too busy
working constantly to make ends meet.

Was I addicted to the random rushes of confidence and community that
I nurtured, enough to return year after year, even when obstacles seemed
insurmountable? Maybe I was hooked the first moment I felt the rewards
of my high expectations positively impacting students' lives. Perhaps I had
been chasing that high my entire career.

My journey began in 1973, after reading the groundbreaking book
Death at an Early Age (1967) by Jonathan Kozol, which highlights the fail-
ures of public schools to believe in and educate the mostly minority inner-
city youth in Boston. It was then that I accepted a student teaching position
at an alternative K–12 school in Roxbury, a neighborhood on the outskirts
of Boston. Living with the founders of Rounder Records in a collective
home in Somerville, I would leave the house on bicycle to ride to Harvard
Square where I would chain my bike and take the MBTA subways and then
catch a bus to Roxbury Center. There I would disembark and walk nearly
10 blocks to reach the school an hour and a half later. I made this daily trek
never questioning my commitment and promise to be at school every day.

The Warehouse School, housed appropriately in an old warehouse, was
designed to address the dissatisfaction with inner-city public education by
following an open classroom method of instruction popular in the 1970s.
Derived from the one-room schoolhouse model, students were taught in
multi-age, multi-level classrooms in large open spaces with a team of teachers who grouped students for instruction depending on skills, interests, or

subjects taught. Enrollment included students who could not make it in the traditional school setting and were motivated by the arts. Children came from all backgrounds and learning abilities. It was there that I experienced my first rush of the rewards of teaching.

As is true of most student teachers, I began unsure of my role or what impact I could have. Thanks to this innovative environment, I was able to work openly in the morning with the younger students and I taught a variety of social studies classes in the afternoon with high school students. I designed a classroom that integrated creative dramatics with historical fiction and poetry. Students' responses were enthusiastic, but I couldn't help wondering about the disengaged high school boy who often stood in one corner of the room seemingly disinterested in the antics of the class. I recall teachers advising me not to have high expectations, as Carl was very bright but mildly autistic.

One day, while presenting haiku for a creative dramatics exercise, Carl tentatively handed me a haiku he found in one of my books to have me act out in front of the class. Instinctively knowing that good teachers have to be able to model what they expect from their students, I complied with all the openness and feeling I could find. As a student read the haiku aloud, I incorporated facial expression and movement to portray the poet's words. This activity became the impetus and inspiration for putting on a theatrical performance. The students chose "Waiting for Godot," by Albert Albee, and to this day I do not recall why. It was their motivation and interest that I grasped onto, never questioning their ability to understand the themes of this philosophical play.

On the day of auditions, all the students gathered in our open space, sitting along the windowsills and folding chairs. Excited conversations played out scenarios of who should get what part. It was the more popular, outgoing students who anticipated being chosen for the cast. In the corner, rocking gently, Carl sat silently reading the script. "Maybe Carl wants to audition," I heard with slight giggles of disbelief. Casting aside my colleagues' earlier advice, I encouraged him to read.

At once, Carl jumped up and went fully into character, holding the room spellbound, ending in thunderous applause. Everyone agreed he should have a part. While the entire school got involved with creating the sets, the four actors and I worked after school and weekends rehearsing their lines. My once awkward student became a natural member of this collective effort. The bonds created through hard work and laughter made anything possible. Our project took on a life of its own as the high level of engagement for this performance was palpable.

A few days before the performance, we still hadn't rehearsed the last scene. On the night of the performance, something magical happened. The students' understanding of the play and their own personal interpretations helped them ad lib the last scene with such mastery, even I could not tell if they were following the script or not. After a long-standing ovation, students and faculty presented me with flowers and gifts and a short speech expressing their appreciation. This accomplishment hooked me to the power of teaching and my role as a facilitator of learning.

ACHIEVING MAGIC MOMENTS

I seemed to live for these small victories, the magic moments, when understanding lit the room. Too often it was smothered by the preoccupations and chaos in my students' lives that made learning feel like the greater distraction, as they grappled with their personal struggles. What started as idealism in my youth to make a contribution to the future by working with youth became a stubborn pursuit to create learning environments that support growth.

My persistence was fueled by an understanding that teacher expectations are perhaps the most important factor for fostering achievement. During my student teaching days, I was influenced by William Ryan's book *Blaming the Victim* (1971), which refutes the persistent stereotypes and lies about race, poverty, and the poor. It challenges the belief that minority and economically disadvantaged children perform poorly in school because they are "culturally deprived." Ryan's book convinced me that teacher expectations correlate to achievement and that students could be victims of false assumptions. I kept this revelation conscious throughout my teaching career. I could never look at a child and not see potential; my focus became pinpointing potential and harnessing it for good.

I want to return to Marcus's letter to me to underscore the importance of student writing. His letter continues, "You know how you made me let go [of my hate]? Writing has changed my life because of you." Writing remained my most invaluable teaching tool with all students K–12. Early in my career, I became determined to integrate writing workshop in every learning environment across the curriculum. The only way to overcome the barricades blocking my students was an education that stimulated self-discovery and built confidence by believing and affirming that each child has a positive purpose to pursue. I have used writing throughout my entire teaching career to reinforce learning by making it reflective, rewarding, and relevant. Students not only solidified their learning in journals and essays, but also they discovered something about themselves when sharing their thinking, favorite family stories, or their own life lessons. Each year, I published my students' work as a recognition and celebration of their efforts and the value of their words. Each year, I hosted an authors' party to give voice and power to their words. Each year, students were transformed and validated by their words, and in the process they found a glimmer of hope and a belief that they matter.

For many of my students, reading their writing before an audience was the first time their work was acknowledged as meaningful. I had to coax students with the promise of bonus points and built-in multiple incentives, along with my belief that public speaking is an important skill that will prepare them for their future. More than any standardized test, presenting completed work was an authentic assessment that encouraged strong literacy skills encompassing opportunities for listening, speaking, reading, writing, and reaching out to a real audience for a real purpose.

We are told that our job as teachers is to impart knowledge, but our true role is to facilitate the process of discovery, to help students interact in the real world, to find the strength and courage to meet the challenges of their future. Russian psychologist Lev Vygotsky, whose work is embedded in education theory and taught in many teacher colleges, guided my beliefs on child development and learning. He constructed the concept called "tools of the mind" (Vygotsky, 1978). According to Vygotsky, children need to learn more than a set of facts and skills; they also need to master a set of mental tools by interacting in their social environment to take charge of their own learning. When new skills and concepts are taught on the edge of emergence, where learning transitions from what the student knows or can do to a concept or skill that is new or unknown, described by Vygotsky as the "zone of proximal development," they not only acquire new knowledge, but also they progress developmentally.

That was the purpose and goal of my student publication projects and authors' parties. Project-centered learning for real or authentic purposes, similar to the role-play Vygotsky observed in young children, was the engine that drove my students' development and learning. Standardization of content and testing alone were not productive with my students, as they negated engagement, which is at the core of all learning. I had to meet my students first where they were in order to set them on the path to achievement. In time, the tests took care of themselves, as a majority of my students were able to pass because they had learned the content in authentic ways. By first motivating my students with content that spoke to their interests and known experiences, they could then transfer the reading comprehension strategies and writing structures taught to more difficult, grade-level texts. If we cannot help students make connections between what they are learning and how it might have applications to their own lives, we should not be surprised when students do not develop the higher-order thinking necessary to apply their learning in the testing environment, nor develop strategies for problem solving in new situations.

REFLECTING ON WHY I TAUGHT

I was well aware of the energy it takes to be a good teacher, yet I constantly marveled at the multitude of decisions made in the moment to promote learning. I learned I did not have to sacrifice the interests or developmental needs of my students while teaching the content of my courses. The power I had was the power of choice over *how* to teach. By explicitly modeling what good readers and writers do and using a project-centered approach, I was able to adapt the curriculum to meet individual needs and interests while building community and real opportunities for learning.

In addition, cross-curriculum connections and interdisciplinary education were not just terms I learned about in teacher training programs; instead, they became essential elements of effective curriculum design and daily lesson plans. Everything connects, whether we are teaching history, integrating literature, designing math word problems, or discussing current events. If students are not invested in the assignments, if the content does not relate to them on any level, then engagement cannot be achieved. If students cannot see themselves as part of history, literature, or science, most go through their school days as if in a fog, grasping for meaning or searching for the light that might guide them out of their cloud of confusion. When teachers validate each child's culture and experience, when teachers inject facts and stories that connect the past and present to the future, when teachers design real opportunities for students to work collectively with others, students can then explore how their lives are woven into the fabric of society and begin to imagine how they too can contribute to our world.

All this does not answer how I was able to remain in public schools and make it to full retirement. I have seen many talented teachers leave the profession when the demands of education reform make it harder and harder to find fulfillment in their jobs. We all know teachers are not in it for the money, so what was it that held me to the task?

My answer begins to emerge as Marcus's letter reveals, "You have showed me something, something I haven't seen in a long time. Do you know what that is? It is love." Reading this, my emotions dissolve, unable to read on through my tears, knowing the truth of my journey lies deeply embedded in his words. Having high expectations, integrating topics and projects that connect to my students' lives, and celebrating their accomplishments were correctly perceived by Marcus, and I hope, all my students, as love. There is a quote by Martin Luther King implicitly embedded in my student's letter, "Darkness cannot drive out darkness; only light can do that. Hate can not drive out hate; only love can do that." At the risk of sounding trite, I believe I was motivated by a deep respect and compassion for youth that at its core can be defined as love. That is how I held fast to my career.

I naturally found joy being with young people and I treasured each regardless of what they brought. I always told my students when they tested my patience or bent the rules that I knew they were evolving human beings. Making mistakes is part of the process of discovering who we are and what we believe. I wanted my students to feel respected and safe to explore, learn, and grow. As a teacher, I had the capacity to influence child development and impact the future like no other profession.

Then I find in Marcus's letter something that goes to the heart of why I taught all these years, from my first student teaching experience to my last day as a public school teacher and all the days in between. I read on, "Remember the story [I wrote], Love Makes Us Stronger? That was not only for other people; it was for you." I know I have helped instill confidence, courage, and the motivation for my students to take charge of and find value in their own education. Marcus concludes, "No matter what people say . . . [I won't] worry about anything but my own well being and education." YES! This is why I taught.

I now believe it was the love felt by my students, defined by my high expectations and an inability to give up on a child, that made all the difference. My teaching career was motivated by an insatiable quest and a dedication to the future by working with youth. I know we cannot save every child, but I think of the Yiddish proverb, "To save a life, you save a generation." My difference in the world is but a ripple on a pond, yet I know I have made a difference, one child at a time. In that way, I have achieved my goals.

CHAPTER 4

Looking Forward Backwards

Teaching Freedom and Democracy in the Classroom

Berta Rosa Berriz,
with Alice McCabe, Jerry Pisani, Amanda Smallwood,
Taryn Snyder, Lesley Strang, Jeffrey Timberlake, and Erica Welch

Before my retirement last June, whenever folks asked me what I did for a living, I would always say, "I am a bilingual teacher of immigrant Latino students in the Boston Public Schools." That was then. Today I am shaping a new life as "Abuelita Tita," a new role in a new state, closer to my son, Tristan, and granddaughters, Naja Zahara and Adena Caridad.

Yet, the pull of my life's vocation is as strong as ever. I am drawn back to the classroom by a recent photo from the proud mother of a former 3rd-grade student posing with the UN Secretary General—the boss at his first job in the real world. Then, one of my student teachers invites me to teach a guest lesson on memoir writing for her English as a Second Language (ESL) students and I learn that she is being honored with National Board certification. She was in my classroom when I was working on my own certification. And, most recently, I am a sounding board for Union School colleagues who keep me in the loop on events, issues, and personalities.

Along with all these sweet moments that only teachers know, I am also reminded of the raw reality facing teachers today: ever-changing administrative mandates; bureaucrats who render teachers' knowledge invisible in the policymaking process; the continuing marginalization of students in under-resourced, segregated classrooms; and whatever may be the latest "magic bullet," which inevitably proves unresponsive and ineffective, with all of these chipping away at the time for quality teaching.

Confronted by this sobering reality, where does a committed teacher find that last ounce of energy, the courage to take on one more—just one more—hopeful project for her students? Where do we go for guidance, support, and affirmation? The obvious answer is: we must turn to those most affected by the work we do, our students, their parents, other teachers, and communities. These are the people who have always played a vital role in developing my teaching practice.

With these words, then, I want to share reflections on my passion for the craft of teaching, as well as a few of the many lessons I have learned in my 33 years in Boston's public schools. Last, I will share my 4-year adventure as a founding teacher leader at a teacher-run, parent-friendly K–8 public school—a testament to finding a new way out of "no way."

STUDENTS AND THEIR PARENTS: NEGLECTED RESOURCES

Over the years, my students have left me with many stories—stories that express their fears, hopes, and aspirations; stories told in their own voices, capturing what they have learned in class and beyond. Sometimes, they have called me at home or visited my classroom to add a new chapter to their story. Sometimes it's a chance encounter on the streets with former students, now young adults, writing stories of their own children.

There was this wide-eyed and curious 8-year-old with dark hair in pigtails, a new arrival from the Dominican Republic, who entered my 3rd-grade bilingual classroom without a word of English. But she was determined to learn. Years later, she shared how a classroom writing project in autobiography had kept her focused through high school and into college. Or that young man mentioned earlier, the only son of a dedicated African American single mom, whose passion for social issues was kindled in that same 3rd-grade cohort, eventually leading to his job at the United Nations.

Through my students, I relived the joys of dawning awareness, nurturing connections to families and communities, and taking a stand with each new school year.

Contrary to the popular portrayal of inner-city families as unaware, indifferent bystanders alienated from their children's education, my students' families were actively invested in the learning process. In my classroom, parents were welcomed as respected resources, often overcoming demanding job schedules, the burdens of single parenting, and limited English skills to share their wisdom and knowledge with my students.

There was the time the boys and girls in my class were having a heated argument over physical education (PE) class. It turned out that the PE teacher decided he would only teach the rules of baseball to the boys in the class. The girls could entertain themselves with jump rope games by the dumpster. José's father came into our classroom on his day off to facilitate the conversation among the children. As a result, José and Meyshia composed a letter to the principal on chart paper that included suggestions from both girls and boys. The letter the children crafted advocated for both boys and girls to be able to learn to play sports during physical education class. Although girls were included in the games as a result, the principal and the PE teacher came to speak to the children while I was absent that Friday. They chastised the children for daring to question the authority of the teacher. It was a bittersweet victory that resulted from their activism, a victory that I hope will seed further acts of courage.

Through the parents of my students—valued sources for feedback, encouragement, and inspiration—my connection to home, culture, and community are continually refreshed.

TEACHERS: ALSO IGNORED RESOURCES

Teachers love to learn. Our students challenge us to find ways to enter their realm as curious, playful collaborators in their exploration of the world. Where one child might only find focus in hands-on life science, the culturally rooted ways of knowing of another require the big picture for all the juicy details to fall into place. Then there's the child who needs to sing and dance and rhyme to gather meaning. From my very first classroom to the present, it has been clear to me that race and culture are both invisible in Boston Public Schools (BPS) decisionmaking and, as a result, become an obstacle to access to learning for our non-White, non–middle class students.

The first time I stuck my head out of the water of my classroom practice to reflect on what was taking place both inside and beyond the classroom walls, I realized some of the strategies that I was using in my bilingual special needs classroom were the focus of current research. For example, researcher Anne Wheelock was interested in doing research on how my colleague Beth Handman and I used accelerated content-area instruction to engage a broad range of learners. Working collaboratively at the Mackey Mosaic Middle School, we combined my bilingual special needs 6th-graders with her 6th-grade Advanced Work students in a team-teaching project around an enriched curriculum. We called our work TeamStream (Wheelock, 1990), a new approach to building integrated learning communities.

Later, the Lucretia Crocker Fellowship year (1989) marked the first time research and critical reflection became an integral part of my teaching method. Particularly for this TeamStream project, I studied conflict resolution and cooperative learning with Educators for Social Responsibility (ESR) to engage my young scholars in social-emotional learning and build their capacity to effectively participate in a diverse learning community. The most eye-opening aspect of this inclusive classroom was the similarities shared by young scholars tackling above-grade-level work. Clearly, student enthusiasm and participation in our blended 6th grade was indistinguishable across so-called ability groups—at a time when inclusion was not yet even a buzzword in academic circles.

At different points in my career, I used professional development opportunities to learn new strategies for reaching that "one student," the one who I just couldn't reach in the usual way. For example, while preparing for my two-way bilingual classroom, I soon realized that teaching in a multilingual/multicultural environment would present a new challenge. Until that point in my career, I had worked almost exclusively with Latino students and their families, so I needed to deepen my knowledge of the African American community, not only to better reach my culturally diverse students, but in order to bridge the long-standing cultural schism between Latino and African American people in my school's South End neighborhood. I followed the Black Story Telling festival from city to city to learn all that I could about African American traditions, stories, language, and arts (http://www.nabsinc.org/).

With Community Change, Inc. (CCI), I worked on various anti-racist projects within our schools and in the community. CCI was born out of the civil rights movement and in response to the Kerner Commission, which accurately named racism as "a White problem." CCI has done what few organizations are willing to do: shine a spotlight on the roots of racism in White culture with the intention of dealing with racism at its source, as well as with its impact on communities of color (http://www.communitychangeinc.org/). The first project involved a 2-year grant to study historical and sociological aspects of race in the United States. Each school involved in the grant then developed an anti-racist/anti-bias committee to apply what we were learning to everyday situations at our schools. I learned much about my own identity, personal biases, and group privilege. I also studied the histories of liberation movements among oppressed peoples in the United States and around the world. This challenge to become more self-aware was key to reaching others across our differences, one of the most human aspects of teaching.

Chafing at the narrow professional development offerings then available from the district, my colleagues and I organized an informal, teacher-led study group where we read works by Lisa Delpit (1995) and Antonia Darder (1991) to better understand the significance of cultural identity in the teaching–learning process in urban inner-city schools with overwhelmingly African American and Latino students. During the first year we read these books, we discussed the questions they raised about our practice. In the second year, we designed an action research project around these questions. This experience eventually led me to my doctoral studies, where I conducted research on the relationship between the process of becoming bicultural and teachers' assessment of students' academic progress.

Beyond the classroom, teacher knowledge is a powerful resource for schools, districts, and the nation. Yet, rarely are teachers included in the most critical policy decisions concerning public education. On the school level, teacher knowledge and experience is rarely utilized in so-called "leadership teams." Instead, principals and administrators are compelled to implement the latest greatest "teacher-proof" curricula, test-preparation strategies, standardized tests, punitive discipline measures, and one-size-fits-all quick fixes for the "achievement gap."

Most teachers do their best to conform to each new policy in good faith—at least until compliance becomes complicity. One of my colleagues noted her own disturbing realization that due to her fidelity to a new math pacing guide, "I was moving so fast from one lesson to the next that when I looked back at my class, I realized that none of them was keeping up with me. I had lost the entire group and had to backtrack. I didn't even know at what point in the unit I lost each one. But I had covered all of the material on schedule."

No one considered that the math curriculum required grade-level literacy and prior knowledge of particular math concepts. What about new immigrants, then? Where was the scaffolding for the language or various methods for approaching the same problem, including traditional algorithms?

Then there is the scripted literacy program, again with a pacing guide, that uses only decontextualized excerpts from literature, never an entire text, sacrificing the big picture and inhibiting efforts to fully comprehend its parts. So what attention is given to those students who may not have had exposure to various literary forms enabling them to fill in the missing chunks? How about those of us who need the big picture in order to comprehend fragments of knowledge?

Are we teaching children? Or are we merely teaching a curriculum?

It is no surprise to those of us who *teach children* that the learning-opportunity gaps remain. We are compelled to fund our own classroom libraries, to invest in our own ongoing professional development, and, worse still, to shut our classroom doors in an effort to use all that we have gathered to teach children.

I have come to cherish the wealth of knowledge that each child brings to the learning project. It is the only place to begin, creating possibility each year anew in a web of relationships, with no script, constructing access to new knowledge through caring, careful observation and assessments tailored to each student. The learning happens within the intellectual conversation, getting to the other side of dissonance and discovery in a learning community. Providing a rich learning environment in the classroom and beyond is the essence of teaching. We are teachers. We know how to do this. Yet, rarely are we asked to share what we know by the self-appointed "experts" who influence the deliberations on education policy.

THE BTU TEACHER-RUN SCHOOL PROJECT

To be honest, when I was approached about building a school where teachers would enjoy the "freedom to teach," where students would be challenged to step up and discover their own potential, and where a diverse and engaged school community would have a voice in its own future, I could barely contain myself. I was teaching 5th grade and had only 5 years or so until my retirement. With doctoral research behind me, classroom teaching gained new meaning. The classroom is my favorite geographical location. None of the other roles I have played—resource specialist, literacy coach, bilingual department administrator—hold the same allure, challenge, and joy. What if teachers could really plan a school where they could teach with freedom, support, and recognition?

The Boston Teachers' Union (BTU) wrote a commitment to open a teacher-run school, emphasizing school-based management and shared decisionmaking, into its 2006–2010 contract. The autonomies granted over hiring, budget, curriculum and assessment, governance, and the school calendar suggested that a "pilot school" format held the most promise for this effort. Yet, past experiences of painful isolation and official retaliation still bubbled just beneath the surface of our enthusiasm as we contemplated the essential principles that would guide our new school.

Engaging ideas such as centering decisions on curriculum and instruction in teacher knowledge, shared leadership, and peer accountability, and providing a broad, challenging liberal arts education to all students, slowly took shape. More important, these principles soon ignited the imagination of teachers joining the Union School faculty, often taking surprising forms in our classrooms. For example, Lesley Strang, K1 teacher, initiated a collaborative research project on "making learning visible" with other early childhood teachers. This small group applied an approach based on Reggio Emilia, highlighting how children's learning can become evident to teachers through observation, documentation, interpretation of artifacts, and listening closely as little ones learn in groups.

Lesley reflects on the essential quality of the learning project she initiated.

The Freedom to Teach

Lesley Strang

The freedom to teach is why I teach now. I deeply believe that all children learn when they are in a classroom where they are known, appreciated, cared for, and allowed and encouraged to be curious. Creative, hands-on, engaging curriculum and thoughtful, observant teachers are keys to making this happen. In my first year of teaching at the Union School, I went to training on the power of observation inspired by work done in Reggio Emilia. From the moment I left the conference, I did my best to sit and quietly observe my scholars in action—every day if possible. I can often be found sitting quietly in the block area with a clipboard and pen listening and recording how my 4- and 5-year-old scholars are learning, solving problems, and making connections . . . I learn more about my students from sitting quietly and listening than by being told when to administer a certain assessment that may or may not be appropriate for my scholars. A scholar should be known as a whole child—not just how he or she scored on one day of testing in one area. Observations have made me a better teacher.

The belief that teachers are knowledgeable and are great resources allows teachers to be their best selves. Gone are my days of dreading administration and instead, I look forward to meeting, talking, and learning with and from my colleagues. I truly love coming into my classroom every day and being open to all the learning and magic that is going to happen.

Another teacher, Jeffrey Timberlake, proposed readings from *The Mindful Teacher*, a book he had contributed to, and he led rewarding and revealing conversations on reflective practice. The reading invited reflection on the very issues that promote joy and fulfillment in our vocation as teachers and proved most useful in the early stages of building our school community. Interestingly, this project brought out the diversity of our teaching faculty. One of our conscious moves at the Union School was to create norms that frame faculty interaction in supportive ways.

Here is Jeffrey's take on moving ideas forward in contrasting school communities.

Becoming Mindful

Jeffrey Timberlake

The freedom to teach creates trust and moves ideas forward. A top-down model of leadership can be stifling and sever the lines of communication. In 2008, I joined the Mindful Teacher Project (MTP) developed by Boston College Professor Dr. Dennis Shirley and BPS classroom teacher Elizabeth MacDonald. The MTP project brought teachers across the district to discuss challenges within our schools, across the district, and within the country. For 3 years, the MTP nurtured
my teaching mind and heart as I struggled in a school that placed more value on MCAS scores than it did on the social and emotional learning of its students. I distinctly remember describing my participation with the MTP to an administrator at my previous school, who barked that I could continue, "As long as it does not interfere with your commitment to our schoolwide goals." From the important work of BPS teachers and the leadership of Dr. Shirley and Ms. McDonald, *The Mindful Teacher* (2009) was published. One day, I was flipping through its dog-eared pages and thought: "Why don't I bring this text to a Faculty Team Meeting at the Union School?" I proposed the idea to teachers at our school and everyone agreed to read the book and have a book discussion with its authors at our school. I remember thinking, "They said yes. Teachers want to do this." Later a veteran teacher shared with me, "The only reason I agreed to read this book is because the suggestion came from you. I trust you." Over the past 2 years, this teacher and I had sometimes disagreed with one another, but our respect for each other remained constant due to

our school's 48-hour rule. This norm encourages staff to communicate with one another when interpersonal problems arise. The 48-hour rule has helped to create a school climate where it is okay to disagree. A teacher-led school brings together teacher leaders with strong opinions about best teaching strategies. Communities everywhere experience conflict. It is part of the growth process.

I became a "lead teacher" in the school. For me, this role was always much less about pursuing my own initiatives than about creating space for others to lead, building mutual support, and promoting solidarity. The grade 3/4/5 team is shaping this value of solidarity as the teachers move through the everyday situations within their collective classrooms.

Taryn Snyder, grade 3; Alice McCabe, grade 4; and Erica Welch, grade 5, speak of their 3/4/5 team as the "single most important factor" in sustaining their human and professional selves.

Creating Collaboration

Alice McCabe, Taryn Snyder, Erica Welch

Our team consists of three classroom teachers and includes the staff of the Learning Center: two interventionists, an ESL instructor, and our Literacy Collaborative coach. The team's work is essential for coordinated planning and learning but serves an arguably more important purpose in supporting us as professionals and as people. My team members are the first people I turn to for help in any situation and their advice is always spot-on. We are incredibly fortunate to share with each other a deep belief in the collaborative nature of teaching and an environment of trust that enables us to open our classrooms and our practices to each other without fear of judgment. This is essential for our own learning, but what we have learned after 2 years together is that it benefits students and families and the rest of the school community as well. We view our students collectively and they in turn know that they can come to any of us for help or support. As students transition to higher grades, they are joining familiar classrooms with teachers they know and trust.

In addition to our formal planning times, we talk about teaching and students informally throughout the day. It is not uncommon for us to reach out to one another in the evenings or on weekends to ask questions or offer support. When Taryn was teaching fractions in 3rd grade, Alice sat in on lessons and taught alongside her to help. Erica regularly stops into 4th grade to reinforce Alice's teaching and ensure that student learning is closely aligned to prepare them for 5th grade. Alice conferences with Erica about students in 5th grade, sharing background information and problem solving to support her former students as they continue to grow. A high level of trust is needed to engage in this level of collaboration, and we treasure the respectful and supportive relationships that allow it.

Perhaps the most precious aspect of a strong team is that we know one another as individuals and as teachers. We care for one another personally as well as professionally. Together, we constitute a shared repository of our hopes and dreams for our students and our school. When the challenges of the world threaten our hope and our vision, our team members remind us of the teachers we want to be. At the heart of all our work is a deep respect for our students and their families and a belief that all students can learn and grow at our school. Teachers can become disillusioned by the constant pressures of testing, crippling budget cuts, the challenges our students face in and out of school, and the relentless demands on our time from every direction. Despite our training, professional development, and pedagogy, the day-to-day demands of teaching can be crushing. Even the best-trained and most dedicated teachers will fail if they become isolated. A trusted team enables us to reflect honestly on our practice, to receive productive feedback, and to renew our efforts and our hopes every day.

For me, the most attractive feature of our school is this notion of the freedom to teach. It is this value that enables passionate teachers to develop unique approaches to our students. When we say that we teach young scholars, not a scripted curriculum, we mean that the careful assessments of student learning needs drive all instructional decisions. Within our Union School classrooms, differentiating instruction through the arts, the use of literature in guided reading groups, writing to learn, and other child-centered approaches create access for diverse learners.

Early on, we wanted to extend academic support services to scholars in need of targeted instruction before referring them to special education.

For this reason, I call the Lower School Learning Center the heart of our teaching and learning community for the lower school. Learning Center teachers include specialists in special education, a broad range of literacy interventions, mathematics, and ESL. Rather than remediation, Learning Center teachers use accelerated instruction to bridge learning gaps. This is key to the success of the Learning Center both with students and teachers.

Learning Center teachers service scholars through both push-in and pull-out approaches. This makes the relationship with the classroom teacher key to scholarly progress. In order to nurture the relationship between classroom and Learning Center teachers, we constantly have to fight the typical culture of the closed classroom door. Opening our doors to our colleagues is at times a vulnerable stance that rewards risk taking with professional growth. As a lead teacher, it is at the Lower School Learning Center that I found a home for my ongoing teaching practice.

Amanda Smallwood, Literacy Coach, reflects on the magic of open classroom doors.

Open Classrooms, Open Minds

Amanda Smallwood

Having the opportunity to share teacher knowledge and collaborate with others is what initially enticed me to apply for a position at the Boston Teachers' Union School. In my previous 9 years of teaching, I never had the opportunity to work in a school that actually created time for teachers to collaborate. I was intrigued by the vision of a school that was based on teachers working together.

I spent my first 2 years at the Union School as the 2nd-grade teacher. In my third year, I left the classroom as the primary teacher and began my "field year" as a Literacy Collaborative Coach. I was fortunate to be able to co-teach with our kindergarten teacher, Jerry Pisani. We quickly figured out that we had a similar vision around teaching. When kids have fun at school, they want to be there; when teachers know students well and incorporate their interests, strengths, and needs into the learning, kids excel. Jerry and I rapidly became a cohesive team.

When I reflect on that year and I think about why it was so successful, I realize that it was because of our collaboration and commitment to working together. Something important happened for me that year. It felt like a little bit of magic. We carved out the time to prepare things thoroughly. We dedicated ourselves to planning for the many differing needs in the classroom. We formed a strong and enthusiastic working relationship that was the undercurrent of everything that happened in the classroom. There were countless Google docs created. There were numerous late-night texts and early-morning phone calls about great books to add to text sets or a new approach or strategy for one of our students. Jerry and I dreamed, planned, and taught in the ways that we had always wanted to, and we left no stone unturned. We labored over the best mentor texts, the most unique approaches, and the coolest ways to display student work. We did it right. And we could, because we were working together. Collaborating. We divided up the work, valued each other's strengths and talents, and supported our own growth as teachers. These tremendous shifts in my practice would not have been possible had I remained isolated within the walls of my own classroom.

One of the challenges of being a lead teacher was protecting my teaching time from the demands of administrative responsibilities. The time I dedicated to teaching actually sustained my spirit as only relationships with children can. Because my work formed part of the Learning Center faculty, it was there that the decision to work with the more advanced readers took shape. While looking at the data on student needs, it seemed that we placed a big focus on children with gaps in their learning. Naturally this needed to be the case, particularly because we were free to service scholars with gaps without special education designation. But what about the most advanced readers? How would they have the opportunity to deepen their critical thinking as competent readers through the arts? These questions guided my teaching work at the Union School.

Laura Davila Lynch, the Union School art teacher, wrote an arts expansion grant for integrating the arts with content-area studies. The faculty named the grant CIMA: Curriculum & Interdisciplinary Mapping with the Arts. CIMA supported interdisciplinary curriculum maps for visual arts, music, and core subjects where Union School students demonstrate need for intervention and enrichment. Imagine my excitement with this arts integration project, as the arts are an integral part of my life as well as my teaching philosophy and methodology.

I designed two projects for 2nd- through 4th-graders that centered on accelerating learning strategies from my bilingual and sheltered English practice. The personal entry point is a key to inspire a sense of belonging in school. Reading and writing biography/autobiography foster a deep understanding of social studies concepts such as everyday people's relationship to history and the significance of family stories, beliefs, and values for the social, political, and economic conditions of a society—that is, that who we are and what we do shape history. The CIMA Biography and Portraiture study focused on the different patterns of life stories within a specific context or moment in history. This unit made connections between the deep comprehension of biography and portraiture art, an approach to biography that aims to enliven a more authentic sense of self and others. Together we read two biographies of history makers who lived during the same time in United States history: *Revolutionary Poet: A story about Phillis Wheatley* (Weidt, 1997) and *George Washington Spymaster* (Allen, 2007).

Although all scholars in my guided reading group had similar achievement levels, I wanted to ensure that they all had a common understanding of the art of portraiture. We carefully observed and critiqued portraits of Phillis Wheatley and George Washington. Scholars noted how portraits of Phillis usually included a quill pen, books, and the inquisitive look of a thinker. Portraits of George had him standing tall, dressed as a statesman or general, with details depicting his stature as a leader. As we read the biographies, scholar artists responded to the reading for that day with a detailed drawing they might want to include in a portrait of their chosen historical character.

At first the children seemed overjoyed not to have to write a response to the reading. Instead, a small drawing would capture their understanding of an important aspect of the personality demonstrated through the action in the biography. Conceptually, they struggled to make a connection between the idea and the representation of that idea in a small drawing. In other words, through a close reading of explicit text, scholars were challenged to make logical inferences through art while having to support their representations with specific evidence. The portraits and accompanying artist statements by Jakhari Freeman on Phyllis Wheatley and Morgan Stenvenson-Swadling on George Washington speak for themselves.

Portrait Artist Statement

Jakhari Freeman

Phillis Wheatley is like me because she likes to write. At first, I thought my artwork was terrible. But Ms. Davila kept on pushing me and pushing me and pushing me to success. In a couple of days, I really liked my artwork. Phillis Wheatley's words are like weapons making the world a better place.

A portrait response to the reading of *Revolutionary Poet: A Story About Phillis Wheatley*, written by Maryann Weidt and illustrated by Mary O'Keefe (January 1997, Creative Minds Biography).

Morgan Stevenson-Swadling

Notice the compass. Now think about George Washington and his traits. Bravery, guidance, and leadership may be some of the words that pop into your head, right? George is also a leader, and so is a compass. A compass symbolizes bravery and wilderness. Agent 711 was George's spy name. A spyglass deciphering a letter depicts the hard-working spies. So, look at my portrait and see George Washington in my eyes.

A portrait response to the reading of *George Washington Spymaster: How the American Outspied the British and Won the Revolutionary War,* written by Thomas B. Allen (2007, National Geographic Society).

A second unit involved poetry as biography. As a teacher of immigrant students, I found poetry to be a literary genre that offers a great deal of possibility in developing language. Poets are astute communicators who can compose meaning while painting a picture with words. Getting at the heart of a poem was the big challenge of the teaching design for the Poetry, Style, Language, and Meaning Unit. To understand a poem is to understand the poet. The idea here is that poetic themes spring from the poet's way of life. Again, I want to make the point with scholars that everyday life can be an inspiration for writing, learning, declaiming. Who you are matters. Your knowledge is valuable to the story, the poem, and for making the world.

Scholars reviewed a range of poets and selected one poet to get to know well just by reading poems, nothing else. Through clues from the subject matter of a series of poems, scholars were challenged to recognize aspects of the poet's life experiences. Once they chose a poet, scholars gathered the heart of meaning for each poem that spoke to them. Ambri Huston was taken by the work of Langston Hughes. Ambri read and reread poems from two collections of the poetry of Langston Hughes (1996; Roes, 2013) before she picked out her favorites. Ambri selected the "nut stanzas" from several poems, illustrated them, and created a PowerPoint presentation that included an original poem of her own. She created pencil drawings in response to the central idea she found. Finally, she wrote a poem that names what she learned about the poet from his poems. The resulting PowerPoint presentation was both captivating and revealing.

Drums
I dream of drums
And remember
Nights without stars in Africa
Remember, remember, remember!

Mother to Son
Well son, I'll tell you:
Life for me ain't been no crystal stair.
It had tacks in it
And splinters,
And boards torn up

And places with no carpet
   on the floor—Bare.

Genius Child

This is a song for the genius child.
Sing it softly, for the song is wild.
Sing it softly as ever you can—
Lest the song get out of hand.
This is a song for the genius child.
Sing it softly, for the song is wild.
Sing it softly as ever you can—
Lest the song get out of hand.

Hughes (1996)

The Poet Langston Hughes
By Ambri Hurston

The poet Langston Hughes
   remembers
When his mom used to say,
"Life is not no crystal stair."
The poet Langston talks
Like he was alive when black
And colored were slaves.
The poet Langston liked
When his aunt read him stories.
The poet Langston probably
Was a genius child
And people were jealous
Because he was smart.

REFLECTION ON THE IMPORTANCE OF THE FREEDOM TO TEACH *NOW*

The word *now* is in the front of my mind as I reflect on these lessons. The approaches I've discussed reference teacher knowledge, authentic literature, Common Core State Standards, and the thinking that students bring to school. This kind of teaching taps the learners' imagination, invites the discourse of everyday life, and implies thinking about shaping a better way of life. In both the biography and poetry units, students were challenged to build independence and raise questions for close reading through a unique artful interpretation. Jakhari exposes Phillis Wheatley's intellectualism through a thoughtful gaze at her desk adorned with the tools of a writer of her day. Morgan places tiny clues in the buttons of George Washington's coat to signify his undercover story as a spy. Ambri empathizes with Langston Hughes through her own challenges with family struggles and being "smart" in school. This personal reading approach of quality literature builds curiosity that transforms reading to children's play, a game that, instead of demanding a prescribed answer on a multiple-choice test, elevates children's thinking as a source of social conversation and status in the classroom. This playful thinking drew different kinds of responses from each scholar. In an environment where thinking is valued over reproducing the "correct" response, academic identities are nurtured and self-efficacy is built. For example, when Ambri designed a presentation to share with her classmates, comfort with talking about ideas enabled her to entertain questions and comments during her talk, all 21st-century skills named for college readiness in the Common Core Standards.

At the Union School, teachers make a deliberate decision to do away with segregated student groupings. The diversity of our student body generates a broad range of learning styles even within similar academic groupings. The makeup of my reading groups reflected this broader diversity of our school—mostly, students of color representing a broad range of socioeconomic backgrounds. In our guided reading group, each scholar's life experience becomes a resource in the search for unique answers of their own making. Although these ideas have always been part of my teaching practice, it wasn't until I worked at the Union School, where the freedom to teach is valued by teachers and families alike, that I was able to openly work with these ideas in my teaching. The freedom to teach expands opportunities for teachers as well as for our young scholars to grow and learn.

Although discussions on unifying our approaches and values to teaching children may pose threats to clarity, solidarity, and learning from within, it is the toxic climate of education reform that might ultimately bring our school down. In a climate where only test scores matter, annual budget cuts reduce our capacity to respond to the troubled students dumped on our doorstep, mid-year, and often without adequate information or support. It is precisely in these most difficult times that the mobilization of teachers, families, and the community to defend what my mentor and mother of my intellectual family, Eileen de los Reyes, would call our "pocket of hope" becomes most critical (de los Reyes & Gozemba, 2002).

The teachers' voices in this essay refer to the essential human element in the art of teaching children. Teachers talk about observation, mutual respect, collegial support, creating possibility for each child, opening the door of the classroom to families and peers, leadership that honors the work of teaching, and becoming leaders in shaping a school culture. Tapping into our passion for teaching and the knowledge and creativity that is enlivened in the teaching process is precisely why it is essential to teach *now*, despite the pervasive climate of teacher-bashing and anti-unionism, undeterred by the unthinking abuse of students through the overuse of standardized testing and destructive disciplinary policies. We must teach because we know that if a student has even just a single year with a caring, passionate teacher, motivation and engagement from this one year can sustain a career of learning. My passion for teaching is now, more than ever, stoked by the dogged efforts of valued colleagues who are also looking for "pockets of hope" in the often bleak and disheartening landscape of our public schools. It is this hope that drew my colleagues to the teacher-run school-making project.

Jerry Pisani, K2 teacher, captures the collective voice of teachers at the Union School.

Hope, Every Day

Jerry Pisani

When I came to the BTU Pilot School I found a space where I was honored and respected enough that my own growth was as important as my students' growth. We allowed space for teacher knowledge, but we also made space for teachers to learn from and with each other. It was the promise of working with a group who cared about personal growth for all stakeholders that was life-giving. We could each work with and learn  from colleagues, form partnerships with community organizations, get to know our scholars and their families, and share who we were and who we wanted to be as a teachers and, through all that, honor, value, encourage, and celebrate the sometimes messy uncharted trials of growing. I don't think that there is a more hopeful place to be in than one that holds untold potential. And that is where I was and where I hope to be and where I hope to bring my students every day.

TEACHING TO DEFINE IDENTITY

Part III includes four teachers who, although working in starkly different contexts, understand that teaching has helped define their professional and personal identities. In the first essay, sisters Jennifer Burgos-Carnes and Vanessa Burgos-Kelly recount their own struggles with identity as they were growing up, and they explain how these struggles helped them decide to become teachers so other children might not have to go through the same turmoil. Although they had different trajectories, their shared struggles are a poignant reminder that sometimes people become teachers to rectify mistakes made with them as children. Vanessa and Jennifer also provide us with an example of how a strong cultural identity can make the difference between hope and despair, both for themselves and for their students.

In Chapter 6, teacher Missy Urbaniak, by recounting the challenges and joys of working in a one-room schoolhouse on the prairie, provides a vivid picture of what it means to teach in a rural setting, from warding off rattlesnakes, to having children from several grades and the same family in the same classroom, to being the person responsible for everything that goes on in the school. Hers is a powerful example of a different way of teaching that—although not immune to some of the same pressures felt by teachers in bigger schools—nevertheless honors the values upon which U.S. public education was founded: family connections, individualization, and teaching the whole child. Part III concludes with Pamelyn Williams's essay on the divergent path that brought her to teaching, and the children who keep her there. Now firmly identified as a teacher, Pamelyn started her career in a very different profession. Luckily for the children she has taught since changing course, her story is about serendipitous choices and happy endings.

CHAPTER 5

Somos Maestras:
Our Journey to Self-Confidence,
Our Passion to Inspire Others—
Two Teachers Write About Identity, Advocacy, and Activism

Jennifer Burgos-Carnes and Vanessa Burgos-Kelly

"*Mis hijos, siempre sigan adelante,*" always go forward, our parents have always told us. Growing up as military brat daughters of a Puerto Rican father and a Dominican mother, it seemed like we were always on the move trying to figure out where forward was.

JENNIFER'S STORY

As the youngest of three, I always looked up to my big brother and sister for guidance. My brother was 13 years older than me and moved out when I was fairly young. My sister and I are about 3 years apart, which made it easy for us to grow up being very close to each other. I've always considered myself one of those people who tries to learn from others, so as I grew up, I often looked up to my siblings for support and encouragement.

When I think about how education has influenced me and why I wanted to become a teacher, I always look back to 2nd grade. Second grade was a very significant year in my life. This was my final year living in Germany as a child. I think that is the reason I remember it so vividly. It was in 2nd grade that I had a teacher whom I try to model myself after to this day. This teacher constantly reminded me of how special I was for being able to

fluently speak two languages. She was the teacher who
invited my mother into the classroom and allowed me
to translate for her as she shared with our class our
family traditions and celebrations such as Three Kings
Day. It was my 2nd-grade teacher who also put a map
up in the classroom and highlighted all the places that
were represented in our classroom and congratulated
me in front of the class for being bilingual. I remember
a lot about my 2nd-grade year because this was also the same year that my
sister began teaching me about the importance of being Latina. I used to
giggle when we'd be in the store and she'd stop me from getting the blonde
"All-American" Barbie and instead convince me to get Teresa, the brown
Barbie doll who looked more like me. It was these experiences that helped
me realize at a young age that you should be proud of your culture and want
to share your uniqueness with the world. That summer I was devastated
about our family having to move to South Carolina. I remember saying to
my parents, "South Carolina?! No one lives there!" Little did I realize how
much my life would change.

Third grade was another one of those years I remember a lot. I don't
think South Carolina was ready for an 8-year-old Latina going into 3rd
grade. School began to change for me at this point. I thought I was 100%
confident in my skin, but it was the move to South Carolina that made me
forget who I was and where I came from. I remember being asked, "What
color are you?" This is a question I never knew how to answer. I'd simply
reply by asking if they meant my actual skin color or where I was from.
I remember a group of girls arguing with me on the playground during
recess about how really I was African American like they were because being
from Puerto Rico meant that I was not White. I always knew I could speak
Spanish, and I knew I came from Puerto Rico, but I never felt that race was
the only thing that defined me. All these feelings and questions about who I
was or what I was were beginning to confuse me.

As I started moving through elementary school and into middle school,
things kept feeling more complicated. I had come from a place where cultural differences were accepted, to a place that seemed like race was the main
attraction. I began to question my culture and realized that a lot of things
during this time period seemed to be about Black and White. I wasn't sure
where I fit in. Because I never felt like I was ever truly being myself, there
was a period where I thought I needed to assimilate with one group of students, then I'd try another group of students. There wasn't anyone else like
me in my class. I don't even remember there being a Latino population in
my school.

Middle school didn't get any easier. As I struggled with my personal identity my sister was starting Latin dance clubs in high school and making a name for herself as a proud Latina. I felt like I wanted part of that action but wasn't quite sure where to begin. I went into U.S. history class in 8th grade when the teacher had us doing round-robin reading from our textbook. At this moment I began thinking to myself, "This is going to be my 'Latina breakout' moment." We were reading about Latin American countries. I was so excited because the paragraph was about Monterrey, Mexico. It was my turn to read and as I began, I came to a pause, took a breath, and in my Spanish accent I read "Monterrey, Mexico." Shortly thereafter, the teacher said, "Excuse me?" I repeated again in my Spanish accent "Monterrey, Mexico." At this point I was a bit unaware of why she said "excuse me" but then it became clear when the teacher corrected me and said "No, it's Mont-el-ray, Mexico" in a very southern American accent. This was the moment where my Latina bravery once again shut down. I found my chance to show my peers that I could speak *español*, and my teacher made it very clear that this was not acceptable in her classroom.

These types of experiences kept happening to me throughout middle and high school. I remember there was a student in my junior-year English class who said, "I heard you speaking Spanish the other day. Where are you from?" This was one of those moments where I felt pretty cool until he responded with, "Oh, did you have to swim here?"

As a child and through the end of my elementary and middle school years, I never felt comfortable in my own skin. I want to make it clear that not everyone in South Carolina has made me feel awkward in my identity, but I will say that it was being here that truly made me think about race and culture in ways I wasn't quite ready to see. I understand a lot of that comes with age as well, but I feel that much of my hurt came from teachers who did not create a learning environment suitable for all students in their classrooms. None of my feelings of confusion changed until I made it to college.

When I got to college, I had a professor who began to peel back my layers of hurt. It almost felt like she had known me my whole life and knew exactly what I was hiding. I'm not sure what she saw in me, or how she saw it, but from the moment I walked into her classroom, it felt like she did everything in her power to again ignite the passion I had for my culture. She pushed me out of my comfort zone and made me take chances I know I wouldn't have taken on my own. She constantly found opportunities for me to showcase my strengths, proving to me once again, just like my 2nd-grade teacher, that teachers can make a difference. It was in college that I finally felt I knew myself again. I was ready and proud of who I was and where I came from and I could openly express my love for my culture.

Why I Teach

I am never surprised by the responses I get when asked "So, what do you do?"
As soon as I answer that I am a 3rd-grade teacher the conversation always
ends in the same way. "I applaud you!" or "I don't know how you do it! I
couldn't do it." It amazes me that there are so many who are well aware of the
difficulties of being a classroom teacher, yet we live in a society where teachers
aren't as valued as I feel they should be. I agree 100% with the voices of those
who've asked me. Teaching is a challenging job. It is not easy by any means. The
moment you feel like things are finally falling into place something or someone
throws you a curve ball. Yet, even though I am sure there are many teachers who feel exhausted, or undervalued, stressed, underpaid, misrepresented, I
mean, the list can go on . . . there is still a fire, a passion, a desire in some of us
to keep going. To some of us it's what we believe we will achieve, the greater
good, the spark that hits that *one* student that keeps us wanting to keep going.

I've been teaching now for almost 4 years. Along with other "newbie"
teachers, I assumed that the longer one teaches the more natural it will feel
and the easier it gets. Over and over we prove ourselves wrong. It almost
seems like the longer you teach the more you realize how difficult the task
really is. You've got people pulling you in all kinds of directions. It's not only
about your vision and what you feel you can do for your students. There are
the lawmakers, the district, the administration, your colleagues, your grade-
level teams, and the parents. The interesting thing is that at the end of the
day we all want the same thing. We all want what's best for our students.
What makes it difficult is the vision. How do we all go about accomplishing
the same goal when we are all trying to reach it in different ways? How does
that happen? How can we all want the same things yet at times it seems like
we are pulling apart what everyone has worked so hard for? One year we
have this program that research says will produce these results, the next year
it's another program, and another, and then finally we strip all three programs for a new one that will do something that no one really understands
yet. Then we design this test that will prepare them for that test, which will
show how they will perform on the end-of-year state standardized test. And
while you prep them for these tests, don't forget to teach the state standards,
but also teach the Common Core Standards because soon those will become
our state standards, but wait . . . they may not be implemented by our state
due to funding, but let's go ahead and go in full force and later if we need to
go back to state standards we can, but we'll be ahead of the other districts
because we went ahead and started the implementation. Confusing, right?
Exactly! Teaching is like a football game. You've got to keep up with the

game, make the right plays, and know that you are doing it all for the trophy at the end.

Honestly, I can go into detail about all the stresses that go into teaching. I can talk about how we are supposed to start our school day at 7:50 and dismiss students by 2:20—which everyone feels makes teachers so lucky. But then I would also have to tell you that we often have teachers who pull into the parking lot well before 7:00 in the morning. We have some teachers who don't leave the parking lot until after 8:00 in the evening. I could tell you about how if a teacher leaves school before 5:00 it is often with a bag of "goodies"—also known as lesson plans, papers to grade, letters to write, projects to work on, and so on. One might remind us that we have summers off and winter break. Well, let me remind them that we also have something called recertification, professional development, graduate school, and many other teacher trainings that occur over the summer.

Although it may seem as if I am going on a rant about the challenges teachers face . . . let me explain that although I am sharing all the things we are responsible for, it is only to inform, not to complain. As inservice teachers, we quickly become well aware of what is ahead of us. We go through experiences following master teachers that open our eyes to things we did not prepare ourselves for freshman and sophomore year of college. Somehow, "we teachers" . . . we look past all of that.

There is something amazing that occurs deep within your bones when you get back from winter break and begin working with your students again. All of a sudden it seems like everything you worked so hard for during those first 4 months of school has come to light. The beginning of the year can be scary. You leave the end of the previous year with 3rd-graders who are ready for 4th grade and begin all over again with 3rd-graders who just left 2nd grade. That may not seem like a difference, but boy, is it a difference! You work long hours planning and prepping to get them ready for 4th grade. There are moments when you feel like you've tried everything and you're just not sure that it's working. Right when you feel like you want to give up, it's time for winter break. You take your break, refresh your mind, plan ways to boost up for the new year . . . then you walk into the classroom to greet your students and it's a sudden rush. Everything you worked so hard for in the beginning, it finally clicked. It's like the students took that time off and their brains clicked in all the right places. I call it the "Rubix Cube Effect"—everything just clicked into place. This is the reason I teach.

Sometimes I can't sleep at night in excitement of what I am going to work on with my students the next time. I wake up sometimes to write down ideas that spark my mind mid-snore. I know that all I do, stressed out or not, will pay off. It's for moments when students say "Man! I wish it weren't Friday!" or "I wish I could spend the night at school!": Moments like this remind me why I do all that I can do be the best teacher. There is a desire inside of me to help these children see in themselves the things that they may not be able to see unless someone leads them in that direction. It is my ultimate desire to start the year with students who may not believe in themselves and see those students turn into individuals who are inspired to try new things and know they can accomplish anything they set their minds to through hard work and dedication.

I teach because I cannot think of anything more rewarding than to help nurture the mind of a child who may one day grow up to be the next Albert Einstein. And even on those days when I want to hang up my teacher bag and call it quits . . . all it takes is one look at our class picture to remind me of how remarkable each one of my students really is. It's because of these children that I continue to teach at a time where educational reform is at the forefront of politics nationwide. I've not been a teacher for that long, but I cannot wait for the day when I am casually walking and I hear my name and it's one of my former students. I cannot wait to hear of the amazing things that they've been able to accomplish in their lives. There are many different types of teachers. I've had them all—some you wish to forget, others you wish to find again. I hope to be the one who truly inspired. I continue teaching because I dream of that moment.

VANESSA'S STORY

My elementary years as the middle of three were scattered among various places around the world: Virginia, Panama, the Netherlands, and Germany. I finished my middle and high school years and am now settled with my family in South Carolina. My earliest memories of school were mostly of what must've been ESL class because I remember being pulled out of my class to practice my days of the week and months with an Asian girl who barely spoke English.

As a child and until college, I always felt unique. My uniqueness seemed like an asset when my 3rd-grade teacher let me share an oral report on Puerto Rico. When we read stories that had Spanish words, she would ask me how to pronounce them phonetically. When we would go back to visit family in Puerto Rico and the Dominican Republic, I was an American who spoke English, ate hamburgers with fries, and listened to hip-hop.

I would come back to the States with a renewed awareness of my *Latinoness*. I felt important because I translated for my mom when my father was on his military tours during Desert Storm and Operation Just Cause. Even though my mother spoke little English and my father wasn't home much due to army assignments, they both made it clear that the expectation is that we would go to college.

The novelty of living dual cultures started to wear off during adolescence, beginning with a 5th-grade teacher who ran short on patience when I didn't understand how to multiply fractions. She snapped, "I don't know what else you want me to do, do I need to say it in Spanish!?" That was the start of my indifference toward school.

We moved to South Carolina when I was in 7th grade. Right away the infamy of racial relations in the South showed when one of the movers made a comment about how many "n*****" were in the neighborhood" and how "he can't stand them"—the first time I heard the term used outside of fiction.

My first day at school, I didn't know where to sit at lunch. Walking into the cafeteria, I could clearly see how the students segregated themselves. A classmate asked "What are you?" I responded "a girl," confused as to why she didn't notice that right away. "I mean, are you White or Black or mixed?" she clarified. I let her know my dad is Puerto Rican and my mom is Dominican. When she asked me if Dominican was a part of Mexico, I knew the next couple of years were going to have many instances of clearly classifying myself as Latina for others who wondered if I was Asian or biracial at first glance.

After moving to different middle schools and then into freshman year of high school, I found myself gravitating toward anyone else who was Latino. I didn't have to explain to them that I wasn't Mexican or where my accent was from. The area where my parents settled was rapidly developing and the Hispanic population was beginning to grow. The questions changed from "What are you?" to "Why are you here?"

I had a group of girlfriends who were either Puerto Rican or Mexican and we started a Latin Dance club at our school along with other students who were taking Spanish class. My Spanish teacher encouraged us, which gave me a reason to at least show up to the second half of the school day. At this point, I had explained so many times what I was that I was fixated with showcasing my culture in as many ways as possible. When some peers stopped my friends and me walking in the school hallways to scold us to "Stop speaking Spanish; you are in America and English is our language," my obsession with spreading Latino culture grew. I would draw my flags everywhere and buy anything that had my flags on them. I was told by school officials to abstain from wearing the flags during my high school graduation because that year there was the controversy of the Confederate flag hanging at the State House and they thought it might "offend" people to see any flags except the U.S. flag.

In my senior year, even after I shared that I was interested in law, the guidance counselor suggested I start speaking to army recruiters to prepare for life after graduation. The expectation of continuing my education was not reflected in my school despite the fact that I had taken Advanced Placement classes that gave me college credit before graduation. High school left me with the impression that schools are factories whose job it is to maintain the status quo.

College was not in my plans right after high school. At one point I worked three jobs at once, including at an after-school center. I decided to go back to school to become a teacher because working all day and night and still struggling was not appealing. Working with kids felt right. Once I made it into the education program at the university, I realized that again I had to go through the explanations of being Latina. By the internship year, I was the only non-White preservice teacher in my cohort. Whenever they needed a "diverse" perspective or quota met, I felt like I was the token Brown girl.

Some professors at the university would teach cultural awareness only to be followed by my White classmates' grumbles after class about how they felt the lectures were blaming them for the achievement gap. My smiles and nods suppressed my disappointment that these future educators, undeterred by the attempts of some professors to provide background about how our educational system continues to fail some students, don't understand that it's not about who's to blame, but how we can fix it.

Why I Teach

My first year in the classroom was eye opening. I dove into teaching wanting to create an environment where all students learn from one another, where they ask questions and express ideas in a variety of ways. By grace I was given my most desired position: being a social studies and language arts teacher. The class consisted of 16 5th-graders of culturally diverse backgrounds. I was excited to work with a school population that was about a third Latino as a result of South Carolina being the state with the second-fastest-growing Hispanic population between 2000–2011 (see www.pewhispanic.org/2013/08/29/mapping-the-latino-population-by-state-county-and-city). The school was adapting to recent changes in demographics, culturally and socioeconomically. The staff was mostly made up of newly hired induction and young veteran teachers. I was zealous in trying to integrate U.S. history and English language arts, collaborating with the other teachers and maximizing my ability to communicate with Latino parents at the school.

At the end of that year I still felt passionate about being in the classroom in spite of how much the focus on standardized test scores was increasingly becoming a measure for instructional effectiveness. Teaching standards and curriculum programs were evolving faster than my ability to master content. The second year I was pregnant and went down to 4th grade. Trying to figure out how to be a mother put the classroom down on the priority list. I found myself intensifying the time spent on testing strategies and passing out more multiple-choice assessments. At the same time, the passion for the classroom was beginning to fade.

My fourth year I changed schools and went from being the other half of 5th grade as the social studies/language arts teacher to working in a team of six. This new school had different demographics and a mostly repositioned staff. The school had a significantly smaller Latino population, so what I saw as my unique asset was becoming less relevant. The vigor of data increased as testing consumed more classroom time. The classroom environment was tense and the students were more aggressive. That was the year I truly questioned, "Why do I teach?" I am sure it is not for a passion to pass out #2 pencils and walk circles around students filling in bubbles. I realize that tests are needed for accountability and standardized government testing is continuing through Smarter Balanced (see www.smarterbalanced.org). Testing is a requirement in most classrooms. However, the learning to pass any "test" relies on experiences upon which students can draw but experiencing a lot of "tests" results in less time having real experiences. When I think back on the moments when I really enjoyed school, I realize it was when instruction was an adventure. I remember when my 6th-grade teachers created an ancient Egyptian environment with period costumes while students shared their projects, and an audio-visual class that let the students create music videos.

I redirected my efforts into creating relevant experiences more often while still being aware of the appropriate tests. When the students create and share, they apply their learning in an environment where they feel valued. There's satisfaction in hearing kids share that they really enjoyed a unit of study versus mumbles when there is another silent testing session. Being allowed to create projects through a variety of publication formats and seeing the spark in students' eyes when they share their hard work is more gratifying than showing them a number on a table and labeling them "on grade level." It's rewarding to be reminded that the memories that were created are strong enough to trigger random contacts from former students. The passion for teaching rekindles.

Toward the end of my secondary education I had many experiences in the classroom when I felt like I was just taking up space until the next period, but I also had teachers who created unforgettable learning experiences. A student's potential can be weakened or enhanced by classroom experiences. I became a teacher because I wanted to impact the lives of students who may feel, as I did, that school is an uninspiring place. I wanted to become a positive role model for Latino students who may rarely see a Latino in an educational role. My focus on serving in a classroom with a large Latino population shifted after moving to a school where there isn't one. I grew to realize that all students should have more positive role models in their lives.

Even though for a while I started seeing the students as test scores and viewed my position as a certified testing supervisor, after reflecting on answering the question "Why do I teach?," I am reaffirmed that I teach so that all the students who come into my classroom are exposed to authentic learning experiences that help them realize the value of exploring, asking questions, and having the confidence to share their ideas because they start to see the value of collaboration, regardless of differences.

AS TEACHERS TODAY

It's because of our experiences and the consistent encouragement from our parents that we decided that being educators is the path we needed to take. We became the first in our family to finish college. Our parents continue to have high expectations and encourage us to strive for excellence throughout our careers. After years of reflection, we realize the power a teacher has. A teacher can break you, or a teacher can help you realize your potential.

In spite of the fact that today's educational climate is tense due to high-stakes testing and changing expectations for the classroom, an effective teacher is invaluable. Modeling tolerance and high expectations is vital in order to have a positive classroom environment. The classroom may be one of the few places our students are exposed to rich, positive learning experiences and are encouraged to persevere regardless of the obstacles outside their immediate control.

We teach because we hope that when our students are asked, "What are you?" they all are aware, no matter where they came from, that "We are lifelong learners."

CHAPTER 6

Snowdrifts, Rattlesnakes, and the Children I Love

The Life of a Rural Teacher on the Prairie

Missy M. Urbaniak

7:00 A.M., DARK AND DRIVING

Just before 7:00 A.M. my 7-year-old son and I climb into the car and head off on our morning commute: 25 miles of winding, hilly, mostly gravel roads that, on a normal day, take at least 30 minutes to navigate. Today, snow covers the ground and the sky is still dark and I know it will take more time. A few miles from home I realize that the snow is deeper than I first  thought and the overnight winds had blown it into icy drifts. Turning back for the four-wheel-drive pickup would mean being late, and, anyway, I have my cell phone, so we continue on. Most mornings my son and I talk about what the day will bring, discuss books, or practice spelling words, but today with each passing mile, I find myself becoming more and more focused on the road and not feeling quite so chatty. I light-heartedly whisper a few prayers to keep us going down the road.

I know that the first 7 miles of road heading south will be mostly blown clear of snow and drifts. It's those next 4 miles after the turn west and then back south again that are always more difficult, mostly because of the small, clustered hills that catch the snow. Also because it is not a mail route, it is narrower than the other gravel roads I drive on, and it is also the last road plowed by the county road grader. By the time we reach those 4 up-and-down miles, the sky is beginning to lighten, and I can see the unplowed drifts I will face. I can also see headlights in the distance, and I know instantly that it is Mrs. Baker on her morning commute as well. She faces a 50-mile commute each day, mostly paved highway, but nevertheless treacherous on a day like today when those 50 miles are deserted and covered with drifts.

It is then I see what is between our two vehicles: a massive drift. It is definitely wider and probably deeper than any other I have driven through this chilly morning. In a matter of seconds several thoughts flash through my mind. First, this drift is potentially higher than the clearance of my Ford Taurus, which means the car could easily become high-centered, that is, the front wheels might make it over a hump of snow or dirt but the back wheels might not. The result is that the center of the vehicle would be resting on the snow so that the tires spin, but the vehicle could not move. It is difficult to tell just how deep the snow is in the dim light. The wind is from the west, so the drift is higher on my side of the road than it is on the other side. I would fare better to drive more in the center of the road rather than staying in my lane. But Mrs. Baker is coming! Too late—I'm already past the point of stopping, and if I stop, there is nowhere else to go.

I am reminded of the childhood song "We're Going on a Bear Hunt" that I sing with my students, and the chants of, "We can't go *over* it, we can't go *under* it, we have to go *through* it!" Yup, there is no way around it, I have to go THROUGH this drift, and I had better do it quickly because I don't want to risk a collision with Mrs. Baker. At least, I tell myself, if I don't make it through, someone is here to help; also, she is in a four-wheel drive vehicle. I grip the steering wheel, aim the car for the center of road, tell my son to "Hang on!" and punch the gas. We sail through the first few feet of the drift, snow flying up from both sides, blocking my view out of the side windows. The noise in the car is deafening as the underside scrapes along the hardened snowdrift. I continue to hold the gas pedal down; if I let up, we're stuck for sure. Slowing slightly, and fish-tailing a little, our car manages to burst through to the other side of the drift. Mrs. Baker has slowed to nearly a stop on a clear patch of road, no doubt watching me. I fly by her, remove my white-knuckled hand from the steering wheel just long enough for a quick wave (it would be poor manners not to wave—one always waves on a country road), breathe a sigh of relief, and continue, too afraid that if I slow down I'll never get going again. Plus, now that I have cleared the way, she can drive in my tracks and make it through the drifts. "You're welcome, Mrs. Baker," I chuckle to myself.

As my commute continues, I cross one paved highway for a brief moment and then drive for another 8 or so miles of snow- and drift-covered gravel road, although none of these drifts is like what I encountered earlier. Then I reach the only 3-mile stretch of paved road, just enough smooth pavement to mock me each day, and, finally, I turn onto the last mile of gravel. I have reached my destination: a one-room schoolhouse, covered by drifts, with doorways that must be shoveled clear before the students arrive. My son and I stomp through the drifts to reach the door, retrieve the shovel, and begin scooping. It is fully light now and students will arrive soon. Once inside, the phone rings,

"Good Morning! Hereford School, this is Mrs. Urbaniak. How may I help you?"

"Oh, Missy, I'm so glad to hear your voice! I just wanted to be sure you made it to school all right." Mrs. Baker chimes. "My husband drove me to school today."

I blush, embarrassed that there was an audience to my erratic driving.

"He thinks you're some kind of Nascar driver!" she comments.

"Well, I had to get to school," I thought, "after all, I'm the only teacher for these nine students."

A SMALL ONE-ROOM SCHOOLHOUSE IN A VERY LARGE DISTRICT

For the past 5 years, I have been a rural teacher for the Meade 46-1 School District in western South Dakota. Our district encompasses a startlingly large geographic area: approximately 3,100 square miles of hills and prairies, it is the largest school district in our state. Our K–12 enrollment is 2,583 students, most of whom attend school in Sturgis, Piedmont, or Whitewood. But, there are also six rural school sites east of Sturgis that accommodate approximately 90 students. The district and administrative buildings are based in Sturgis, 50 miles from my school. It is 100 miles from Opal School, the most isolated of the rural schools. The principal for the rural schools is also the principal of the Whitewood School, where her office is located another 10 miles to the northwest of Sturgis.

For the first 3 years of my tenure as a country teacher, I taught at the Hereford School. During that time I had 8, then 10, and then 9 students. I'll never forget walking around while my students worked at their desks that first day. "It's so quiet!" I kept thinking. I was used to teaching a full, bustling room of 22 to 28 5th- or 6th-graders, as I had for the previous 5 years in Sturgis. Now, I had one 7th-grader, two 3rd-graders, and four kindergarten students; one of whom was my own son. I also had the luxury of a full-time paraprofessional, thankfully one who was more experienced in this setting than I was. She would become my saving grace over the next 3 years. And those eight students who were so quiet on the first day? They soon showed me that a few country kids can be even louder than a classroom full of town kids!

For the first year, my husband, three boys, and I lived in the Hereford teacherage, a single-wide, two-bedroom trailer house provided by the district for the teacher to live in so that he or she could be near the school. So, for that first year I could just step out my door, and I was in the schoolyard and in a few short steps I was at the schoolhouse door. Just a few weeks into my second year of teaching at Hereford, my family and I moved 25 miles away to my husband's family's ranch near Fairpoint, South Dakota. For 2 years, I drove that winding, windy, gravely commute with my son each day. I frequently met Mrs. Baker heading to the Atall School from her home in Sturgis. She has since retired, and I have taken her place at Atall, which is just a blessed 5 minutes from my home. I am now beginning my third year as the teacher of the Atall School.

No one is sure of the origins of the name Atall. Most likely it was named by or for a homesteader in the area. The school sits in a pasture belonging to one of the families whose children attend our school. When looking out the windows, only open prairie can be seen, and only a few buildings are visible on the horizon. Most of the windows and the front door face east, two windows face south. The building itself has a small entryway with hooks for coats and backpacks, and two classrooms with a hallway and restrooms between them. The schoolyard boasts two small cottonwood trees, a basketball court, and an old metal playground set complete with a swing-set, slide, teeter-totter, and merry-go-round. Until just this summer, the old one-room schoolhouse also sat in the yard. Recently used for storage, several of the students' parents and grandparents attended school in that building. The previous two schoolhouses before that one also remain in the area, now privately owned by neighbors and used as storage. We are also fortunate to have a full basement. This proves helpful in cold or rainy weather when recess outside is not ideal. It is also reassuring in case of tornadoes or strong thunderstorms.

A few times a year, herds of cows are moved down the gravel road in front of the school. Riders on horseback and four-wheelers push the cows and calves along the road between the fences and right past the school, heading for the corrals down the road where the cowboys will work the cattle. If it happens to be recess time, we call the students inside so that the cattle will not be spooked by the noises of the children, and if a cow were to wander into the schoolyard, none of the children would be in any danger. All of the students are growing up on ranches, the great-great grandchildren and in some cases the great-great-great grandchildren of settlers who homesteaded the rolling plains of western South Dakota. They are used to cattle drives and horses and being around cattle.

Bulls or a herd of cows often graze in the schoolhouse pasture just on the other side of a barbed-wire fence that is the boundary between our schoolyard and the pasture ground. Some mornings, I pull into the yard to find that a calf has rolled under the wire and is now grazing near the slide or the swings. This is not a cause for concern, because the family will soon be bringing their twin daughters to school through that same pasture. It is shorter for them to come that way than to drive around on the gravel road. The girls are accustomed to bouncing across the pasture as they ride to school on a four-wheeler or in a tractor. Whoever is delivering them will chase any stray calves back under the fence or through the nearby gate if necessary. Most days, the cattle start to drift away as the students begin to arrive. Skittish white-tail deer and cottontail rabbits frequently nibble on the grasses in the schoolyard, but they, too, quickly depart as cars and pick-ups drop off students for the day.

Rattlesnakes are not so accommodating, and one morning, there was one under the steps as I hauled my supplies into the school. I was alone, and it was not a school day, but I did have to make several trips into the school and back to bring in supplies from my car. Luckily, the wooden steps only have small slits between the boards, so the snake could not bite me through the slits. I went about my business, ignoring the angry rattling and hissing that were set loose each time I stepped on a board. It is almost unforgivable to live on the prairie, come across a rattlesnake, and not proceed to kill it. So, I was honestly a little grateful that because of the shadows, I couldn't quite see the snake, didn't have a clear shot at the snake nor a weapon, and was therefore absolved from having to kill it.

Porcupines are also fond of the space under our steps at the Atall School, and my son and I were greeted by a rather fat one on a calm morning last fall. I was hesitant to try to shoo him away from the step, so, once again thankful that the slits between the boards were small, we just went ahead and went inside. I met each student at the base of the steps that day and let them know the situation and then quickly ushered them into the school. Eventually, while we watched through the window, one of the dads chased the porcupine away after dropping off his daughters.

TEACHERS WHO TRAVEL

As with any teaching position, my job has advantages and disadvantages, not to mention the gray areas, those "sometimes-this-is-a-good-thing-but-sometimes-this-is-a-bad-thing" areas. For instance, most days, the only adults I see at work are the paraprofessional (no idea what I would do without her!) and the "traveling teachers." These teachers are the music, computer, speech, and special education teachers who travel from rural site to rural site. We also have a counselor and librarian who travel and make occasional stops at our schools. There is no on-site administrator, administrative assistant, school nurse, resource officer, guidance counselor, librarian, special education director, curriculum director, playground supervisor, food service worker, or maintenance department worker. We have access to most of these individuals largely through email, but they are 50 miles away from my school and even further away from the other rural sites. So, on one hand, one could say I am spared from well-meaning, but sometimes distracting interactions with these professionals. But, the flip side is that I end up taking on the roles of these individuals in their absence.

For instance, if someone calls the school, the phone rings right in my classroom, right in the middle of our lesson or whatever we are working on. Usually, this is an important call from another rural site, our principal, or another school official. But, at least once a week, and sometimes as often as three or four times a day, we get a phone call that goes like this:

"Good Morning! Atall School, this is Mrs. Urbaniak. How may I help you?"

"Yes, may I speak to Mrs. Rosenboom?"

"I'm sorry, she isn't here right now, her office is in another building."

(I usually just leave out the part about that building being 60 miles away.)

"Oh that's all right. May I speak to someone who is in charge of ordering at your school?"

or

"May I speak to your library media specialist?"

or

"May I speak to someone in your physical education department?"

or

"May I speak to someone in your technology department?"

or

"May I speak to someone in your maintenance department?"

I am always left wondering, should I just say, "Yup, that's me! I do it all!"?

Sometimes, I do try to explain the situation.

"I am the only teacher here. This is a one-room school with only eight students."

However, this response usually leads to silence on the other end of the line, most likely as they contemplate whether I am I simply lying, playing a joke, or if they have somehow accidently reached a school in the center of some strange cult. This silence is usually followed by more questions that just end up wasting more of my precious classroom time. I have had some people who simply couldn't understand what I was saying and continued to ask for someone else as if they could not believe that I really was the only teacher in the building with one aide and eight students. I try not to be rude by laughing. I try not to get upset. But, the fact is that just a few seconds ago I was in the middle of an important lesson, and now my students are instead watching me talk on the phone to someone in Alabama or New York or Texas who is also just trying to do his or her job. Nonetheless, all concentration—mine and the students'—is lost.

Some may not find our school setting or its isolation ideal. Working in this setting does have its advantages. I feel I am allowed to teach more authentically. I have more autonomy in my classroom due to necessity. Curricula are not generally written with my setting in mind. Therefore, I have the freedom to adapt and I have to be allowed to make adjustments in order to make the material and the methods fit the child or children I am working with. I am of course not entirely free from restrictions such as standards and standardized testing. I do my best to use these as guidelines, and to not let them dictate the day-to-day routine of our classroom.

Being in a unique situation also provides a unique resource: the students themselves. I have right there in the same room a mixture of ages that begs to be taken advantage of. Younger ones can't help but be excited about what they will learn in the future as they watch the older ones. Older students are given the opportunity to set good examples, be strong role models, and look after the younger ones. Teaching a younger student is the ultimate learning experience for a student in 7th or 8th grade. And, oh how those kindergarteners and 1st-graders shine when it is their turn to show the big kids something! There is power in students helping and teaching each other.

There are also disadvantages. For instance, I am concerned about mandates that stipulate exactly what children should learn and at what exact grade level they should learn it. Mostly this worries me for the students who are in a grade by themselves. I will have three such students this year. Learning is social; it requires communication and conversation. It is becoming more and more difficult to provide that in my setting when I am required to teach students in one grade a certain skill, but not the same skill as the other students in the room. I have been fortunate that either my students who are in a grade by themselves at least have one other student who is in a grade above or below them. Only once have I had a student who was completely isolated: she was a 7th-grader whose nearest classmates were two 3rd-graders. Fortunately, she was a strong student and had not been isolated in this way for her entire elementary education.

Another area in which I feel the downfall of our isolation is in the lack of contact with my fellow rural teachers. Being the only teacher in the building means I do not have another classroom teacher to "bounce ideas off," consult about planning, or share other concerns. The other rural teachers and I have only two staff meetings a year with our principal, and this time is mostly dedicated to scheduling events that involve all the rural schools. We also have seven professional development days, but these are usually governed by the district, and we are assigned workshops in which to participate in or meetings to attend. Time to plan and share and discuss with these ladies who share this unique teaching assignment is virtually nonexistent. When the traveling teachers come to teach music or computer, they take groups of students, not the entire school. This time is helpful to me because then I can focus on the younger or older group, depending on which group is away having another class. However, this means I am rarely afforded any time without students in which to plan lessons or record grades.

I cherish the relationships I have with the paraprofessional whom I see and work with daily, and with the traveling teachers who visit weekly. I regard their opinions highly because they know the ins and outs of rural teaching and their weekly visits are the only constant source of camaraderie I enjoy. I have hopes that the increasing use of technology will alleviate this isolation. Unfortunately, the main issue standing in the way is time.

MANY TASKS, MANY TOOLS

I have become used to the all-encompassing role of a rural schoolteacher, and, for the most part, I am comfortable with it. I heat the students' lunches in a microwave while the paraprofessional monitors recess time. The students eat at their desks while the paraprofessional and I eat at a classroom table and assist them with all the opening up and cleaning up that goes along with young children eating lunch. I make sure they eat all or most of what mom and dad have packed for them. Hmm, lunch break, what's that?

I arrive at school early on snowy days so I can have the sidewalk and steps shoveled before the students arrive, and I chuckle (and, I will admit, sometimes curse) at the thought that technically this is considered my "planning time." I keep a first-aid kit near the door and have used it often. I keep a hammer, screwdriver, and staple gun in my desk drawer and I use them often, too. I keep my cell phone in my pocket when we are all outside; most days I have cell phone reception at the school.

I have also become accustomed to what it means to teach in a little-school-house-on-the-prairie-type of situation. We have accidentally run out of propane to run our furnace, so the students wore their coats in the classroom while we waited for the truck to arrive. Just as I keep a winter-survival kit in my car, I keep one in the school. It contains nonperishable food, candles, flashlights, and blankets in case we are ever stranded at the school without power during a winter blizzard. We have frequently lost electricity due to a wind storm. During my first year at Atall, we had no power the morning of the Christmas party. School was to be dismissed at noon, but with no power, we had no lights, no heat, and no pump for the running water. So, we had our party a little early, in the dark, with no festive holiday music that I had planned to play on the CD player, and no one could use the restroom because we couldn't flush the toilets or wash our hands. It was a smash!

THE FIELD TRIP DESTINATION

In May this year, a school bus of about 40 4th-grade students from an elementary school in Rapid City (about 75 miles away) came out for a field trip. They stopped only briefly at our school before continuing on to visit our neighbor to learn a little bit about cattle, sheep, roping, and life on a ranch. I spoke to the group for a few minutes and tried to explain what it is like to have school in the country. My students also shared their thoughts, and I saw a lot of nods and smiles around the room. I was just thinking, "Wow, this is great, I think these students are starting to understand." Suddenly one girl from Rapid City raised her hand and after I called on her, she asked, very seriously, "Do you guys ever go to restaurants?" Hmm, maybe they don't understand. My students assured her that, yes, we go to restaurants and that one of their mothers even works at a nearby small restaurant in Union Center. We also mentioned that even though it is 75 miles away, we go to Rapid City often for groceries, clothing, parts, and other items.

Sometimes, I really do forget just how different we are from schools in cities and towns. I was reminded when one student from Rapid City asked, "Where are all the desks? Where are all the other kids?" We explained that this was it, there were only seven kids who lived close enough to go to school here. We explained that for most of us, our nearest neighbor was a half mile away, and that we don't talk in terms of blocks and streets out here, we use miles and gravel roads. Most of us cannot see any other houses around when we look out of our windows at home. There are places on our ranches where you can't see any sign of humans: no houses, no roads, not even power lines, and maybe just one fence and that is all, as far as you can see. I think, maybe by the end of the day, the students from Rapid City were beginning to get an idea of what life is like in the country. I learned later that as the bus was pulling away from the nearby ranch one of the boys asked, "Is this where they filmed *The Walking Dead*?"

YES, ALL GRADES K-8

The question I most often get when someone realizes I am a rural school teacher with students in grades kindergarten through 8th grade all in the same classroom is, "How do you do it?!" I have to give the students a lot of the credit. For one, they don't know any differently. Being in the same room with brothers and sisters and kids who are five grade levels ahead of them is just part of their normal day. Never having attended rural schools as a child myself, and coming from 5 years of teaching in town, I am the one who had to get used to it.

Mostly I had to get used to adapting the lessons. I was used to teaching only reading and spelling. Now I had to teach all subjects. I leaned heavily on ready-made resources I would normally have tried to avoid. One of the first lessons in the math textbook for 3rd grade was on estimation. The textbook asked students to estimate—a very necessary, valuable skill. But as I looked deeper I realized the basis of the lesson was on the following questions posed to the students: About how many students are in your class? About how many students are in your grade? About how many students are in your school? Hmm, when the answers to those questions are supposed to be roughly 25, 100, and 500, but for your school they are in fact 1, 1, and 10, it's kind of hard to make the lesson meaningful. Needless to say, textbook companies do not have rural schools in mind when they create their lessons. I was on my own.

The question of how to plan lessons for reading, writing, math, social studies, and science for five or six grade levels spanning K–8th grade while meeting standards each day requires flexibility and creativity on my part—especially because the schedule also includes all of those things that most other classroom schedules include: recess, lunch, music class, computer class, and library time. I will readily admit that there are days when all of this means that the best I can do is tell the students to turn the page and work on the next lesson in the textbook. Those are my worst days, and I try to keep them to a minimum, but they are a reality. On my best days, we are fully engaged in a multidisciplinary study of volcanoes or chocolate or Fort Meade or Dr. Seuss or Cinco de Mayo—all students working on the same topic, but at their own level and in their own way. But, these days require tons of front-loading: me spending lots of time before the lesson trying to match standards from different grade levels to activities that are appropriate for an age span of 5- to 13-year-olds and still engage my students in their learning. So much work, but so worth the extra effort. The students love these days, and I do too.

WHY I TEACH NOW

I was fortunate to grow up with, and to have wonderful memories of, two great-grandmothers who were one-room schoolhouse teachers in the same county in which I now teach. I am fascinated by the era in which they taught. Both women were always spoken of highly and I remember both of them as kind and caring. A cousin of mine, the grandson and student of one of these women, often speaks of how she made her students feel respected. It seems like a small thing, but I have learned that having and showing respect for the students is vital and not always easy. I have never forgotten this simple lesson from my family history of teaching on the prairie.

Looking to the future, I see a year full of changes. This year promises to be my most challenging yet. I will have 10 students, up from just 7 last year. They are in six different grade levels, and three of them have individualized education programs (IEPs) and receive special education services. This will be the most grade levels I have taught at one time, and they will span kindergarten to 8th grade. Three of the students will be kindergarteners who will attend school all day, every day, a change the district made last year from half-time to full-time kindergarten. The twins will be in 3rd grade. There will be one 4th-grader and two 5th-graders, one of whom is my son. There will also be one 7th-grader and one 8th-grader. But these are not the only changes for me. The district is also implementing a new math curriculum this year, a purchased textbook series that all teachers are expected to follow. We are also fully implementing the Common Core State Standards in English language arts and math. The students will take a new online assessment aligned to these standards in the spring. This also means a new report card with new standards and a new system of grading. My head spins just thinking about the work to be done this year. Change is not always easy, but

I have high hopes that most of these changes will be positive ones. There will be bumps along the road, and maybe even a few more snowdrifts to burst through.

When I think about where I teach and why I teach, I see two of my great loves: the students and the land. I see silly smiles and frustrated frowns. I see joy as they discover something new. I see pride when they finally master a new much-anticipated skill or accomplish a long-held goal. I see how innocent and trusting they are, how pure, and honest, and good. Yes, our little school is isolated. Yes, my job is demanding. But there is nowhere I'd rather be. This little school on the prairie has given me a sense of place, of history, and a connection to something bigger than myself. Any contribution I make is just a drop in the bucket compared to what I have gained. I see these open prairies as an ideal place for children to grow and learn, an ideal setting for an education away from a complicated world. And I want to be a part of that.

I'm not completely comfortable with every situation or decision I must make as a rural teacher. I err on the side of caution in matters of safety and well-being. These students are my neighbors' children, most of them are 4H members in the club I belong to, I have taught some of them for 3 years now, and one of them is my own flesh and blood. I do not look at these children and think, "These are students." I look at them and think, "These are *my* children."

CHAPTER 7

Journey Down a Different Path

Pamelyn A. Williams

In July 2001, I moved to New York from Michigan. I left a position as a researcher with a regional marketing research firm. I had worked at that firm for almost 1½ years assisting clients in learning about their consumers and how to market to them by analyzing surveys and conducting focus groups. Following this career path was a by-product of a teenage dream I had to research how African American consumers shop and what marketers and advertisers need to do to attract them to purchase their brands. I pursued this interest by studying psychology in undergraduate school and consumer psychology in graduate school. I worked in advertising, banking, and marketing research. When I moved to New York City, I was intent on finding a job in one of these industries.

New York City is home to the top advertising and marketing firms in the world. I expected to easily secure a marketing research job in the Big Apple. I had interviewed with numerous companies, but to no avail. My aspirations to land a dream position in advertising or marketing were slowly dying. I was about 6 weeks into my job search, and my job prospects were still dismal. Job interviews were few and far between in the marketing and advertising fields. I was disappointed by the kinds of opportunities in my field and further discouraged with the "thanks, but no thanks" reply from interviewers. I was fortunate to secure temporary work conducting family interviews for a multi-state prekindergarten family and social environment study for the University of North Carolina at Chapel Hill and cultural strategies for a parenting project with the New York University School of Medicine Child Study Center.

While working these temporary jobs, a friend insisted that I look into becoming a substitute teacher. It was a way he made income while looking for a job in his field. The idea of substitute teaching was not a far-fetched notion because I was surrounded by educators and I had taught a couple of graduate courses. My mom was an assistant professor at a university and my grandmother was an administrator of an elementary school in south-eastern Virginia. In addition, I had taught a couple of graduate courses for a semester at a university in Wilmington, North Carolina. However, I held on to the idea that I could find a job in marketing research.

It was critical that I find work because my family was pressuring me to contribute financially to the household. Reluctantly, in the fall of 2001, I began the substitute teaching application process for the New York City Board of Education. Why did I have an internal battle going through this process? Reflecting back on this transitional period, I think it was because I feared the unknown and did not have a personal connection with anyone in the area who was teaching. I thought it was extremely risky to work in an area where I did not have a support structure.

TAKING THE PLUNGE:
THE NEW YORK CITY TEACHING FELLOWS PROGRAM

A short while after submitting the substitute application, I was riding the subway and noticed a black-and-white ad with two simple questions on it: "Do you remember your first grade teacher's name? Who will remember yours?" The ad was for the New York City Teaching Fellows (NYCTF) program, a fast-track teacher certification program for career-changing individuals.

I do recall my 1st-grade teacher's name, Mrs. Rudy. She was great! On my first day of school, I entered Mrs. Rudy's classroom late, and crying. I did not want to be there; I just wanted to go home with my mom. Mrs. Rudy calmed my nerves by reassuring me that everything would be fine and I would have a great time in school. She was right; I did have a great time. She brought in her pet cocker spaniel for "show and tell" and I played with him along with my classmates. I will never forget that day because I acquired a love for cocker spaniels. Since then, I have had three cocker spaniels—Victor, Tiffany, and Malik—as family pets.

After the subway ride, I went home and researched the NYCTF program. According to the NYCTF website, the program was launched in the spring of 2000 to address the most severe teacher shortage in the New York

City public school system in decades. As an initiative of the NYC Board of Education (now the NYC Department of Education), the Fellowship recruits and selects successful professionals and recent graduates from across the country. Its mission is to recruit and prepare high-quality, dedicated individuals to become teachers who will raise student achievement in the New York City classrooms that need them most. The prospect of having a steady job with a full salary and benefits while earning another graduate degree was more alluring to me than substitute teaching. I am not much of a risk-taker, but something inside of me said, "Go for it!"

I attended one of the NYCTF informational sessions. It was great to meet like-minded professionals who shared the same aspiration: to switch careers and make a difference in the lives of those who needed us the most, the students of New York City. I heard that there were thousands of applications submitted for this cohort, but fewer than 1,000 Fellows would be selected. Those odds did not sound favorable, but I remained optimistic. After completing the application process and an interview, I received a letter in the mail from the Fellows program. I WAS ACCEPTED INTO THE PROGRAM! Yes! I was ready to embark on a new career in teaching! I was excited about this transition in my career because I would meet new people and receive training, a master's degree in childhood education, and mentor support. I had a job and was ready for a new challenge.

The summer of 2002 kicked off the NYCTF summer intensive training session. My graduate studies and training occurred on the campus of Lehman College in the Bronx. Training consisted of learning about the NYC Board of Education, completing paperwork, and getting fingerprinted. Then, summer school started in July. I shadowed a veteran teacher named Ms. R. for 8 weeks in a Bronx middle school. I co-taught math to 13 7th-graders who had not passed the math state test during the regular school year. I was often reminded that this training was not a true teaching experience because there are two teachers present and the class size is extremely small. I absorbed as much of the "real" experience as I could.

Ms. R. was a mother figure to the students, dressed professionally, and set high expectations for them. She was kind and patient with me. She even took time out of her schedule to review a reflective paper that I had to submit to the NYCTFs. After the students were dismissed, I trekked back to campus for graduate coursework in childhood elementary education. This was a grueling experience simply because of the time I had to commit to working summer school during the day, studying and completing assignments for graduate school, and attending Fellows' meetings.

My summer school experience taught me that middle school students were often unpredictable and moody, and did not take advice from me too well. I felt that I could be more effective with younger children, preferably kindergarteners or 1st-graders. The placement decision was out of my hands. The NYCTF program decided placement based on the needs of the schools.

At the end of the summer intensive training, Fellows in my cohort reconvened for a meeting. I heard that some Fellows quit the program; for some, it was not what they thought, whereas others were belittled by staff and/or students. I was sad to hear the reports, but remained optimistic about my experience and knew the next step was to find a job. I updated my résumé and replied to the question "Why teach?" This was part of my response to the question in 2002:

> I am ready to take on a new challenge and believe I possess several characteristics that will enable me to become a successful teacher. These characteristics are passion, a sense of urgency, and commitment to education.
>
> Teaching is a rewarding career. The reward comes when a child "gets it." "Getting it" occurs when a child is able to read a passage and understand its meaning, respond to questions that they otherwise may not have known the answer to, or can help their classmates with assignments. I want to help children "get it." I want to give back to a greater cause: the education of children and their success.

I was pleasantly surprised that I had a strong position about teaching and on public education, especially because I had little knowledge or experience in this field. I was taking a journey down a different path, but I felt comfortable on this route. I was meeting new people, learning about childhood elementary studies, and interacting with students and their families. My family was proud that I had found a job and that it was providing me with a sense of purpose and satisfaction. I felt good about myself.

MY FIRST YEAR

With résumés in hand and a clear reason for my desire to teach, I was ready for my first NYC Board of Education job fair. I stopped by many tables and circled around many more. I made a connection with an administrator from the school where I had completed my summer school assignment. She was excited to meet me and even informed me that her assistant principal and I attended the same university. What a great feeling! In a matter of moments, I was offered a coveted position as a kindergarten teacher in the South Bronx, New York, and I began my teaching career in the 2002–2003 academic year.

As a first-year teacher, I encountered many difficult teaching situations. The majority of them occurred during the first 3 months of the school year. To understand the dynamic of the specific incident below, I will describe the composition of my classroom.

My classroom was approximately 22"× 27". Pour into the room a teacher's desk, 2 area rugs, 12 tables and 30 chairs, 3 student desks, 2 computer desks, 4 cubbies, several bookshelves, 27 students, and me. There was little free space to move around without bumping into an inanimate object or a child. It was like being in a small elevator with 27 other people when the maximum occupancy is 15. My summer training intensive experience came back to me quickly. Having a small class size and with two teachers is not a true teaching experience. A small classroom jam-packed with furniture and 27 students with one teacher was my reality.

The physical makeup of my classroom was nothing compared with my encounter with a student I will call Napoleon. My preservice training did not prepare me for a student like Napoleon—how to teach him, protect him, or communicate with his family. I was thrown into the roles of social worker, guidance counselor, and security guard.

Napoleon had a physical impairment that caused him to walk with a limp. He possessed little of the academic knowledge valued in school and he exhibited poor social interaction skills. On the third day of school, he cursed me after I asked him to put his supplies away. On another day, he walked across student desks, crawled on top of bookcases, and jumped off like Superman. His actions turned the academic learning environment into a circus, with the other students becoming the spectators. After a couple of months of keeping a running record of his behavior, meetings with administration, and meetings with Napoleon's foster mother, he was removed from my classroom and placed in a different school. This experience was unnerving and left me feeling exhausted at the end of each day. Napoleon consumed my conversations with family and friends, many of whom asked me why I would stay in that job and put up with Napoleon's behavior. My response to family and friends was simple: My responsibility was to teach all of my students, including Napoleon.

As I reflect back over my first year of teaching, one student makes me smile over and over again. I will call him Ray. Ray was a happy-go-lucky child who stole my heart. He was respectful of adults and his peers, smart, and adored by his mother. He did his schoolwork, dressed impeccably, and was a model student. What I found amazing about Ray was that at the ripe old age of 5, he served as the translator for his mom, who spoke only Spanish. My most cherished memory about Ray was when I asked him how he learned to speak English. He replied by saying " . . . I watch Sesame Street." His response was so matter-of-fact, simple, and to the point. Ray was a pleasant student; his smile was contagious.

My students taught me that teaching is more than just learning how to decode, add and subtract numbers, or investigate things in the environment. They showed me what makes them happy and sad. They expected me to give them kudos when they passed a test or understood a concept. Once they felt secure in the classroom, they were willing to take risks and tried their best to be successful with the given task.

I enjoyed working at this school in the South Bronx. The majority of students were respectful of adults in the school and maintained a youthful innocence. There was parental involvement. Families participated in parent–teacher conferences, chaperoned trips, and supplied treats for various in-classroom celebrations. My colleagues kept me grounded, which helped me maintain my sanity throughout my first year of teaching. They encouraged me, offered me advice and support, and gave me critical feedback. We bonded well, so much so that we often ate out, shopped for clothes and school supplies, and attended family celebratory events together. This was my extended family and they helped me to grow personally and professionally during my first years of teaching.

BEING "EXCESSED" AND NEW ADVENTURES

After 3 years at this school, my comfort and familiarity with my colleagues, families, students, and staff was turned upside down. I was "excessed" at the end of the 2004–2005 school year. *Excessed!* This unsavory word means that the administration can release staff with the least seniority, usually due to budget cuts. I had to find another job over the summer or go into the substitute pool.

There was no way I would go into the substitute pool. I enjoyed the comfort of working in one school and establishing relationships with staff, students, and families. So, I invited myself to a NYC Department of Education job fair. I was turned down at the door with the explanation that the event was only for first-year teachers. I no longer felt the security or sense of confidence I had felt when I was going through the NYCTF program. Fortunately, the administrators at my former school supported me through this transitional period by sharing job opportunities with me. With their support I interviewed for a couple of teaching positions and I decided to pursue a job with grades K and 1 in a new school opening in Harlem.

After interviewing with a panel composed of Harlem community leaders and the school administration, I was offered a position as a kindergarten teacher at the Thurgood Marshall Academy Lower School (TMALS) for the 2005–2006 school year. Nine years later, I am still teaching at TMALS. During that time I have watched my first kindergarten class graduate and move on to middle school. I currently teach 1st grade.

While working at the school, my experience has grown exponentially. I have participated in numerous workshops and professional development opportunities. I am better equipped to use data to frame my instruction and hone in on students who need specialized academic intervention. I have been trained on how to use reading comprehension programs such as Accelerated Reader by Renaissance Learning, Inc. and ReadWorks. I am versed in the literacy shifts and math practices of the Common Core Learning Standards.

At TMALS, I have had the opportunity to bring some of my passions into the school community and classroom. I brought the CookShop Classroom for Elementary Schools program for K–2 classes to my school. This nutrition education program, sponsored by the Food Bank for New York, helps students and families develop knowledge of and a love for healthy foods. The school participated in the National Education Association's Read Across America national campaign that promotes reading among students, families, and staff on Dr. Seuss's birthday. On this special day, I invited high school students from our sister school, Thurgood Marshall Academy, to read a selected Dr. Seuss book to classes.

I have been a dues-paying member of the United Federation of Teachers (UFT), the New York City affiliate of the American Federation of Teachers, since my first year of teaching. In 2010, I decided to take a more active role in the union and ran for chapter delegate at my school. I was elected as the delegate and attended union meetings and brought back news and information to chapter members. Fellow members at my school elected me chapter leader in 2012. My primary role is to be the link between members and administration and union officials on matters such as citywide union issues, school budget, and school morale.

In 2012, I was selected for a fellowship with the Institute for Urban and Minority Education (IUME) at Teachers College, Columbia University, and Community School District 5 Manhattan/New York City Department of Education called the Literacy Teaching Initiative. The initiative is led by Teachers College professor Dr. Jodene Morrell. As a Fellow, I learned about conducting action research, an approach used by educators to examine their existing practice and identify elements to strengthen their teaching practice.

The basis of my first action research project, "Identifying Characteristics of Student Engagement Through Poetry," grew out of a need to keep all students engaged and maintain the momentum for a complex literacy unit on poetry. I wanted to make sure that the lessons and activities for this poetry unit were relevant, personal, and upbeat.

The next action research project was a collaboration with a doctoral researcher with the Literacy Teachers Initiative Project of the IUME. We decided to examine how incorporating multicultural complex texts into a structured literacy system (The CAFÉ) increases student engagement and ensures rigorous instruction, and how action research can improve teacher reflection and practice. We had the opportunity to present our research at the New York State Reading Association's 2013 conference.

AN EVOLVING EDUCATIONAL PHILOSOPHY, OR WHY I TEACH NOW

During my first year as a graduate student at Lehman College, I wrote my educational philosophy for a childhood elementary education course. The essence of my philosophy is intact. An excerpt of what I wrote follows, although I have modified it slightly by adding reflections of my current teaching career.

> Education is like a puzzle. There are numerous pieces to the puzzle—students, teachers, the school, the community, family, government, and curriculum/ standards. A certain amount of time and effort must be exerted in order to fit the pieces together effectively. My goal is to put these pieces together in order to form a picture of a knowledgeable and well-rounded student. But, where do I begin?
>
> Ultimately, students learn best through the stimulation of their senses. I believe that these learning experiences become cemented in my students' schema when their senses are stimulated and they make connections with what they have learned. I remember a former student stopping in the staircase to ask me if

I remember when we made stone soup in 1st grade. I was excited that she could recall this event. I enjoyed bringing the story *Stone Soup* alive with the help of my students. We collectively placed ingredients in the crockpot to make our version of the soup. This activity evoked all senses and made an indelible mark on my students. It became a classroom tradition.

The burden of teaching my students the standard-based competencies is not my sole responsibility. However, the local political regime is holding teachers solely accountable for students' academic learning and successes.

Most American children are a product of nurturing environments that foster high educational achievement. As a result, they tend to thrive in primary, secondary, and postsecondary schools, ultimately becoming productive citizens in society. On the other hand, there are children, primarily from disadvantaged socioeconomic communities, who come from environments not conductive to learning and that unfortunately cause these children to focus on meeting their basic needs just to survive. Constant preoccupation with meeting these deficiencies can distract a child from his or her capacity to learn in the classroom. I am aware that many of my students will come from this type of environment. It is imperative that I provide them with a safe community conducive to learning.

Besides teachers, other individuals and organizations must work together to strengthen the knowledge and learning experiences of all children. These include the school and district, the family, community and government agencies, corporations, and religious institutions. Like teachers, these entities play a vital role in the successes of students and they should be evaluated on their performance as well. It holds all vested parties in the sustainability of public education accountable for students' academic and social development. This idealistic concept may never take off the ground. In the interim, I will try my best to incorporate each component into my classroom environment.

The essence of my educational philosophy is as meaningful to me a decade later as it was when I first wrote it. During my 12 years of teaching I have worked at two schools and taught kindergarten and 1st grade, and I have worked with many students and their families. I have seen changes in national, state, and citywide educational policies, curricula, and the implementation of the national Common Core Standards. There has been a movement to hold teachers more accountable for student performance. This has resulted in a change in the teacher evaluation system in New York City. What anchors me in the midst of these changes is this part of the educational philosophy that I wrote in 2003: " . . . if we take the time to invest in the education of all children, then we will have a more productive society that is socially responsible and can solve the problems of the future."

I continue to teach because I still have the desire to educate children. I believe all children should have access to a quality, rigorous academic program that also fosters social development. I will continue to strive to work toward providing children with a nurturing and stimulating environment in which they can take risks and develop the necessary skills to be successful in the world.

TEACHING TO SUSTAIN HOPE

Hope, the *sine qua non* of teaching, is the common theme of Part IV, and includes three essays along with a mini-essay and poem. In the poem and mini-essay, Christina Puntel, a high school English teacher in the Philadelphia Public Schools, offers a poem about "teaching in the now," as well as a mini-essay that describes her teaching life and passion. Christina's poem exudes justice, one of the requisite values she holds onto for "teaching in the now." Mary Jade Haney, an elementary school teacher in Columbia, South Carolina, describes the determination that "creates spaces of hope" and that led to pursuing her own education in spite of—or perhaps because of—the discouragement and neglect she faced in her own early education. Rather than accept this kind of treatment as inevitable, her experience compelled her to demand the best for her students.

Greg Michie is a long-time teacher who had pursued a doctorate and became a teacher educator and well-known writer, only to return a few years later to his beloved middle school classroom, something few academics have done. His essay documents his first year back, exploring the question of "Why teach *now*?" in heartbreaking detail. A moving reminder of how difficult the situation has become, his essay also provides moments of hope that help transcend the dreary nature of what goes on in too many public schools because of the pressures of standardization.

John Levasseur, a chemistry teacher in an urban high school, writes about teaching as his lifelong pursuit. Thrilled to be in the "typical American high school," John reflects on what it means to teach chemistry to students of diverse backgrounds, some of whom have become disenchanted with schooling. But the purpose of education, as John reminds us, is *happiness*, so he doggedly continues to inspire, cajole, and demand the best from his students in spite of some of the conditions that make it so hard.

CHAPTER 8

Teaching in the Now
A Mini-Essay and a Poem

Christina Puntel

In 1998, I graduated from a small, Catholic college in Philadelphia and found myself miraculously employed as a bilingual special education teacher in a small, bilingual school in West Kensington, Pennsylvania. The summer before I began to teach, the 2.5 blocks around our small school became the site of an aggressive effort to "rehabilitate" the neighborhood, with police blockades at every corner. Operation Sunrise, so named by the police department, was an intensive campaign in 1998 to set up a blockade around a small part of West Kensington in order to rid the neighborhood of dealers and drugs. You had to show ID to police to come in and out of the neighborhood where my school was. The American Civil Liberties Union (ACLU) watched it carefully because there were definitely aggressive police actions. It did not rid the neighborhood of crime. The school saw so many initiatives come and go, while remaining a diamond in the rough, a real community anchor. I showed my ID at the corner of Somerset and walked a block up to Cambria to watch a night movie projected on the side of the school, as Operation Sunrise surrounded us. *Vampiros en Havana* brought out families and lots of little ones sucking down hugs and sitting on those blue school chairs looking up at the side of the building. I was welcomed, open arms, kisses on both cheeks, and later teamed up with an amazing veteran teacher to create magical musicals and dance performances.

My classroom practices are greatly informed by the Philadelphia Teachers Learning Cooperative (PTLC). This group of teachers has been meeting for over 30 years in each others' homes after school on Thursdays. The founding teachers of this group were introduced to Patricia Carini and her colleagues at the Prospect Center in Vermont. Through my immersion with PTLC, I learned to describe children and their work using the Prospect Processes. When we describe student work and our own practices through these oral inquiry processes, we develop a relationship with the maker, the work, and with each other. From the teachers in this group, I also learned how to provision my room so students could learn from what was around them, not just from me. Silkworms, gingerbread houses, zillions of books, choice time, poetry. Spanish. English. And parents. Making limeade, helping at choice time, teaching me how to teach. Always the classroom piano. Always music.

Now, 1998 feels a world away. Operation Sunrise came and went. Even though I don't teach there anymore, I am so thankful I spent the first 6 years of my teaching life in a neighborhood school, where parents and grandparents were right outside my windows. I spent lots of time outside school with my students, and parents spent lots of time in my classroom. It was a very good education for me as a young teacher.

Now, it's 2013. I am now teaching students in high school Spanish classes. What remains? A commitment to paying attention and to reflection. "Teaching in the now" is a stance. It is a stance rooted in presence, in being present to the moment, to myself, to my students, to the content in front of us. Teaching in the now means a commitment to reflection and development. Reflection, taking the time to rethink the moments in my day. Development, taking the time to make something new happen, to remake the moment. I hesitate to say "professional development," as this term has been taken away from us to mean something imposed on us. When I say teaching in the now means a commitment to growth, I mean I must make time to make sense, question, revise.

Writing poetry about my practice is one way I come to an understanding of what I am doing right now. Ever since reading Adrienne Rich in high school, I realized poetry opened me up in a unique way. Adrienne Rich wrote, "a wild patience has taken me this far." Part of the wildness and the patience for me is the poetry. I am thankful to have this space to share some of that poetry, and thankful to colleagues, students, parents, and my own family for the inspiration to stay in the now and be awake and alive in the moment as a teacher in Philly.

> what does it mean to teach now? all the found poems
> i sift through at night, i can't capture in words
> the sound of my class when my husband and son come
> to deliver supermarket flowers to me on my thirty seventh birthday
> we are in the middle of flipcam filming a spanish music video

when they walk in . . .
there' s a collective *maestraaaaaaa*,
and then all at once, the whole class busts out with
happy birthday to you! happy biiiiirthday to you!!
when i asked my son what he thought we were doing when he
came in the room, he said: a party.
this is what it sounds like to teach now.

there's the way darius runs in
to check out these gorgeous football plays on my donated
computers before he goes to practice, i'm teaching my
seventh period class and he's back there, clicking on links
from this weekend's game, cougar pride.
sometimes i let kareem sit back there with him,
and darius glances over and helps him with his
verb conjugations or coaches him along in a dialogue.
that's what it looks like to teach now.

music—wall to wall music. mil gracias juana molina
and calle 13 and charles mingus y celia cruz
y mala rodriguez and all of the island of puerto rico
for gifting us music to melt these four walls. the first time
i played alika's jengibre my own body melted in front of the
smartboard. *la realidad de roots es infalible.* this is what it feels
like to teach now, melting walls into sound.

outside the walls, it's philly. outside philly, it's the world.
we go out each day, together. this is what it's like to teach now:
researching genocide in guatemala, gordina choreographs
what she reads into a dance, dedicated to the partners of the
desaparecidos, and to all the bodies in the well in dos erres.
when we do the chapter on *la escuela*, we googlechat with mi
compañero en Guate about the education scene there,
70,000 students out of school, 70% of them are girls
the numbers don't tell the real story. we have to dig deeper.
Oxfam, Millenium Development Goals, and a month later, the chapter
on *la escuela* is so close to our hearts, we're dreaming the stories at
night, in Spanish, and wake up suddenly able to roll our r's, philly
accents gone.
POOF.

when i say i teach now, i promise i will teach justice.
Chile. El Salvador. Nicaragua.
when i say i teach now, i promise i will teach truth.
Sugar. Dominican Republic. Triangle Trade.

i'm saying at night all of this glistens, all of these images and sounds
    twinkle it's like some crazy light show, music, fireworks, emmezileen
    lebrón in first period, página 214 the whole thing. i'm writing it
    down for you so you can know i feel us all here in these moments.
    sun down, preparing for tomorrow. keep the lights burning like this.
    hasta la mañana.

CHAPTER 9

Creating Spaces That Breathe Hope

Mary Jade Haney

In Lak'ech (I Am You or You Are Me)

Tu eres mi otro yo.	You are my other me.
Si te hago daño a ti.	If I do harm to you.
Me hago dano a mi mismo.	I do harm to myself.
Si te amo y respeto,	If I love and respect you,
Me amo y respeto yo.	I love and respect myself.

Mayan-inspired poem, "Pensamiento Serpentino"
Luis Valdez. (1971).

I TEACH TO RECLAIM THE EDUCATION I RECEIVED AS A STUDENT OF COLOR IN THE PUBLIC SCHOOL SYSTEM

Reclaim, in one dimension, means *to reform*. I want to reform and *re-form* the education I received as an African American in the public school system. I *create spaces* of success for all students each day as I look into the eyes of the students and families of the rural communities in which I teach. I see myself in these students. I hope for their future. I hope for their dreams. *Dum spiro spero. While I breathe, I hope.* I want to inspire growth, creativity and inquiry each moment in the lives of these students, always beginning by getting to know the students and their families. Each student has always led me to the *funds of knowledge*—that is, to use the talents, skills, and experiences they have outside of the school building. As these experiences grow, I am able to make more meaningful connections to the curriculum for my students.

I believe parents and other family members are our students' first teachers and it is our job as educators to value their contributions within our classrooms and schools. Knowledge of our students can only enhance their learning experiences across the content areas. As I reflect on my own early years of education, I wonder why some teachers believed in me and others did not. Did they take the time to really get to know me beyond their classrooms? Did they even believe I could be successful?

I TEACH TO EDUCATE MYSELF SO THAT I CAN EFFECTIVELY EDUCATE

Each year I aspire to learn something new about myself and how being a teacher can inspire, empower, and in some cases disempower me as it relates to educational reforms and mandates that are beyond our control. Politicians sometimes put mandated practices in place with a sincere intention to help students, but, unfortunately, these practices—often cloaked as interventions and student assistance—do more harm than good.

From the walls of my classroom, I inform educational reform for the students and families I serve. As teachers, we have ample opportunities to use our professional judgment, and one path for me has been action research. Action research has assisted me in these endeavors by allowing me to build relationships of trust with students and their families. For example, I collaborated with a professor from a local university to create a space for our Latina mothers and their children to value home and school literacies. However, before engaging in action research with my students and families, I explored my own beliefs through a self-inquiry project. I began to study myself through a reflective journey focusing on what energizes me as an educator. I began to pay attention to myself as a teacher of color. I strongly believe working in education is my divine purpose. The self-inquiry project motivated me to stay the course through the tough times of educational reforms that seem unjust for the students and families I serve. I am learning to create spaces and re-create myself in order to influence as well as support and sustain my passions as an educator while serving students and their families. I was born to teach and I will give no one permission to discourage me from doing what is best for children and their families.

Action research helped me continually reflect on my instructional and cultural practices. I tailor my personal professional development based on the needs of the students and families I serve each year. Using these foundations, I try my best to make sound decisions to govern my daily motives and actions as I educate children.

In my classroom, *my world*, the most important people are not the policymakers and textbook companies; they are my students and their families. This is how I navigate the stormy seas as I try to calm the national storm that rages against teachers like me. I urge my colleagues to continually seek ways to support their own professional growth and build classroom curriculum based on the needs of their students and their students' families.

I teach to inform the future through reliving the past and supporting the present. I intentionally design instruction based on historical events that have affected the lives of my students, their parents, their grandparents, and other family members. I believe it is equally important to know who we are, where we are from, and what connects us as human beings. When students learn how we connect culturally and socially, learning becomes an engaging and enjoyable experience. For example, we invite family members who lived during the civil rights movement into our classroom as we study that time period. We have family members who come in and share their experiences of having taken part in the Great Migration of African Americans from the South to the North.

My students and I discuss reasons why it is necessary to take advantage of every opportunity to do their best at school, at home, in the community, and in the world. Together, we understand that I cannot teach them without their participation, motivation, and determination. As we engage in a variety of culturally relevant experiences, I also share my personal stories as we make meaning from these and other historical perspectives in order to gain a better understanding of how history collectively shapes our futures.

I TEACH TO IGNITE AND INSPIRE
THE PASSION FOR LEARNING IN THE HEARTS OF ALL CHILDREN

As I entered my classroom one morning, I noticed something attached to my classroom door. It was a yellow sticky note that read, *To: Mrs. Haney. From: Anaya. One day I'm going to be just like YOU! YOU are my true inspiration! Love: Anaya C. J.* This note came from a student who was not in my classroom, but who knew me only as a reading teacher because I regularly visit all classes. I did not have any direct conversations with Anaya at any particular time, proving that teachers and the words we speak are powerful. Even though the note didn't give any specific details, the word "inspiration" conveys a message that motivates me as I write the reasons for why I teach.

I photographed this small note because I sometimes need to see and read it. Anaya had no idea how powerfully this response affected me as someone who truly cares about students striving to reach their fullest potential. Written from the heart of a child, the note demonstrates that my teaching and life lessons are not in vain.

I TEACH TO DEFY THE LABELS GIVEN TO BRIGHT CHILDREN WHO ARE OUTLIERS

In general, society and schools will quickly place labels on those students who fall "below average" based solely on standardized test scores. If students have other challenges in addition to low test scores, their chances of success are limited even further. These tags and labels convey a deficit perspective and continually alter educational opportunities for too many of our students. I remember all too well the devastation and humiliation I suffered as an 11th grader.

As I began to think seriously about my own future beyond high school, I vividly recall entering the guidance office to request a college application (this was before the Internet). My future educational goal was to attend a 4-year college and obtain a bachelor's degree. The guidance counselor denied my request with the following response: "You are not college material. You will not make it in a 4-year institution. I suggest you take a trade." I respectfully listened to her reasoning and, in my determination to get what I came for, I again requested a college application; she again refused. The message was clear. I left the guidance office demoralized and confused, yet determined to save myself. Because I had been tagged, labeled, and tracked since elementary school, at that time I was not even provided an opportunity to apply to a 4-year college.

I was a student in remedial classrooms and speech for the majority of my elementary, middle, and high school educational experiences. One of my best years in high school was the year I accidentally ended up in an honors English course. There were only three African American students in that class. To this day, I don't know how this happened, but I remember reading *Beowulf, Hamlet,* and other classic literature. We read *I Know Why the Caged Bird Sings* and wrote several research papers. It was an exciting year because I was finally learning to love and appreciate literature.

Unfortunately, later during my senior year in high school, I was placed back in a remedial English class, not because I could not do the work but because, based on my standardized test scores, I should not have been able to complete the assignments. The irony was that my work was exemplary. Nevertheless, the teacher questioned my integrity and she did not believe I had completed the assignments on my own. She accused me of cheating and, because she had the power to do so, she set a course to prove her theory with lies and deceptive behaviors. For these reasons, I was removed from a rich learning environment and sent back to a remedial classroom.

When I create spaces for authentic reading and writing experiences, all students are expected and invited to participate regardless of test scores, labels, or any other deficits that categorize brilliant students as low achievers or struggling learners. From my own personal experience, I have learned that if students have teachers with high expectations, they will rise to the challenge, meet goals, and exceed them.

I TEACH SO THAT I WILL SEE MY STUDENTS IN THE FUTURE AS SUCCESSFUL ADULTS WHO WILL IMPACT SOCIETY IN POSITIVE WAYS

When I see my students again, especially after they have graduated from high school, it inspires me to keep on teaching. When she was a college student, one of my former 5th-grade students shared with me that she chose to be an early childhood teacher solely because of the memories she had as a student in my classroom. She said she wanted to give back by teaching at her former elementary school. Even though she tried to give me all the credit, I refused to accept it. I assured her that her success was due to her own determination.

There was also a time I don't want to remember. About 10 years ago, on the night before the first day of school, I was at a 24-hour copy shop, preparing for the next day. Two of my colleagues and I were held at gunpoint in a robbery. When I looked up, there were three young men with bandannas over their noses and mouths holding guns, telling us and the other two customers to quietly move to the restroom. Of course we did exactly as we were told and we sat on the restroom floor as they held the cashier at gunpoint, demanding the money from all the cash registers. As I sat on that floor with a weapon pointed at my head, a gun that could have ended my life instantaneously, I had a sobering thought: "If I can make it through this situation alive, I will always remember this day. Maybe one of these young men recognized me or one of my colleagues as his former teacher or maybe one or more of them noticed the instructional materials and realized that we were teachers and didn't want to harm us."

As teachers, we will all see our students again. The question becomes, "How do we want to see them?" Do we want to see them as successful college graduates with goals and dreams, or do we want to see them as criminals who conceal their identities behind guns and bandannas?

After this daunting experience, my sister, also a teacher, and I began to offer a summer camp to children in 1st through 5th grades. We created *Camp Top Shelf* with the premise that if you want to succeed in life and desire nice possessions, you must prepare for it and work hard. Our focus is to help students see that being on the "top" requires hard work, focus, perseverance, and excellence. *Camp Top Shelf* is offered from 1 to 2 weeks. The camp counselors are young student volunteers from local middle and high schools; however, because we have no funding, they do not get paid but instead receive a certificate for their service learning hours as well as guidance in planning for their own futures. Our goal is to inspire these young people in various ways, from researching careers to learning the importance of community service. We have no operating costs because we ask local churches in rural communities to allow us the use of their facilities so that we can serve their children and their families through culturally relevant literacy and learning practices.

We will see our students again; how do we want to see them?

I TEACH BECAUSE I AM IN A PROFESSION THAT BALANCES THE UNIVERSE

I believe teachers balance the universe because we make all professions possible, even our own. We need to guide students as they plan for their *one and only life*.

THEREFORE, I KEEP ON TEACHING . . .

I have been teaching for 17 years. In that time, I have taught 4th-graders, 5th-graders, and 8th-graders, and arts integration to students from preschool through 5th grade. I am currently a reading teacher and a reading interventionist at a public elementary school. I also teach undergraduate early childhood education courses at the local university. Over the years, I have seen the pendulum in public education swing back and forth, forth and back. I have learned a very important lesson, and that lesson is "duck and cover."

Decisions and reforms in public education often harm children in ways that we see long after the damage is done. As a teacher, I passionately stand on my foundational beliefs about teaching and learning so that even though my flame may flicker, it never goes out. We all have untapped literacies that could inform ways for students to be successful. I completely understand that change is not in the system, it is within me. This is how I operate as a 21st-century teacher, looking from the inside out, at myself first before seeking to support students, teachers, and families.

As a teacher, my greatest desire is for students to become self-regulated determined learners. Therefore, I create a variety of opportunities and spaces for them to acquire knowledge through inquiry as they pay attention to themselves and others. I encourage them to think critically—asking questions, seeking answers to those questions, connecting their prior knowledge to newly acquired knowledge.

I also surround myself with like-minded colleagues who love their students and enjoy their work as educators. When collaborating with my colleagues, we create spaces for students to engage in a plethora of enriching learning experiences. Some of these have included all-night literacy learning engagements at our school where students and their families enter the building in the evening with sleeping bags, a toothbrush, pajamas, and an extra set of clothing for the next day. During these experiences, families, teachers, and students learn together while building supportive relationships. Additionally, we invite the community to support these authentic experiences. During one particular event, a local astronomy team created an observatory on the school playground and students, parents, and teachers identified constellations and objects such as the Seven Sisters in the midnight sky. Because our school is located in a rural area, the night sky was beautiful and the students were full of excitement as they viewed it.

In 2005, I coordinated a learning opportunity where students, parents, and grandparents traveled to Canada via motor coach. All participants wrote daily responses, reflections, and observations. Some were even inspired to write poetry, capturing each day in their Writers' Notebooks as they viewed the powerful and majestic Niagara Falls, visited a butterfly pavilion, and exchanged U.S. dollars for Canadian currency, among many other experiences.

In another one of our learning engagements, we traveled to Orlando, Florida, and spent the night at Sea World learning together about killer whales, dolphins, and other sea creatures. These experiences opened our students to unique and challenging learning environments that could never be duplicated in a classroom setting during regular school hours.

Some of my colleagues and I have collaborated to create spaces of arts integration for social justice. We have a drama team of 1st- through 5th-grade students who created a Flash Mob performance in order to invite the public into our schools to read with and to them. These students have performed on the steps of the state Capitol building, the main branch of our public library, a local Barnes & Noble, as well as opening for various education conferences. Their goal for this school year is to travel throughout the country presenting their Flash Mob performance. This journey will take them out of state this spring. They will begin at the state Capitol and travel north, stopping at the north side of the White House for a newly created Flash Mob performance, with their final destination being Boston, Massachusetts.

We have also collaborated with teachers, parents, and a local university to create a 2-week-long summer camp at our school for 1st- through 5th-grade students. This was the second year for *Camp Discovery* at our school. This past summer, we collaborated with a university professor who created a course for her graduate students to engage the elementary students as readers, writers, thinkers, and speakers. Because of this partnership, these young mathematicians, scientists, artists, dancers, musicians, authors, and singers were successful, valued, respected, supported, and celebrated.

I partner with families and seek available resources to support the success of the whole child. My life as a teacher reminds me of my life as an elementary school student with Ms. Reid and Mrs. Brooks. These two teachers often collaborated in order to give their students the best 2nd-grade school year ever. During this time the effects of integration could still be felt, and now, as an educator, I cherish this experience that I so fondly recall. Ms. Reid and Mrs. Brooks reminded me of a Black version and a White version of Aunt Bea from *The Andy Griffith* show. These educators came together and loved us with all of their hearts. They worked together in order to educate us through culturally responsive perspectives. This was a time when the faces of students in the schools were changing and both parents and teachers were at the crossroads. Their mannerisms spoke unconditional love, care, and concern as they taught us. Their creative ways made our school life worth living.

One of my most memorable experiences was recess, where both classes would hold hands and form a huge circle in the middle of the playground. Once we formed the circle, we let go of each others' hands and stood in place. These two beautiful teachers stood in the middle of that circle and made eye contact with smiles that spoke to each one of us. Their unspoken words said, "We are so glad you are here and we are so glad to be your teachers." I'll never forget one of the activities that often followed this daily ritual, weather permitting. We would sing:

> Little Sally Walker sitting in a saucer,
> rise Sally rise and wipe your weeping eyes,
> fly to the east, fly to the west,
> fly to the one that you love the best.

Both of these teachers, with the kind mannerisms of Aunt Bea, also taught us the east from the west because they used a compass during the song. The one thing I visualize as I recall this moment is that these teachers didn't end the song until they *flew* to each one of us. The love and care from these teachers made me feel like I was the only child in that huge circle of two classes who stood on that playground day after day until my 2nd-grade year ended. A special space was created for us in this public school through collaborations from two educators from two different worlds. It was clear that they wanted to have an impact on our lives beyond books, pencils, and papers.

I have come to understand from my experience and the work of Paulo Freire that *what you love you won't let fail*! I teach because, just as these two teachers became the wind beneath my wings many years ago, I am continually inspired to guide my students. As we also "fly to the east and fly to the west," I want each one of them to know *I love them best*.

CHAPTER 10

Same as It Never Was

On My Return to Teaching

Gregory Michie

The sounds were familiar. The squeak of gym shoes shuffling up freshly waxed steps. First floor, then second, then third. The muted chatter, growing louder as it got closer, of 7th- and 8th-graders on the first day of school.

The sights, too, were familiar. Comfortable even. I knew this school, these halls, these classrooms. I'd taught here for nearly a decade in the 1990s. Hundreds of kids from this South Side Chicago neighborhood had been students of mine during that time. I'd been well known in the community.

But that was then.

Now, as the first group of arriving students rounded the corner on the third floor and headed my way, I was reminded that I wouldn't be able to simply pick up where I'd left off years earlier. Other teachers received warm "hellos," smiles, or at least nods of recognition from the kids. Not me. I got a few curious looks and sideways glances, but most students just walked past me like I was a bulletin board that had been left up too long.

It was a surreal feeling. Kind of like a sci-fi story where the protagonist returns home one day to find that everything looks just as he remembers it—his house, his family, his dog—but no one knows who he is or why he's there.

Of course, it wasn't altogether surprising that I'd feel this way. I knew when I decided to go back to teaching in public schools after 12 years as a college professor that things would be different. But that morning, I felt like I'd stepped into an alternate reality.

It wouldn't be the last time.

*   *   *

The previous spring, I'd begun telling a few friends and university colleagues that I was considering a return to the classroom. Responses ranged from knotted eyebrows to weak smiles.

"Why?"

"Seriously?"

"You know about the new teacher evaluation system, right?"

"I'm not sure there's a place for teachers like you anymore," one said, citing the crush of standardized testing and other intrusive mandates.

I had plenty of doubts of my own.

I'd been asked many times over the years—mostly by my undergraduate students—if I thought I'd ever go back to teaching kids. My answer was always the same: Maybe. And I meant it. Being a public school teacher had been a huge part of my identity, and sometimes I felt a strong urge to reclaim it.

But with each year that went by, I realized I was becoming more and more comfortable with the relative privilege of life as a professor. I could take hour-long lunch breaks! I could go to the bathroom whenever I wanted! I could go to weeklong conferences! It was an addictive freedom, and the more I had of it, the less enticing a return to the daily grind of schools sounded. I'd been 27 when I started teaching the first time, but now I was pushing 50. Would I even have the energy for it? Would I still be able to connect with the kids? Could I find ways to challenge the reforms I knew were choking the life out of so many classrooms?

Despite my uncertainty about returning, the truth was that I'd never fully embraced my role as a university faculty member. When I presented at research conferences or sat on dissertation committees, I often felt like a fraud—a cut-rate actor playing the part of an academic. I had nightmares about being asked to explain the theoretical framework behind my choice of breakfast cereals. I enjoyed the challenge of working with new and prospective teachers, and I did my best to help guide them on their teaching journeys. But I could never shake the nagging sensation that I was an imposter who would soon be found out.

Beyond that, I also began to question what sort of difference I was making as a teacher of teachers and writer of articles and books about education. I believed it was important work, and I knew that education scholars could be vital voices in the public dialogue about policy and practice in U.S. schools. Still, as No Child Left Behind morphed into Race to the Top, and as corporate reform efforts flooded districts around the country, I felt increasingly distant from the real damage that was being done to public schools. The waters were rising, and I wasn't even close enough to help stack sandbags.

In April, I got a call out of the blue from the principal at my old school. She said a few teachers were retiring and asked me to put the word out at my university. I said I would.

"You wouldn't be interested in coming back, would you?" she asked with a laugh.

The stars, it seemed, were aligning. If I didn't make the jump now, I told myself, I might never do it.

*   *   *

I thought I knew what I was getting myself into. True, I hadn't had a classroom of my own in over a decade, but I'd spent countless hours in other people's classrooms during that time. I knew that teachers were under intense pressure to raise scores, and that—thanks to a new Illinois law—my "performance rating" would be tied to standardized test results. I knew that the district was scrambling to align everything, perhaps even the daily lunch menu, to the Common Core State Standards. I knew that I'd probably hear far less in the coming year about democratic education or social justice than I would about current buzzwords like "text complexity," "accountable talk," and "close reading."

But even though I understood all this going in, experiencing it from the ground-level perspective of a teacher was still jarring. At our school's first faculty meeting, we spent an entire morning doing "deep dives" into test score results from the previous year, comparing our school's "growth" numbers to those of other schools in our network. As each PowerPoint bar graph blurred into the next, I struggled to stay focused. This isn't what I came back to do, I thought to myself. I couldn't remember the word "data" even being mentioned during my previous tenure as a teacher. Now, it was the centerpiece of discussion, the tail that wagged the dog.

And the tail wagged often. Chicago Public Schools' color-coded Assessment Calendar designated 23 weeks of the school year as testing windows of one kind or another. (The fact that a calendar dedicated solely to assessments even existed was, in itself, a sign of the times). My 8th-graders were slated to take the NWEA/MAP test (three times), as well as the ISAT, the EXPLORE, the NAEP, district-mandated performance tasks (twice), and, for English language learners, the ACCESS. Even kindergartners and 1st-graders weren't exempt: They would have to sit through two 40-question "computer-adaptive" exams. It's no coincidence, I thought, that the verb "administer" is used to accompany both harsh punishments and standardized tests.

Along with the accumulating mound of tests, a new mindset had spread through Chicago schools like a contagion. The district's "Chief Executive Officer" called the shots, while emails and staff meetings were littered with jargon from the business world. What used to be merely important was now an "action item." Administrators were on the lookout for "quick wins" in their schools. Hiring was done by the "talent office." If all this were simply a shift in terminology, it might've just been mildly annoying. But the irksome words and phrases signaled a new reality in the city's schools: a business-minded approach, with "data-driven" accountability as its hallmark.

Despite the craziness, most teachers I worked with did their best not to be consumed or ensnared by the focus on testing and the web of demands that accompanied it. But I could tell that, for many veterans, the narrowed focus of the past decade had taken a toll. One teacher who'd taught in Chicago Public Schools (CPS) for over 30 years told me he could easily see himself putting in another 4 or 5 years if not for the stifling constraints from above. As it was, he said, he'd probably take an early retirement. "I still love teaching when I close my door and I'm with my kids," he said. "I have a great group—I always have a great group. But all this other junk they put on us? They've taken the joy out of it."

It wasn't only seasoned colleagues who felt that way. "I'm overwhelmed," a novice 1st-grade teacher halfway through her second year told me during a quick hallway conversation. "Really overwhelmed. Even more than last year. I have a to-do list, and no matter how many things I check off, it keeps getting longer. And so much of our time is taken up by testing, because it's all one-on-one. Sometimes I feel like I'm an assessor, not a teacher. I keep think-ing about all these things I learned in my undergrad classes that I thought I'd be able to do with the kids. But I'm not doing most of them. It's frustrating."

This, I began to see, was one of the real differences in how it felt to be a teacher in the 2010s as opposed to the 1990s. Not that moments of excite-ment, wonder, and genuine engagement didn't still occur in classrooms—they did. But dark clouds loomed overhead. Tension was thick. People who'd dedicated their lives to teaching and to their kids felt overburdened, dispirited, disregarded.

And that was before our school got put on probation.

*   *   *

In choosing between carrots and sticks to enforce their high-stakes account-ability structures, corporate school reformers have typically chosen sledge-hammers. School closures and "turnarounds" have been a standard feature of the reform playbook, and in Chicago, each spring brings another round of contested closures—almost always in low-income African American or Latino communities. In most cases, the first step in the process is probation, which basically serves as a warning to the targeted school community: Get your test scores up quickly, or else. It isn't always a death sentence, but when our principal delivered the news, it sure felt like it. Anxiety levels ratcheted up a few more notches, accompanied by a somber sense of dread.

The saddest thing about it, to me, was how quickly the "probation" label shifted the way some of the adults at our school viewed our collective work. If, the day before, you'd asked individual teachers whether they thought our school was a "good" one, most would have said yes without hesitation. After the probationary designation, though, some seemed to accept the notion that we'd somehow been wrong about ourselves all along, that the board's formula for measuring school failure was infallible, that we were on a wayward ship that needed immediate course correction.

Even if you didn't buy into that line of thinking—and I didn't—it was hard not to feel added pressure. If we weren't able to climb out of the probationary cellar after the first year, we'd be much more likely to be "turned around," which would mean a complete reboot, with all teachers and administrators losing their jobs. I was a little worried about how that could affect me personally, but I was more concerned about what it would mean for the community. Our school was over a hundred years old. Generations of immigrant families had sent their children through its doors. It was a valued and valuable asset in the neighborhood, a site of hope and a safe haven. I didn't want to see it be overtaken by a gung-ho charter operator or a battalion of Teach for America recruits.

Besides, being "turned around" wasn't the only threat. Like many other schools in the city, we were already facing noticeable enrollment declines thanks to the glut of new charter schools opening every year. For a decade, district dollars that could have been used to increase funding for struggling neighborhood schools had been diverted to establish unproven charters, some of which were brazen in their efforts to entice families to pull their children out of neighborhood schools. The week before the school year began, representatives from a nearby, soon-to-open charter had passed out promotional brochures to parents right across the street from our school.

Budget cuts and layoffs were also impacting schools across the city. Many no longer had librarians. Others, like ours, had a social worker who split time among four or five buildings, so students with urgent needs—like Juana, who cut herself, or Sulema, who had been sexually abused—often had to wait a week for a session. Teachers tried to fill in the void, of course, and the Chicago Teachers Union leadership fought to stem the losses, but the bottom line was that teachers were being asked to do more with less. At one march against proposed budget reductions that I attended, a teacher held a sign that read:

> Dear students,
>   Due to recent budget cuts, please bring the following supplies on the 1st day of classes:
>   toilet paper
>   paper towels
>   markers
>   1 case copy paper
>   hand soap
>   books
>   pencils
>   teachers
>   teachers' aides
>   nurse

All of these larger contexts swirled through our hallways and class-rooms each day, and while I tried to set them aside and focus on the kids in front of me, it was sometimes difficult to do so completely. In my social studies classes, it was easy enough to ignore the fact that we were on pro-bation and needed to improve our test scores (or, to use the corporate ver-nacular, to "hit our growth targets"). Because social studies wasn't a tested subject, nobody really cared about it. Our school had "vertical teams" for reading, math, science, and writing, but not social studies. When schools crafted their improvement plans every 2 years, they could choose from a menu of district-approved "focus areas" to direct their attention, but unlike other academic subjects, social studies wasn't even on the list. It was freeing, in a way, because I could pretty much teach whatever I wanted. But it was troubling as well. If our schools were supposed to be preparing democratic citizens, how could we relegate social studies to a curricular afterthought?

My reading class was a different story. Because reading and math scores largely determined every school's fate, the stakes there were high. I'd decided before the school year began that I was going to teach reading the way I believed was best for the students—test scores be damned: a workshop approach with lots of student choice, shelves full of great books, challenging articles on current issues, and plenty of time for discussion and independent reading. In the "old days" of the 1990s, I never would've even considered revising my methods based on how I thought it might impact test scores. But in this new environment, second thoughts crept in. As much as I believed in the plan I'd laid out, I worried that the results wouldn't show up where it mattered. In the middle of otherwise fruitful lessons, I'd hear whispers in my head that I'd rarely heard before: *But is this going to help their reading scores?* I hated to admit it, but it was true.

*   *   *

"What does Coates mean," I asked the 30 8th-graders in my reading class, "when he writes, 'We cannot protect [our son] from our country, which is our aegis and our assailant'"?

The students looked at their papers to locate the passage I'd read. "I don't even know what *aegis* or *assailant* mean," Gabriel said.

"Yeah, I actually didn't know what *aegis* meant when I read it, either," I said. "I had to look it up." I projected the definition on a screen at the front of the class: shield or protection.

We were reading a short online essay by author and journalist Ta-Nehisi Coates, written in response to the jury's verdict in the Michael Dunn trial. Dunn, who is White, had been charged with first-degree murder in the killing of Jordan Davis, a 17-year-old African American. Davis and three friends had stopped at a gas station in Jacksonville, Florida, one night when Dunn demanded they turn the music down in their SUV. A verbal exchange ensued between Davis and Dunn, who pulled a gun from his glove compartment and fired 10 shots at the teens, including one that killed Davis. Dunn insisted he'd seen a gun in the teens' vehicle, but none was found, and no other shots were fired. The jury found Dunn guilty of three counts of attempted murder, but failed to convict him on the more serious first-degree murder charge in Davis's death.

"An assailant is like somebody who attacks somebody else, right?" asked Beto. I nodded.

Eva jumped in. "So I think he's saying that, for Black people, America is like their protector and their attacker at the same time."

"That's kinda like irony," said Gabriel.

"Kind of," I said. "Why would he feel that way?"

"'Cause even though we have laws, they didn't protect Jordan Davis," said Eva. "Michael Dunn still didn't get convicted. So he's saying African American parents can't protect their own kids from stuff like that happening."

"'Cause the jury's racist," Kevin said, anger rising in his voice. "How could they not convict him? He didn't even call the police to tell them what happened. The article said after he killed Jordan he went back to his hotel with his girlfriend and ordered a pizza." Students around the room agreed. If the jury had been pulled from this group of kids, the outcome would've been different.

We spent another 30 minutes on the essay, analyzing Coates's argument, breaking down unfamiliar allusions, and making connections to the students' experiences as the children of Mexican immigrants. Coates's suggestion that White racism is not merely an individual foible, but part of the fabric of America's history and heritage, made sense to most of the kids, even if they didn't grasp every nuance of his essay.

"If Jordan Davis woulda been White and Michael Dunn woulda been Black, he woulda got convicted of everything," Kevin added. "People would be thinking of this totally different."

As our discussion wound down, Lisette glanced at the clock. "Didn't you say we were gonna read today?" she said, waving a copy of Marie Lu's *Legend* in front of her.

"Yeah, you did!' another student agreed. "We didn't read yesterday, either."

We had been reading the entire period, of course, but they meant a different kind of reading: independent reading, at their own pace, with a novel of their choice. It was the centerpiece of our class, and I was convinced it improved the students' reading and vocabulary skills as much, if not more, than any direct instruction I provided. The best way to become a better reader, I believed, was by reading.

A couple of minutes later, I sounded a hand chime and the students—except for a few—buried their heads in books of various genres. Some were reading paranormal romance. Others realistic fiction. Still others manga or a dystopian thriller. But no matter what book they had in their hands, it was a book they chose—and a book they could also choose to abandon if they decided they didn't like it.

At the beginning of the year, I'd told them that they would each be required to read 3 books per quarter—12 for the year. At the time, I considered this ambitious, even risky. Most of the students had read just a few books the previous year, and some had read only one or two. But by the end of the second quarter, several students had read as many as 20 books, and almost all had read more than the 6 that had been required up to that point.

More important than the numbers, though, was the fact that most of the students were enjoying reading more than they ever had before. They asked insightful questions when we did Skype sessions with favorite authors, and recommended titles to one another—sometimes spontaneously.

"I love this book!" Kevin said suddenly, to no one in particular, looking up from his copy of *Eleanor & Park*. "It's heartwarming!"

If you don't realize how remarkable Kevin's words were, you probably haven't taught middle school. For a 14-year-old boy—a boy who came into the year loudly proclaiming his dislike of reading, a boy who had made a name for himself as one of the "cool kids," a boy who loves basketball more than anything and who dreams about playing in the NBA—for that kid to announce to the entire class not only that he loves a book (a book that is, in fact, a romance) but that he finds it *heartwarming*? Amazing.

But it didn't matter, not to the people who counted, the people who liked to count things. I was gratified that most of my students would be leaving my class with a greater love of literature, and with more confidence as readers, but those changes couldn't be easily measured. They wouldn't be part of the formula used to determine whether our school stayed on probation. The only thing that mattered was whether I got the kids' test scores up. If I didn't, I'd be seen as a failure, and so would my students. Nothing heartwarming about that.

*   *   *

So, why am I teaching *now*? Are my aims different in the age of Common Core State Standards and value-added measurements? Have my beliefs been hacked by the new realities of Chicago schools? Has my return to the classroom brought with it a revised philosophy? As I was thinking about these questions, I took a break from my writing to mindlessly check my phone, one of my many well-tooled procrastination techniques. Scrolling through my Twitter feed, I paused on a Tweet from Stephanie Rivera, a graduate student at Rutgers University and education activist. The Tweet consisted of two words—"Why teach?" alongside a photo of a book page with a paragraph highlighted. I tapped the photo to enlarge it and immediately recognized the words. They were mine, from the final pages of *Holler If You Hear Me*, my memoir of my first go-round as a teacher, published in 1999:

> At the core of our work [as teachers] is the belief, despite the distressing signs around us, that the world is indeed changeable, that it can be made into a better, more just, more peaceful place, and that the kids who show up in our classrooms each day not only deserve such a world, but can be instrumental in helping to bring it about. Their voices are abiding reminders that there is something to hope for in spite of the hopelessness that seems to be closing in around us—something tangible, something real, something in the here and now.

I hadn't reread those words in a while, definitely not since I'd returned to CPS, and it was odd, not to mention surprising, to see them staring back at me in a tweet. Reading them again, the critical part of me thought they sounded a little too flowery and idealistic. But a more generous part of me was struck by how much they still resonated all these years later. Sure, my approach has evolved, my beliefs have been tested and refined, my years of experience have helped me to continue to grow as a teacher. But the core of what I believe about teaching, and why I teach, remains constant: All kids—especially kids our public schools have too often failed—deserve an education that honors and validates who they are, that makes room for their questions and concerns, that challenges them to think deeply, that helps them find meaning in a sometimes hostile and confusing world.

Realizing this vision has never been easy. But what has made it even more difficult are the number of obstacles placed in the way, the layers of demands and constraints piled upon teachers, the narrowness of focus promoted by misguided efforts at school reform. In my earlier tenure as a teacher, I used to say that trying to hold on to one's values and beliefs was like teaching in the ocean's undertow, with a constant, sometimes imperceptible tug pulling you in the direction of conformity and compliance. These days it's more like teaching in a tsunami.

But I see signs that the tide may be turning. In Chicago and across the country, teachers' unions are embracing a renewed focus on issues of social justice. Grassroots groups of parents and community members are organizing to question district policies and advocate for public schools. Students and teachers are boycotting standardized tests. Teacher-bloggers are ensuring that teachers' voices are a vital part of the public conversation about education. There's plenty more work to do, of course, but a lot of good things are happening.

In a few weeks, I'll begin the third year of my return to the classroom. I still don't know if my school has been removed from the probation list or not. Some days I still feel like a stranger in an unfamiliar land. But as summer slips away and July becomes August, a nervous excitement for the upcoming year is building. I've been around long enough to know that it will be tempered soon enough. This year, like the previous two, will be filled with challenges. But it will also be filled with possibility—and with moments, like Kevin's bold proclamation of love for a book, that make everything else worthwhile.

CHAPTER 11

Teaching Chemistry, Impacting Lives

John Levasseur

"Do you like cowboy movies?" I asked Charles, a student in my high school chemistry class, who had become frustrated with the fact that I would not direct a question to another student until he gave a quality response. He had heard my spiel and had been my student long enough to know that in my classroom responding to a question with "I don't know" or a shrug of the shoulder would not suffice, and would instead spark my ire.

"For an 11th-grade high school student to respond to any question with '*I don't know*' is a lie or a cop-out," is a statement that has reverberated throughout my classroom and into the hall again and again during my career. "Even if you do not know something, you have come too far and know too much not to be able to add something intelligent to this conversation even if you respond by asking a clarifying question. As far as the shoulder shrug goes," I added, "it is simply beneath your dignity. Let's be honest, what you are really saying is: '*Ask someone else; I cannot be bothered to think*.'" I continued, "If I move on to another student now I will be saying to you that I believe you're not worth bothering with, and I am not going to do that."

A mantra that I say to myself in uncomfortable situations at school, and I must have called it to mind at that moment, is: "Never surrender the classroom!" For whatever reason, today this young man was digging in. He was not answering and was not going to be engaged in learning or thinking about chemistry. Because I feel that it is a responsibility dodge on my part to allow students to opt out of learning when they are in my classroom,

I wasn't letting him off the hook. The classroom's atmosphere of learning hung in the balance of the outcome of this interaction.

"They all right," Charles conceded to the cowboy movie question, which was the only answer he'd offer other than "I don't know," for the last several minutes while both my blood pressure and the tension in the room increased. "You know those metal things cowboys wear on the back of their boot?" I followed up. "Yes," came the young man's reply. Another student volunteered, "I have always wanted to know what those were." "Spurs," I said in the most dignified calm tone I could manage, "Cowboys tap or kick the sides of their horses if the horse isn't going in the right direction or running fast enough."

"Charles, the pain, frustration, or embarrassment you're feeling is not from me; it is from the cowboy of time." I paused and took a deep breath to let the curiosity percolate. "You see, what you are feeling is the spur of the moment correcting and encouraging you, because RIGHT NOW IS YOUR OPPORTUNITY to learn, and this moment does not want you to miss it, nor do I."

"Okay, mister, what was the question you asked me again?"

AH-HA MOMENTS

That interaction not only improved my relationship with Charles, it also changed for the better the way the class interacted for the rest of the school year. As I recall and cherish the memories from more than 15 years of teaching, this particular instance is one of thousands of fond memories. Many wonderful moments come from responding to, or positioning, a single student or class into an "ah-ha" moment. Of course, not every second of a teaching career is spent at your best, drawing out and addressing the ah-ha or teachable moment. There are many difficult situations, frustrating days, and challenging students, but I believe most of the moments spent in a high school classroom have the potential to be profoundly "teachable" and unquestionably rewarding.

I have wanted to be a teacher all my life. When my friends talked and dreamed of playing professional baseball, I was planning how I would teach the Battle of Gettysburg, if given the chance. While growing up, I am sure I dreamed of teaching every imaginable subject from shop class to English grammar. Great teachers were my heroes and interesting topics were to me more collectable than baseball cards. In college I studied by imagining I was teaching whatever course I was enrolled in and I created lesson plans of how I would have taught the lesson that my professors had presented. As many young adventurous people do, I traveled in an attempt to answer the question, "Who am I?" At the age of 20, I went to Tanzania on an 8-month tourist visa. While traveling through that East African nation I was offered my first real teaching job at an Agricultural Secondary School in Iringa, Tanzania. I clearly remember my first day, first class, how nervous I was and how I had placed such high expectations on myself. I walked in with my box of chalk and eraser, never looking at the children; I headed straight for the shelf next to the blackboard to lay down my burden. As I walked in, the students rose and greeted me with the respectful welcome in the Swahili language, "*shika-moo.*" I summoned the nerve to turn and face them so I could respond. When I responded to those beautiful brown eyes with the words "*marahaba, hamjambo,*" an indescribable warmth came from my own heart and waved over me, as well as a powerful sense that the classroom was my home. It was my ah-ha moment, a moment that turned an 8-month safari into a 2-year sojourn and ultimately a childhood dream into lifelong ardor and career.

TEACHING IN THE AMERICAN CLASSROOM TODAY

When I returned home to Massachusetts, I earned an English as a Second Language Certificate at Worldwide Teachers Development Institute in Boston and attended the Stockbridge School of Agriculture at the University of Massachusetts in Amherst, and in time earned an associate's degree in fruit and vegetable crop production and a bachelor of science in plant and soil science with a minor in biology. Between starting and finishing at UMass, I spent some years teaching English outside of Hong Kong in Shenzhen, China. While in China I decided I wanted to return to the States and teach at the most American high school I could find. I remember thinking, "I'd like to find something like John F. Kennedy High on Main Street, USA." Well, I came close: My current job as a chemistry and English language learner (ELL) science teacher at Central High School on Roosevelt Avenue in Springfield, Massachusetts, seems like the quintessential American high school. For me, teaching at Central High is the "*Big Leagues*" and a dream come true. "Central's student body represents the ethnic diversity and changing face of America, with students newly arrived to this country from around the world, as well as those whose families have been here for generations."

Central High has all the problems and all the challenges that face American education today, but it is for me the ideal school setting. Like many other great high schools, Central has all the strong academic programs, from Advanced Placement science, math, English, and history classes to literary and political debate clubs, television and print journalism courses, exceptional preforming and visual arts programs, and amazing leadership and physical fitness opportunities in both the ROTC corps and sports teams. Although these wonderful academic and extracurricular programs are significant and important, the real reason that Central High is a great school is the significant cohort of passionate, highly skilled, and dedicated teachers and administrators who bring life to the school's programs. When I am having one of those difficult days, I re-inspire myself by watching or listening in on some of my colleagues' classes; there is an irresistible passion for teaching as well as a humanity and self-knowledge that permeates the air of a powerful classroom experience.

It is no longer news that today's classroom teachers and students face a host of difficulties that come from outside the classroom. There is the latest wave of scapegoating public education in America for the nation's ills and its identity crisis as we make the transformation away from being the dominant global economic and military power. Teachers are now, more than ever, charged with enacting a flood of new initiatives from sincere and well-meaning experts that are, let's be honest, simplistic and often contradictory quick-fix solutions to overwhelmingly complex social and political issues. From great universities and researchers comes literature on an assortment of new or old teaching strategies that have proven successful being taught by some capable teachers somewhere; each of these strategies is presented as if it should be employed in every classroom. In addition, there is a seemingly endless stream of mandated testing that interrupts classroom instruction and compels many teachers to simply prepare students to be evaluated rather than educated.

This can be a confusing and challenging time in education. When faced with these noble yet contradictory ideals and teaching strategies that do not fit my personality or classroom experience, I often feel like throwing my hands in the air, embracing the cop-out, and announcing, like Charles, that "I do not know, nor do I have any answers." Ah, but then I feel that sharp metallic poke in my side from time's cowboy and I am reminded that: RIGHT NOW IS MY OPPORTUNITY TO TEACH.

From my favorite book on teaching, *The Courage to Teach* (Palmer, 1998), I came to realize that as critical as content knowledge, teaching style, and techniques are, great teaching comes from the teacher's innermost and true self and that ultimately what we teach is who we are. We have all heard the saying that in real estate the watchword is, "Location, Location,

Location." Well, in teaching it is, "Context, Context, Context." So in this light, and to ensure that my classroom remains mine and a place where I can give my students what I have to offer them, which ultimately is myself, I have felt obliged to define and enact a simple personal scheme for my classes. I teach to my students' needs, the way I feel that I can be most effective in educating them for their successes.

As teachers, we have learned that a diverse student body and staff make for better-educated students. Perhaps we are still learning that a variety of teaching approaches strengthen our students' ability to understand what it means to be, and how to be, an educated person. Due to the circumstances of where, when, and how I teach, I find myself falling under the "back-to-basics" approach at this time. I am forced by the circumstances and context in which I teach to ask myself, "How can my teaching community produce the next generation of rational (root word is ratio) and critical thinkers if we don't successfully teach fractions, the basis of ratios, and the fundamentals of grammar, the logic of the language that creates and organizes thoughts in the mind?" Most of my students are missing these basics when they arrive in my room, and I believe a solid education in these fundamentals is essential to, and builds the foundation of, my students' education. Because a student cannot learn chemistry without understanding the math of fractions and ratios, then I had better be willing to teach fractions and ratios and reinforce that foundation before I attempt to teach chemistry and build knowledge on a shaky foundation. If my students struggle with reading and writing, then it is my responsibility to make room for literacy to share the stage with the content of chemistry. Isn't the origin and definition of social justice giving the tools of success to every student?

WHY WE TEACH: EUDIAMONIA

While an undergraduate, I tried to come to grips with why teaching was so important to me. At the time I was reading some of the works from contemporary scientists and had come to the notion that teaching, the training of the young members of our species by the older members, is a biological imperative because children are so completely dependent on adults. Richard Dawkins, the famous evolutionary biologist from Cambridge University, in his book *The Selfish Gene* (Dawkins, 1989), compares the passing on of ideas, which he calls *memes* (from the Greek word for an idea to be copied, *mimeme*), with the passing of genes to the next generation. Since those formative years at UMass, I have continued to question myself about the power and sway that this curious vocation has on my life.

Why do we teach *now*? Certainly, no one with any sense enters the teaching profession with the intention of making money. No, people who go into teaching plan to make a difference.

The summit of education and teaching is not the ability to answer the question, "Who am I?" as fundamental as that is; nor is the central reason for schooling to increase social justice and ensure a more equitable society, as noble as those goals are; nor is it education's task to produce a qualified workforce of good American or even global citizens, notwithstanding how pragmatic that objective may be; nor is teaching the basic and biological desire to pass on our knowledge, irrespective of how humanistic that goal may be. Those are all means to an ultimate end, and that end is *happiness*. It is as simple as that. Is it really too farfetched and outlandish to propose that we taught in the past and continue to teach for the simplest yet most important thing in life: happiness?

The alchemy of education changes emptiness to fulfillment for teachers; education transmutes fear and despair into hope, and creates exuberance and joy for students. It also offers the potential for peace and security to our civilization by confronting ignorance and prejudice. The great Greek philosopher Aristotle concluded that happiness is the highest human good and the very purpose of life (Aristotle, 1984). Aristotle used the Greek word *eudiamonia* to describe happiness. As used by Aristotle, this term has a greater meaning than simply pleasure. For Aristotle, eudiamonia is the joy, satisfaction, and fulfillment that come from self-realization and a virtuous life of action and contemplation all rolled into one (Kosterski, 1990). It is this happiness, eudiamonia, that I believe comes from and is the reason why we teach.

Henry David Thoreau, a 19th-century Massachusetts Transcendentalist, wrote,

> Obey the spur of the moment. These accumulated it is that make up the impulse and imputes of the life of genius. . . . Let the spurs of countless moments goad us incessantly into life. I feel the spur of the moment thrust deep in my side. The present is an inexorable rider. (Thoreau, 1980)

My hope is that all teachers feel the steel of that inexorable rider, the cowboy of time's spurs, and can join me in remembering: "RIGHT NOW IS OUR TIME TO TEACH!" while we are goaded toward the eudiamonia that life in the classroom is offering to us and our students.

TEACHING TO HEAL

Teaching serves to heal both teachers and students from personal and institutional hurt, and that is the topic of the four essays in Part V. Matt Hicks, a teacher in Georgia, describes how he came to a deeper understanding of both his White privilege and native citizen privilege through his experiences as a teacher and coach with his largely Mexican American immigrant student body. Given the changing demographics in our public schools, his essay reminds us that this change is ubiquitous and likely to grow rather than diminish. For example, who could have imagined, a couple of decades ago, that numerous schools in the South would now have more Latino than African American or White students? Diversity is everywhere, from our most populated urban areas to our smallest towns, and immigration issues are also sure to increase. Matt's empathy, deep care, and understanding of his students' predicaments help define what it means to care for all students, not just those most like us.

In Sharim Hannegan-Martinez's essay, we catch a glimpse of the pain that accompanies a growing number of our students to school, pain that, in Sharim's case, she has learned to deal with the pen and education, and by teaching. Her question, "What matters?" is a good one to keep in mind as we think about the schools we want, the teachers we need, and the kind of education that will heal our young people. Eileen Blanco Dougherty, a teacher of "special children" in New York's Harlem, describes how working with children with special needs and their families is particularly significant now, given the many mandates, restrictions, and regulations with which schools must contend. Knowing that children such as these can quickly get lost in "the system" keeps Eileen advocating for them while also recognizing that it is they who keep her going.

The final essay in Part V is by Chuck Greanoff. A social studies high school teacher in Lakewood, Ohio, Chuck made a career change from psychotherapy to teaching when he realized "I was always a high school history teacher at heart." In his essay, Chuck laments the current state of the marketization of education while at the same time refusing to give in to such forces and arguing instead for professional agency, both in the classroom and outside of it. Through interviews with a number of his students, he describes some of the qualities he has attempted to develop as a teacher. He ends his essay with some of the values and behaviors that have kept him going, and urges other teachers to consider them as well.

CHAPTER 12

Coming into Full Humanity Through Teaching, Sharing, and Connecting

Matthew Hicks

"Coach, put your seat belt on, *wey*."

"Man, he be driving so fast sometimes. We can't do that."

"Coach, why don't you put your turn signal on? Mexicans can't get away with that."

"My dad would be deported if he drove like this."

"If I had a million dollars, first thing I'd do is tell my dad he could drive as fast as he wants, everywhere."

I used to think that my social justice bent came from my place of privilege. That it was forged from the time afforded to me to study social inequities in college, and the guilty heat I felt looking in from the outside. I would be lying to say it felt much deeper than just a pressured intellectual pursuit. I began to question this, though, not long  after I started my teaching career and began to form deep, meaningful relationships with some very special students.

Intellectually, I gained a better understanding of what it meant to be one of the estimated 11.1 million undocumented immigrants in the United States through conversations like this one on car rides home from high school soccer practices. The other coach and I usually spent our evenings carting home the majority of our soccer team after practices. Our rides home generally started the same way: fights over who would sit up front, jokes about how many could squeeze into the backseat, and boyhood ribbing of one another about an errant shot or nasty slide tackle from the night's training session. On the way, though, there were backseat warnings that would deviate from this script.

Their jokes about my White privilege and my citizenship privileges were something I understood to be more than just jokes. From these cracks, I was able to open some doors to more thoughtful, personal discussions with the boys. Over time I became more and more conscious of their status-specific struggles. I became more sensitive to their familial needs and was able to help them as players and young men in more ways than as just a coach. It truly impacted my thinking, though, when another player with whom I had been especially close pulled me aside during his senior season to ask for help finding a way into college through soccer.

Eduardo was better off than many of the other players on the team. He had strong grades and didn't need rides home after practice. He didn't make those backseat jokes. His status needs weren't even on my radar. He and I sat together each afternoon during my planning period researching small, local colleges that he might be able to play for. After some work we found a couple and I contacted their coaches. One showed some interest. So I put the ball back in his hands to finish this communication, but he dropped it. Frustrated, I chased him down the hall between classes and lit into him a bit about not meeting his end of our deal. He dropped his eyes and told me he'd come by later to explain.

The day buzzed by, and I looked up to see a sullen, shame-faced Eduardo standing in my door. All he could say was, "Sorry, Coach. I should have told you."

"What's up?" My jaw had clenched with residual frustration, but my intuition told me to loosen up and understand that I needed to pull back from the verbal assault I had committed in the hallway earlier.

He choked up and sat in his usual chair alongside my desk. My thoughts raced with concern, and my body language invited him further in. "I didn't call the coach back. I'm sorry. There's something I should have told you. I can't go to college. They can't take me on their team. I'm . . . an illegal alien." My mind locked onto his face, his tears. Eduardo. A sweet but tough, near 200-hundred-pound 18-year-old was now before me in tears.

"I'm, I'm sorry. It's okay. Slow down, man. I didn't know. I've never heard you talk about it like the other guys. Your family always appeared better off."

"I know. We are. We, um, were. I'm different." He pulled back tears and through watery eyes recounted his brief story. Eduardo and his family had come here legally on a visa many, many years ago. His parents had been able to keep good jobs for much of his life, a life here that started in early elementary school. This, however, was ripped away after the anti-immigrant, xenophobic policies that came in response to the September 11th attacks. Shortly after the Twin Towers were ripped down, so, too, were the visas of Eduardo's family and thousands of others. Almost overnight, Eduardo's family lost it all. "But, shit, Hicks. This was our home. Hell, I've lived here since I was a small kid. We couldn't leave."

Undocumented immigrants are classified as "international students," regardless of how long they have attended Georgia schools. This severely limited Eduardo's soccer options. College coaches can only take a limited allotment of internationals, and they are generally reserved for overseas, elite recruits. Eduardo was so crushed he told me that he wanted to drop out of school. He felt this way, despite being just a month shy of graduating. His hope was lost.

"Whoa. Hold up. There are still options, buddy. Let's talk about Athens Tech. I know you can go there. You can go there, at least, until we look into other options. Serg, your best friend, Sergio goes there and he is illegal." (I had not yet come to find "undocumented" in my vocabulary and only parroted the words I had heard in the media.)

"Yeah. I can do that. But what's the point, coach? I can go there, get a degree, and then what? Cut fucking lawns!? I still can't get a job."

That stuck in my head. My head pounded. My logos seemed on point. He needed to make a step forward, even if they were baby steps. Education is liberation, right? If I knew anything, then I knew this much. My brain hurt. This was no longer true—not for Ed, anyway. We worked through most of his hopelessness that day. He agreed to make it through the next month to graduation and investigate Athens Tech as a step forward. We did so because he trusted me. The problem was, I didn't know if I trusted myself anymore.

Since then, because Eduardo was one who crossed into our country on a legal pathway, he was able to continue along that pathway. He married a citizen. I attended his wedding and was later honored with a very special request. He asked my wife and me to sponsor him and his wife. Eduardo now has a green card and is on a very solid path. This was a huge load off my mind.

Fast forward a couple of years, and I found myself looking up from my desk to find another student in my doorway, again in tears. Uma, though, was a deep part of my heart. I had coached her for 3 years, taught her in class, and she was to be my intern the next semester. She was brilliant, beautiful, and driven. She had a bright, genuine smile that always made my busy days better. Her tears didn't resonate in my head, they poured straight into my heart. Although we have shared many tears together over the years since, this was the one time she ever cried in front of me about this. She had spent the last 17 years racking up top-notch grades, academic awards, and endless dreams only to now find out that she was undocumented. Her parents, El Salvadorian immigrants on Temporary Protected Status (TPS) visas, had brought her here in 3rd grade. They did so to escape a civil war with two other, even younger siblings on their laps aboard a plane. These were children young enough not to need their own plane tickets, and they now lacked any evidence of their arrival here. Her parents were documented, but their three girls were not. They had hidden this from her for over a decade in hopes that their attorney could fix it or laws would change.

Now that she was pestering them for a driver's license and permission to accept the many internships and job opportunities that had come her way, they finally relented and told her the truth. Her vision of the future seemed lost, her identity crumbled under the questions. Still, she mustered the strength to find answers. Her dedication and her resilience since then have pushed me to do more.

Due to the Georgia Board of Regents ban on undocumented students at the University of Georgia and four other state institutions, she was locked out of her dream school and the HOPE Scholarship. Anti-immigrant sentiment and legislation was growing in Georgia. House Bill 87, modeled after Arizona's SB 1070, now threatened her very safety, and there seemed little hope for anything more than other mean-spirited bills coming in its wake. Still she began to apply for scholarship after scholarship, school after school. She came to me with a litany of questions: how to fill out paperwork, what loans or scholarships she was eligible for, what to do when they asked for social security numbers, etc. etc. These answers were not yet out there. Our counselors knew little. We sought out our own answers. One-on-one meetings commenced, web searches hit walls, and phone calls to admissions' departments became commonplace. Answers were slow but eventually came.

Along the way many of the students I had connected with during HB87 rallies came to me with similar questions. My answers were simple.

"Go ask Uma. She's doing that right now."

"You don't know Uma? Fine. Meet me after school, and we will figure it out together."

From our work together, we learned a lot. I asked Uma, who was now my intern, to compile this information so we could share it with the 132 other undocumented students at Cedar Shoals High School. I gave her a simple outline for a table of contents, and then she blew me away with her product. She took it all in and put together a 40-plus page guide for undocumented students who needed to learn about the local private and public colleges that would serve them, the available scholarships, admissions questions, and much more. I sent it far and wide to counselors around the state and to our own people in the district. Then I asked her to help me use the school's enrichment period to teach a class from this guide.

This was a 3-day-a-week open period at our school where students were able to sign up for their choice of enrichment or remediation classes. I had to do much of this under the table for fear of reprisal from administrators or community members, and, of course, I needed to make sure not to violate any part of the Family Education Rights and Privacy Act (FERPA) or "out" any students. We gave the course a vague, innocuous name, and from there we used our relationships with other kids to bring together 15 aspiring, college-bound, undocumented students who we believed could benefit from this information. Seven of them were now seniors. The deal was simple: We would do all we could to help them get into college with as much schol-arship support as possible. They just had to do the work and find other undocumented students to whom to pass the guide and its lessons.

We started that first year with a small group. Out of this work, com-munity was built, family grew, and so did their dreams, empowerment, and open doors. Seven students left there having been accepted to at least one college. Three students earned six scholarships. Uma earned more than I could keep up with and chose to pursue a full ride at Agnes Scott College. This work was more than just something I made plans for each week. It was no longer an abstraction or intellectual pursuit. It was close to my heart each night as I prepared for school. It was what brought me there each day. Those kids brought me there each day. It's what pushed me.

Once our application and scholarship work was done, we moved into a new project with Tobie Bass, a close community member from outside the school. We set forth on a video project about the students' self-representation and redefining how others perceived them and how they perceived them-selves as undocumented immigrants. And the students got stuck when asked to find an image, find a quote, find music that represented them. So I tried a protocol I had previously used with some thematic analysis work in litera-ture classes. I created a worksheet.

1. I want to tell people _____
2. I care about _____
3. I love _____
4. I hate _____
5. I fear _____
6. I want to change _____
7. We are different because _____
8. We are the same because _____
9. I dream _____
10. I am _____

I brought the students in that day, turned down the lights, and gave four simple commands. "Take out pen and paper. No talking. Trust me. Shhh. I want nobody to speak. Just relax." I tried to speak as calmly as I could. They weren't used to their vociferous, energetic teacher pulling this on them, but they fell right in line. The bottom line was simple, they did trust me. "You are all over-thinking Tobie's and my directions for this video. You've sent some great things. We've had some great discussions. But you are all stuck on trying to find the perfect submission. I need you to let go of that. The truth here will come from the compilation of your pieces. The beauty and answers will come when you let go."

I began to read aloud each prompt. They had 12 seconds to give their instinctual, gut response to each one. Their answers lay there, after all. *Shhhh!* No talking. They dutifully completed the task, and this work sparked a thoughtful, short discussion before the bell pushed them out of the door. I watched them leave. Each of them seemed relieved yet excited to go home to complete their individual task of sending submissions for the video. I liked my decision. My heart was warmed by their unconditional trust in the process, and my gut told me this would help.

It was only a few hours later that my doorway shined with Uma's smile, and, as always, I felt a sense of home and family whenever my intern reported for duty. As I had often done, I put the paperwork for our immigration and education class aside for her to help me with later. I handed her the sheets, which I had not had time to read yet. I asked her to compile their answers on an electronic document, as she had done for me many times before. She grabbed the papers with a confident smile and took them back to her table. As I prepared for tomorrow's literature class, she typed away in the corner.

She glided over right as the bell rang, told me she had emailed me the document, and stood up under me, as she often did. Just for that extra minute. It was her way of showing closeness without words. She hugged me, soothing my heart after a long day of teaching, and then scurried out the door.

I opened the document without much thought, only to have everything tear at my insides. I read through and saw some powerful responses. Then I got to number 5. There were 13 answers on that sheet. Ten were the same. None of those kids saw each others' answers. None of those kids had spoken. I looked at those lines and my stomach wrenched.

> "I fear being separated from my family."
> "I fear being separated from my family."
> "I fear jail. Losing my family members."
> "I fear my father being deported."
> "I fear. I fear every time my dad is late coming home from work."
> "I fear being separated from my family."
> "I fear the law."
> "I fear losing my family."
> "I fear never seeing my family again."

Ten times. Almost word for word, the same thing. The love that had just melted my heart and left the room rained down into my gut. My jaw clenched, my heart sank, and my stomach tightened, because I couldn't handle those words swimming around in my head, pouring down into my heart, and pounding down on my stomach. These weren't the stories filling my Facebook Newsfeed, these weren't the articles I had read online, these weren't abstractions. This wasn't politics. This was my family.

This was Leeidy, whose trailer I'd been to. I'd seen her bedroom window facing the parking area into which her father pulled his red Ford Explorer late each night after his shift at the doughnut shop. As I read, I heard Leeidy's voice and saw her face: her huge, innocent eyes and scrunched up chin resting upon her window sill, awaiting her father's arrival each night from the time she was a small girl.

This was Karen's beautiful, green eyes tearing up as she recounted her own story in front of nearly 200 people at a University of Georgia forum as part of our "Coming Out of the Shadows" Program. She wept and spoke of a 7-year-old Karen who saw her father detained by immigration for 7 months, unsure of when she'd speak to him again, not knowing if he'd ever come home, and then watching her mother use all of their savings to pay for an attorney who might possibly bring him home again.

This was Pastor Jordan, the sweetest young man I knew, who was partially deaf in one ear and put his arm around us to lean in and communicate in his own gentle way each day. He was now telling me about his fears for his father, who was deported the very next year.

This was Hex, tough on the outside but thoughtful on the inside, who had been part of those backseat soccer rides home pulling me aside to ask more serious questions about what he could do to help his family. This was Hex, now man enough to share his deepest fear with me.

These were six other kids who grew up with that burden. It was deeply embedded in them during each waking and sleeping moment. My stomach turned. I went home that night. Their words swam through my head, their words pounded in my heart, their fears wrenched my gut. And I asked myself, "What the heck have I done? How can I open this up and not know how to handle it? How can I carry this burden and sleep at night? How the hell can I ask myself these questions when I have not lived like this? How can I be so selfish?"

I went to bed that night with Karen's weary green eyes, Leeidy's worried face gazing out the window, Uma's smile, and Pastor Jordan's arm around my shoulder. Their fears felt like my own. Now they were. Each had now entrusted me with them and given me a deeper understanding of why I teach. Their honesty and vulnerability had taught me more about myself and humanity than they would ever know.

Teaching is inherently a reciprocal experience. It provides me the opportunity to connect with others, share our lived experiences, and grow together. I teach because I see the humanity revealed in these spaces and through our struggles. At its purest, this is teaching. At its purest, it connects me to who I really am. Teaching for social justice is a part of who I am, on a deeper level now, and the resolve to use my place of privilege to advocate for each and every one of my students is now a part of my very being.

Teaching to Save Our Lives

Sharim Hannegan-Martinez

"My first 'kiss' happened when the dirt fastened its lips to the creases of my ashy *adolescent knees.*"

This is a line from a poem I wrote in October of 2009, 9 years after I was coerced into my first "kiss." Like many young women of color in urban neighborhoods and border towns like the San Diego/Tijuana *frontera* where I grew up, I experienced saturated levels of sexual harassment, violence, and assaults. The trauma of these experiences manifested itself in a variety of ways throughout my adolescence—from drinking, smok-

ing, ditching, and fighting, to blatant self-hate—which I used to isolate and separate myself from other young women of color. For many years, I denied this trauma, even to myself; even as it was being shoved down my throat over and over again, I convinced myself that I had asked for this, that I had wanted this, convinced myself I was not a victim. It was not until my first year of college that I began to have real conversations with other women about the things I had been through. It was in those moments that I learned to name my experience, to name my oppression; it was then that I learned to speak and write with purpose, as articulated by Paulo Freire and Donaldo Macedo (1987). We were women, *finally* allowing ourselves to break. We were Katrinas as the levees cracked and in the midst of that turmoil, in that brokenness, I became literate.

I spent the greater part of my youth searching for light at the end of the tunnel, told that there wasn't one, that I was crazy to dream of light, so I broke in the darkness. My life changed when I found the voice to say that it was dark, that I was afraid, and that I needed light, that I *demanded* it. Finding the voice to name my oppression was the hardest thing I've ever done; I nearly suffocated in sobs, breaking and healing every time I watched a woman rocking herself back and forth, trying to comfort herself, trying to love herself. With these women, I learned how to fight alongside them, rather than against them. Alongside these women, Black and Brown, with crazy curly straight long short lively hair and indignant voices, my pen transformed from a Band-Aid to a bullet. Comparable to Gloria Anzaldúa's description of why she writes (1981), in these moments when I began to speak and write the silenced and unmentionable truth, I began to reconcile my self-hate, heal from trauma, and save my own life.

This is something a school *never* gave me—a choice, a chance, a weapon with which to protect myself, a voice with which to dream and fight and heal. I've been blessed in that I have been able to read and write since I was young, but this is not literacy, in the same way that being able to cut up onions and tomatoes does not necessarily make you a chef. I had teachers who could see me drunk, breaking, voiceless, but they pretended not to see me stumbling into class, or reeking of alcohol. Teachers are either agents of repression or of social change; in my context, they were no better than the police, no better than the abusers I had come to know well.

I am literate: I can name my many oppressions as a young, working-class woman of color; can read the wrinkles on my mama's forehead to know whether we have enough to pay the rent; can decode the corners I can walk on at night; can spot the *migra* from a mile away; can listen for the sound of gunshots and rattling doorknobs; can write and speak and yell truths in a language my *gente,* my people; can understand. I am literate because I can read my world (Freire & Macedo, 1987), and I never learned it in a classroom, but I could have.

Literacy saved my life, which means that by default its absence could have ruined it. Many people ask me why I became a teacher, if my experiences and relationship to schools were negative. That is precisely *why* I became a teacher: because I believed deeply in the power of words, of literacy, of healing, of transformation, of agency, of community, of resistance, and of love, *in spite* of schools. I became a teacher because I wanted to be the type of adult I never had; in a way, I wanted to be there for the 12-year-old me. I wanted to help her heal, tell her that it wasn't her fault, teach her to read and write, teach her how to forgive herself, help her to find her voice. I didn't want her to sit with her pain for a decade, didn't want the scars to harden. I also wanted to prevent it from happening so pervasively, to provide space for young men to redefine and relearn what it means to be powerful and masculine and vulnerable. In a way, teaching was a way of saving, healing, and redeeming myself. Becoming an English teacher specifically seemed the most natural fit: I believe deeply in the potential of language and its relationship to power, in the need for us to be able to tell our own stories in our own words, to claim and re-claim our languages, and to access institutions so that we can transform them. In Isabel Allende's essay "Writing as an Act of Hope" (1989), she says that the greatest truths can be told through the lies of fiction, that we should write what should not be forgotten, and that writing should transform the conscience of its readers. I sought to create a classroom where these ideologies could exist, where young people could analyze the conditions of their reality through literature, write to heal, and become agents of change.

STILL IN THE FIGHT

As I begin my fifth year working in schools and my third year as a full-time high school English teacher in one of the highest-need schools in Oakland, which is by far one of the most beautiful and most disenfranchised communities in this country, I find myself asking, "Why are you *still* teaching?," or "Why do you teach *now*?" In the last year alone, I have had to navigate district-mandated curriculum and high-stakes testing, the strategic displacement of my entire administrative team, the microaggressions that are almost guaranteed when you are one of the only Latina teachers on a campus, a grotesque lack of resources and basic amenities such as bathrooms and functioning windows and ventilation, in addition to the loss of several of our students' lives, countless fights, a significant racial riot, and a shooting in which the .45-caliber bullet ricocheted not 6 feet from our classroom door.

After burying so many children, losing so many to juvenile hall, watching administrators target and police the bodies of Black and Brown children, and feeling helpless and hopeless as I witnessed so many young people I love being pushed out of school over the last few years, it would be a lie to say that answering the "Why do you teach *now*?" question is easy. There are times when the combination of institutional oppression, dehumanization, gentrification, violence, trauma (both historical and contemporary), and the plethora of societal ills feel impossibly overpowering and I find myself asking "What's the point?" More specifically, the question I keep asking myself is not "Why teach?" or "Why teach *now*." but "Why teach now . . . in *these* schools, in these historically oppressive, rotten-to-the-core and unchanging, unrelenting institutions?"

The answer to that question changes for me every day; sometimes it even changes from period to period, but I've decided that as long as I have one reason to stay at any given moment, then we're still in the fight, then we still haven't lost the most critical thing needed for transforming our communities: hope. Still, I wasn't sure how I was going to answer this question today. After an exhausting week with a new administration that insists on legalizing a stop-and-frisk policy on our campus that is resulting in heightened tension and dehumanization, this question felt harder than usual. I sat down to write it, got up, sat down, eventually got up again and, frustrated, I decided to take (another) break from writing and go to the grocery store. As I was walking down the aisle, somebody ran up and hugged me from behind. Startled, I turned around to see one of the students I worked with in my first year as a teacher apprentice in a program called East Oakland Step to College where I had the privilege of training under Jeff Duncan-Andrade and Patrick Camangian—two veteran teachers. After spending a few moments talking to her, her mom and little sister came up and hugged me as well. As she was walking away, she yelled "love you!"

I came home and began to look through the pictures and videos I had from the year I had worked with her as a direct mentor. As I was getting nostalgic looking at how tiny my students were and how long ago it seems, I came across a video of this girl performing a poem she titled "More Scars than Birthdays." It's a poem I think of often, and remark as being a pivotal moment in both my personal and teaching life, but it had been over 2 years since I had watched it and *really* listened to it. As I watched it again, years after the fact and with the question of why I teach now at the forefront of my thinking, I was overcome with grief and compassion and courage and hope and *love*. In this video, in a classroom full of people, this tiny Raza girl stands not 5'1" as she recites, amidst sobs, a poem in which she says:

> If I had a gun pointed at my head, and I had moments left to live,
>   I would see . . .
> a little girl getting raped at the age of four years old/
>   . . . I would see four years passing by before my eyes
> Rape after rape after rape
> I would see an 8 year-old girl with more scars than birthdays . . .

Several times throughout the poem she breaks down in front of her peers, and they alternate between silently respecting her need for time and making comments like "take your time," or "you got this."

I could say that I teach to make sure that young people get these opportunities, or because I think poetry is important and writing is transformative (Camangian, 2011), or because I think speaking publicly is a code of power (Delpit, 1988), or because I think having spaces to radically heal from our traumas is necessary (Ginwright, 2010), and all of these things would be true; they are all part of why I teach. But the main reason I teach, the real reason I have come back after some of the most traumatic experiences in schools (as both a student and a teacher) is because as she walks to the front of the room to perform her poem, she is not alone. A young Black man, her peer, 15 and at 6'3" he towers above her as he stands before the class along-side her. Before this moment they were not friends; they were assigned to work with one another for this project specifically and everybody until now has performed alone, but as he stands next to her, the first thing she says is "He's here because he's going to support me." As she sobs courageously through her poem, he stands there unflinching and unrelenting in his sup-port of her, awkward as it may feel. When she finishes, he grabs her hand and raises it in victory.

WHAT MATTERS?

THAT is why I teach—because I believe, with *every* reason and with *all* the proof in front of me, that writing matters, that love matters, that rela-tionships matter, and that they can help us heal, save our lives, and change the world. I teach because young people are courageous in ways I found unimaginable at 15, and because they heal me profoundly, because they love deeply, and when they are courageous enough to love each other, I feel loved and honored in return. These young people, the young people I am blessed to stand in front of every day, make me feel more human and more loved than I ever thought possible. We owe it to them, it is our duty to fight for spaces *now*, inside these loveless institutions that seem intent on disregarding their humanity, their potential, their worth; it is our responsibility to fight for spaces where they are allowed to be fully human, to be vulnerable and honest, and loving in the ways that are going to save and transform us all.

Arundhati Roy once wrote "Another world is not only possible, she is on her way . . . on a quiet day, if I listen carefully, I can hear her breathing" (2005, p. 75). I teach because the moments I have known this to be truest, the moments I have seen glimpses of the world we have coming and the beauty that she will hold: Those moments have all been in a classroom, those moments have all been in the words and the actions of our babies, of the people who are going to build our future, and our world.

CHAPTER 14

Teaching Jack, and Other Joys of Working with Special Children

Eileen Blanco Dougherty

I met Jack when he was 3 years old. Day after day, for weeks, he would greet me at the door of his apartment with one question, "What train did you take today?" I would always smile and respond with a hello and ask him how his day was going. Jack would talk about the subways of New York City with anyone who would listen and he remembered people by their home subway stop. These conversations intrigued many upon first meeting Jack, but after having the same conversation three or four times, the novelty would wear off. Jack was an adorable little boy with big brown doe eyes; he was full of ideas, but many people saw him as only a rigid little boy who did not care much for conversation or peer interaction.

I worked with Jack four times a week for 2 years. We had good days and we had bad days. I had to work with his family and make sure that his home life did not promote behaviors that would prevent progress. I had to be sensitive to parents still coming to grips with what a diagnosis of autism would mean for their family. I collaborated with his speech therapist, occupational therapist, physical therapist, and other teachers to make sure we were all on the same page in helping Jack reach targeted goals. It was not an easy road, but we saw progress and before we knew it, Jack was asking questions and engaging in activities in ways we had never seen before.

Imagine my excitement when I arrived one spring afternoon and was greeted by both Jack and his mother shouting, "We have good news!" Jack continued, "I am going to kindergarten, the best one!" I looked at his mother, her eyes filled with tears of joy, and I said, "Congratulations!" Jack had been accepted into a public integrated kindergarten class that served four children with autism spectrum disorders and eight typically developing children, better known as the Nest Program in New York City. As I read the acceptance letter, my eyes too filled with tears of joy. I thought of how far Jack had come over the past 2 years and the many meaningful conversations he now had with both his peers and me. I thought of how others were finally seeing him for the amazing little boy he had always been. That acceptance letter was indeed a significant professional accomplishment, and I continue to be inspired to work for other children like Jack.

ADVOCATING FOR SPECIAL CHILDREN

I have worked with children with various disabilities for over 13 years. The disabilities vary but they include cerebral palsy, Down syndrome, and autism. Autism became an area of particular interest to me about 6 years ago when I began working in a self-contained classroom in New York City. I thoroughly enjoyed my time in the classroom and the collaboration between the teachers. It was an extremely positive experience that led me to pursue my master's degree to understand various issues in special education and early childhood education more clearly.

While in graduate school, I learned about the profession of Special Education Itinerant Teachers (SEIT) and I met various such teachers. I was intrigued by the one-on-one work with the children and the collaboration between the teacher, family, classroom teachers, and therapists. I began to investigate this profession as part of my master's degree research project. SEITs service preschool-age children in accordance with the child's individualized education program (IEP). Each session with the student is documented with the goals, activities, and progress of the child, and after various assessments these data are used to write reports about the child. As a SEIT, I was expected to communicate with families regarding the child's developmental progress and parental concerns. Working closely with classroom teachers and other specialists ensured the child's progress. I also participated in Committee on Preschool Special Education (CPSE) meetings to advocate for the needs of the child.

Special Education Itinerant Teachers aid both children and their families in the transition between early intervention and kindergarten. This transition can be a vital part of the child's success, as early intervention usually provides services until the child is ready for kindergarten at 5 years old. Intervention at the preschool age helps prevent regression and assures a solid foundation as the child enters kindergarten in a more structured academic day with peers and perhaps less support. Without early intervention, these children would likely begin formal schooling with an experience of deficit. Early intervention allows children to experience school in the most positive and successful manner, which may define how they feel about school later in their academic career.

I have participated in many CPSE meetings as a SEIT. At many of those meetings, I have sat beside parents to advocate that child's services be met as they entered kindergarten in the public school system. There were many meetings in which I could hear the politics of the system speaking louder than my assessments or louder than the voices of the therapists, teachers, and families. Although there were many times in which I felt confident that I had advocated effectively for the student and that he or she would receive the support needed, there were also times in which I was left wondering what would happen to my student in kindergarten. It was that curiosity that led me to change my path in the field of education.

GRADUATING TO KINDERGARTEN

This September, I found myself in the same position as many of my past students: I entered kindergarten. I was assigned to be a special education teacher partnered with a general education teacher to co-teach in a classroom of 23 children, 8 of whom currently have IEPs. It was my first year teaching outside the preschool early intervention system, and, needless to say, I had plenty of anxiety about the transition. Nothing seemed familiar and there was much that needed to be explained.

It was only 4 weeks into teaching in an elementary public school and I was emotionally drained. I spent day after day trying to understand a system in which the needs of the child are at times quite low on the totem pole compared to the interests of numerous other adults outside the classroom. I was frustrated and quickly disheartened when I realized that my work as an early intervention educator for years did not seem to be able to support my students once they entered kindergarten. What I had feared in many of the past CPSE meetings was unfolding before my eyes.

As a first-year teacher in the public school system I had to be mindful of how I handled situations, but I also had to be able to sleep at night and keep my students at the center of decisionmaking. There were situations in which parents came to my co-teacher and me asking for help and we directed them to seek out a parent advocate who could better navigate the politics of the system. It was not that I did not work hard; it was that the system was one in which the children would inevitably become lost without advocates ensuring that their needs were met. I had to step back many times in order to not get sucked into a negative space of complaining about what was wrong with the system. I had to come to a level of compromise within myself and realize that I still had a job to do, and these children deserved all of my energy.

FOR THE KIDS

During these first few weeks of harsh reality checks, and after many long dinners with mentors and fellow educators, I realized that if I was going to survive, I needed to reevaluate exactly why I made the decision to move into this new realm of education. In the many moments of anxiety, I must refocus and ask myself, "Why do I teach?" As my alarm goes off before the sun is up, I ask myself, "Why do I teach?" While the various levels of education argue over "appropriate" curricula and the early childhood educator in me cannot help but notice the lack of play in the curriculum for my kindergarten students, I ask, "Why do I teach?" In the moments of organized chaos throughout the school day, that same question comes up and I recall one of the many answers that keep me focused: In those hectic moments, the answer is always quick and simple: it is for these kids. When in less frenzied moments, the answer "the kids" is only the beginning.

The children, their families, and what they each have to contribute to this society are all reasons why I teach. Each reason includes more complex descriptions. My role as case manager of students with special needs allowed me to support families to have their child's needs met. Throughout my career, working with my students' families has brought me a lot of joy. It allows me to make sure the child has some follow-through of my lessons at home. It also allows me to form a relationship with parents who need support. Most important, my relationships with families honor the importance that the families have in the children's lives. The families of my students are the first educators that my students have, and I often wish that schools would honor these educators more. I really try to position parents and families as collaborators and essential educators in the success of their children. I have always advocated for, and will not cease to advocate for, my students, especially through their families. I continue to make sure that parents know their rights and how to go about having their children's needs met.

When I am asked to sit in on an IEP meeting for my kindergarten students, I am certain of what the student needs to be successful given the intense academic curriculum he or she faces. I am prepared to justify why this child needs support and I am able to account for each minute of the support requested, as is required of me by those outside the classroom. The support does not look the same for each child; for some it is refocusing on the task before them, for another it might be a sensory break, and another might need the curriculum in a different form. My co-teacher and I are aware of this reality and we honor it to ensure that foundational skills are in place if students are to be successful.

I am blessed to have been paired with a co-teacher who holds similar beliefs to mine as to what kindergarten students need and how we can make our particular group of students successful. In our classroom, the vast majority are students of color, and this fact is not lost on either of us. We know that these particular children have roadblocks that other children might not have, ranging from socioeconomic challenges to language barriers. These differences can be highlighted when the designation of "special needs" is added to the list.

I want my young students to feel successful daily. I want them to know what is expected of them and that I am confident they can achieve those expectations. Nothing makes me happier than seeing students take pride in their work, while knowing that I am just as proud as they are. I teach to help these students know that their success is important and that they are more than capable. I like to think that our classroom can model a society in which their voices matter and in which they can learn to negotiate and be empathetic. I am inspired daily as I see my students learn to engage in these behaviors.

Although I may be in a new setting, one that took weeks to get used to and continues to be an adjustment at times, my reasons for teaching remain intact. I am currently looking forward to my second year of teaching in the public school system. There were many lessons learned that have made me a more confident teacher and more aware of how I can aid my students in being successful. I have formed new relationships with parents and we have fought successfully together to make sure their children's needs are met. My advocacy for my students will never stop. After all, it is because of them that my world is full of laughter and my gray skies have become much brighter.

CHAPTER 15

Teaching in the Invisible Spaces

Chuck Greanoff

I consider myself a very lucky teacher. I am a social studies teacher in Lakewood, Ohio. Lakewood is my hometown, and Lakewood High School is my alma mater and that of my parents. I have been teaching at LHS for 8 years after making a mid-life career change. I previously worked for 13 years as an adjunct psychology teacher at local community colleges and as a practicing psychotherapist for most of that time. Although I spent the better part of 9 years grinding my way toward a PhD at Kent State in psychology, I majored in history as an undergraduate at Ohio Wesleyan, and think I was always a high school history teacher at heart. Helping to restore struggling or even "wounded" clients as a psychologist was gratifying, but left me wanting to play a role in shaping the experiences of young people, not just helping to repair them. After I became certified as a teacher, I chose not to apply for any other teaching position until I heard from Lakewood, and every day since my hiring, I have experienced pure magic. Even the rough days have special moments; even the setbacks offer redemption.

After 8 years in the teaching profession, I've developed what I think is an identifiable philosophy and style, although it is still evolving. I think of my teaching style as "Socrates with a heart." I like to present information and spark dialogue—for example, *Why would subsistence farming, non-slave-owning southern Whites support the planter aristocracy?; What was the impact of the Federal Highway Act on cities and inner suburbs?* Having been a cognitive-oriented therapist has helped me probe for underlying assumptions and prod students to provide evidence for their assertions. I constantly push for critical thinking, understanding the interconnectedness of things, and, above all, helping students develop an analytical disposition.

At the same time, the "habits of the mind" I try to cultivate will only count if students get the sense that our school, and my classroom, are places of warmth and acceptance. Former students have free reign on the candy drawer—as long as they update me on their studies and their lives—and current students are encouraged to bring in pictures of their pets for the pet wall. I want them to laugh and feel safe being sad. Sometimes I miss being a therapist, but I never want to stop teaching. I've found my piece of heaven.

Sadly, a lot of very powerful, well-organized people have a different agenda for our schools, and it doesn't include pet walls, concern for the emotional health of students, or even democratically elected school boards. Recognizing this threat has made me feel very uneasy. Increasingly powerful forces are aligning against "us" (public education) and, as such, many teachers are languishing under a constant battle to retain our spirits. The greatest danger of a depressed spirit is a sense of learned helplessness, a passive acceptance of the "inevitable" evisceration of public education.

As the waves of the reformist agenda came crashing down around me, I came to the realization that I could not, in all good conscience, watch idly as public education was plundered for power and profit. I have always believed that teachers serve democracy in the broadest sense: We seek to cultivate informed citizenship and respect for diversity, as we also promote social justice. We should recognize that the reformist movement is intentionally marginalizing the most meaningful work that teachers do to the point of becoming invisible. As our curricula become constricted in service of the reformist agenda, we need to assert the importance of a broad curriculum— the liberal arts—to both students and society. We want our future engineers to appreciate and enjoy the arts, and our future artists to understand why the bridge they are driving over hasn't collapsed. We want to foster a vibrant, engaged citizenship. All of which runs counter to the precepts of the "reform" movement and its narrow and impoverished rhetoric of "college and career ready."

The attacks are clearly taking a toll, not only on teachers but also on those considering joining the profession. It saddens me when I hear about talented students not wanting to enter the teaching profession, and current teachers looking for a way out. Who can blame them? The good work teachers do daily is practically invisible due to the dictates of the testing/ profiteering machine. Yet, if we "give up the ship," if we don't fight with all we have, what message are we sending students? That the best response to injustice is passive acceptance? Even if and when we lose some battles along the way, we contribute to the democratic process through our resistance.

Now is not the time to become "domesticated (Freire, 1970)." Domestication implies an unquestioning or even reluctant acceptance of the "reformist" framework. In their model, we are stripped of professional agency and become instruments of their agenda. Essentially, in the reformist world we narrow our assessment of ourselves and our students to a test score or scores, ignore the emotional aspects of teaching, and become increasingly passive in our classrooms and community. If teachers don't lead in and out of the classroom and build coalitions with parents and students, we will be reduced from professionals with a voice to technicians and conduits for the profiteers. As we suffer, so do our students and our democracy.

For me, the struggle is very personal. As a social studies teacher, I feel we are not only fighting for a bedrock principle of our democracy—public education—but for our communities as well. As public schools are privatized and children monetized, the commodification of every element of the educational process will inevitably erode many of the bonds that hold our communities together. This is not the future I envision for my community—Lakewood, Ohio—or for our schools.

LAKEWOOD HIGH SCHOOL

Lakewood High School (LHS) is a large (1,800 students) public school in Lakewood, Ohio, an inner-ring suburb of Cleveland. Lakewood is the most densely populated city in Ohio, with a large immigrant community, evidenced by the 26 languages spoken in the halls of LHS. Our housing stock is as diverse as our population, ranging from lakeside mansions to lower-priced rental properties. To the west are the outer-ring suburbs that are more uniformly everything—more White, more affluent, more culturally homogenized, and with higher aggregate standardized test scores than Lakewood. To the east is Cleveland, which, like cities elsewhere, was abandoned by people of means long ago and struggles with test scores near the bottom.

As communities across the nation become more segregated and homogenous, Lakewood is becoming increasingly unique. We not only remain diverse, but also we are one of only two "walking districts" in the entire state; that is, no kid takes a school bus and at the end of the school day, students of all races, ethnicities, and income levels walk home. Around town people often say we "live on top of one another" and therefore have to learn to get along. Insofar as a diverse environment is an ideal laboratory for democracy, it's tough to beat Lakewood and LHS.

Given the dispiriting attacks on public education and the profession, teachers everywhere are often asked, How do you still get up every morning to go teach? How do you find the strength to continue to encourage your young students to become or remain motivated, and to be caring and compassionate members of society? As these questions pass through my mind, I've actually found a new energy for teaching. In particular, I have found a renewed purpose in two places: my commitment to teaching as a democratic act, and my dedication to treating my students as people I love rather than as objects producing test scores. Teachers, and indeed anyone who values public education, can find energy and purpose by reminding ourselves that being agents of democracy and effective teachers are not mutually inclusive; one cannot survive without the other. In fact, we can look to our students for purpose, hope, and reminders of what good teachers do. To that end, I interviewed some of my students and thought back on the most meaningful moments in my career. Their responses, which I share later in this essay, have informed how I define teaching. This journey, and my reflection upon it, gets me up in the morning.

TEACHING FOR DEMOCRACY

The continuous assaults on public education have compelled me to exercise my voice outside the classroom and fight in the political arena. For example, I recently wrote a three-part series for a local newspaper, *The Lakewood Observer*, on the Common Core State Standards. After extensive reading, I concluded that the Common Core and its testing regimen is designed to lay the groundwork for the monetizing of children, the privatization of public education for profit, and the marketing of scalable educational products that can be sold *en masse* to schools all over the country.

With this knowledge, I could not keep my concerns to myself. I had to find a way to expose the reformers and their anti-community agenda to the best of my ability. At the end of the day, political engagement not only strengthens my sense of agency in the classroom but also helps me sleep at night. I know I will be able to answer the question if someday society asks, "Where were you when your local school schools were being taken over by the corportocracy?" My answer will be two-fold: (1) that I engaged directly in the political process and (2) that I never abandoned those invisible moments where real teaching and learning occur, that I taught for students, not for someone else's bottom line.

TEACHING FOR STUDENTS

During this reform era, teachers are bombarded with new data, testing, and reporting mandates. Any notion of forming genuine teaching and learning relationships with students is now officially nonexistent. Although it is easy to lose sight of what really matters and what impact teachers can have on students' lives, I have found solace in my daily routines. For most of my 8 years as a teacher, I've had the privilege of teaching the entire spectrum of LHS students—from inclusion students, to refugees, to AP Scholars. At graduation a few years ago, within seconds of each other I was greeted by an auto-tech student who was thrilled to have gotten a job at a local garage and a writer heading off to Northwestern University. In an instant, I fell in love with LHS all over again. I think communities that lack diversity and a student body that is a fair representation of our country are suffering from a certain type of poverty.

Sometimes, I'm reminded of the structural inequities in our society and of our moral obligation to ameliorate their effects to the extent of our ability. For example, every day last year, four students—or "the friendly foursome" as I would call them—stopped by my classroom, partially in search of chocolate but mostly in search of connection. They came with questions and comments about school, history class, and other concerns. Most teachers would recognize them as "happy kids," violinists and cellists, "high achievers" from "stable" homes with front porches and family dogs. They're as funny as they are intelligent and they have an edge. In short, they were any teacher's dream. As their teacher, I not only push them through challenging lessons and critical thinking, but also through these interactions and through caring that they grow to be good and compassionate people. I find their stories uplifting and they are a big part of the reason I continue to teach.

One day, as I reveled in my own friendly foursome routine, a colleague stopped by with a less uplifting story: One of his students had become homeless. This was a kid with no family dog or front porch, no "stable" home in the neighborhood, and no violin lessons. My caring colleague was taking up a collection for a food card for which I pitched in $20.00. There has not been another day in my 8 years of teaching that has more profoundly affirmed my commitment to teaching. My colleagues rallied to his cause, which was heartening, but most affirming was the reminder that teachers can and should assert their role as leaders of a community. These moments, although invisible to the reform establishment, give our lives meaning.

For me, the juxtaposition of these events reminds me that we need to be fully present—physically and emotionally—for every student. It's more than just ironic; it is criminal that the most meaningful moments of teaching are evaluated the least, or not at all.

Meaning, and the energy it brings, has sadly gotten lost or, more accurately, been made invisible by the reformist establishment. But I've learned that meaning can be found virtually everywhere inside schools. For instance, another of my most memorable and meaningful moments came at a swim meet. On a Friday in February a few years ago, one of my students was beaming with enthusiasm for the upcoming sectional. Her relay had a chance to qualify for the state meet, and she had spent thousands of hours training with that goal in mind. Then, life became cruel. She disqualified the whole relay team by jumping early and then jumped the gun again in her best individual event. She later told me that she spent her Sunday in a fetal position and was inconsolable. On Monday in class, she was distraught, tearing up and putting her head down. I sensed it was a teachable moment, but I didn't know what to say. I offered a few encouraging words, but to what effect, I was uncertain.

The following year, she was just as determined for the sectional meet, and this time, she won the 100-yard freestyle. In her moment of victory, she looked for me in the stands and gave me a joyous thumbs-up, warming my heart. Her grit and commitment—and the joy I get from many students—immunizes me from the increasingly toxic environment in which teachers must function. They remind me of what a special teaching/learning community can and should be: an intellectually challenging, emotionally nurturing environment. Encouragement and engagement will never be measurable on standardized tests but they are the lifeblood of effective teaching; reminding us of our mutuality of purpose with our students, that we are truly partners in this endeavor. My student's thumbs-up means more to me than Bill Gates, the Pearson Corporation, or David Coleman will ever understand.

These stories are the invisible moments of teaching. And amidst the current "school reform" assaults designed to discredit and defund public education, they help me resist the temptation to give up by either quitting or succumbing to the pressures to become a glorified test-prep technician. If I ever need to be reminded of why our schools are worth fighting for and why I still love teaching, it will always be the students, their stories, and the teaching moments they make visible. Within those spaces we share our hearts, our commitment, our lessons, and, yes, sometimes, our money.

TRANSCENDING THE "REFORMERS"

Sadly, to some extent, there can be material consequences for teachers based on their students' "performance" on these standardized tests. The temptation becomes to actually believe and/or value the opinions and assessments of those invested in our failure. I offer this alternative: Let's listen to ourselves and our students. We should never outsource the evaluation of our work to those rooting for us to fail.

Reflecting on my experience and in order to encourage students to reflect on their education, I asked seven former students a set of questions, including *"What qualities do effective teachers have?"* and *"What do effective teachers do?"* To gain a more authentic perspective, I chose students who represented a broad cross-section of our school community. They include (not their real names): Inez, the most tenacious student I've ever had, who came to the United States from Eastern Europe at age 7 and is now attending a highly selective college on the East Coast; Carly, a White student in an Advanced Placement class who wrote the best essay I've ever read but turns homework in late, if ever, and rarely gets A's and who's now attending a local state university; Dennis, a White student in Advanced Placement who was always sleepy in class but still managed to do well in discussions and on tests who is now attending a highly selective liberal arts college in the Midwest; Markus, an African American student, relatively new to Lakewood, who is an athlete and supports all other athletes at the school, and is trying to find a way to afford college; Annabelle, a Latina accepted at Ivy League schools but who chose to attend a state college on a full scholarship; Rebecca, a White student who takes some advanced and some non-advanced classes, who describes herself as "full of contradictions" and "chronically disenchanted"; and Patty, one of our 50 or so refugees (mostly from Nepal and Burma) sponsored by Catholic Charities, who studied relentlessly to pass the graduation tests and succeeded.

To a large extent, their responses to these questions gave me a way to judge myself as a teacher.

Keep Your Enthusiasm for Your Subject

This is the number one factor cited by all the students. Annabelle put it this way: "The most important quality of an effective teacher is passion/interest for the subject they teach." Dennis said: "Be enthusiastic about what you're teaching." Carly was emphatic in stating "Show that you are a person with likes and dislikes." Both Annabelle and Carly talked about how teachers need to share things about themselves—especially as it relates to teaching—without necessarily being too personal: What books are you reading? Where do you get your information? Why do you teach? Carly said she wants to know that teachers have an "intellectual life." They remind us that our power as role models is more potent than just about anything else, including the latest technology.

Form a Relationship with Students by Celebrating *Their* Lives

Whether it's through volleyball games, concerts, plays, or whatever, relationships between teachers and their students are an essential part of teaching. Generally, students remember their time on the field and on the choir rafters more so than their time in our classes. Why not tap into that energy and passion, and fuse it with both your lessons and your relationship with students? Go to their games, plays, concerts. Students have told me repeatedly how much it means to them when teachers attend their events. After all, we are leaders of a community designed to support our students. Standardized tests might be how others judge you, but should not be how you judge yourself or your students. Your commitment to them and involvement in their lives is a better barometer of your effectiveness than anything the reformers come up with.

Recognize That Emotional Fragility Is the Biggest Obstacle to Student Achievement

Remembering this makes our work more authentic because the good we do generally comes not from combing through the inert "data" on standardized tests, either individually or in absurdly designed teacher-based data teams. When we think about our students, we must remind ourselves that our value comes in our ability to encourage them to try their best, and to mitigate the pain of failure by rewarding effort and persistence. Students who have experienced rejection, abandonment, and frustration bring a "risk-averse" disposition that is directly contradictory to success in school. This is where the work of great teachers lies: in leveraging our genuine feelings for students in service of encouraging them to try, and if they fail, to try again.

Patty emphasized that good teachers find a way to "*relate to each student.*" Markus used the word "connect" in just about every response: Effective teachers "*are able to connect with all types of kids.* His happiest memories center around "*playing sports and connecting with new people.*" The reformers, to the extent they consider "connection," think of it in terms of technology and/or new "efficiencies" vis-à-vis raising those test scores. Unlike Markus, Rebecca is not easy to connect with—she dislikes school, most of her fellow students, and most teachers. Beneath her disgruntled exterior, however, is a hard-working student who wants to learn. She made a point of saying, however, that good teachers *"make students feel special,"* especially when they seek extra help/guidance. Experienced teachers recognize that when students ask for "help," they are often testing us to see if we believe in them, have patience, and care about them.

Take the Long View

Unlike reformers who traditionally take the short view—that is, the latest score on a standardized test, and the "growth" of a student on a profoundly narrow "learning objective" over a semester or a year—teachers are more effective when we take the long view. Although forced to attend to short-term goals, nothing should deter us from efforts to positively affect the trajectory of students' lives. As a history teacher, I find that story is the most powerful tool. Marines raising the flag on Mount Suribachi, the March on Selma, the survival of the Pequot against a campaign of genocide: All of these events can inspire students. Inez said that *"the stories of history, the human struggle"* kept her interest up. *Nothing lasts without an emotional charge.* Go for the heart.

Class Discussions Can Be the Most Rewarding or Frustrating Classroom Experiences

Rebecca and Dennis had much to say about class discussion. Rebecca said: "Discussion is a really important tool to get students to think, but some teachers neglect to guide the discussion . . . hold students to a standard . . . demand evidence and sound reasoning." The testing establishment will have trouble making money from this, but we should be nurturing citizenship, not producing bubble fillers.

Above All, Understand That There Is Not Just One Predetermined Way to Be a Great Teacher

Remember that *congruence between the real self and your public persona matters.* Students value a variety of teachers, but the best ones all have the ring of authenticity. Following a script prepared at central headquarters is a great idea if you are a waiter selling chocolate cake in a corporate restaurant:

"Did you save room for dessert?" But you're not selling cake, you're inspiring students. There is no way to be anyone else's version of a great teacher; there's no formula; you can only be *your* best version. If you are the no-nonsense type, many students like that; be your best version. If you embrace all the latest technology, many also like that; be that best version. If you are the quirky, sarcastic, high-energy type . . . you get the idea. Resist pressures to blend into a homogenized teaching mold or lose the power of authenticity.

Whether the friendly foursome, or homeless students, or any of the kids we serve daily, all students deserve our energy, knowledge, and genuine interest in their lives. Yet, we exist in an increasingly poisonous environment seeking to undermine the essence of effective teaching, replacing it with a profit-inspired test-prep dogma. To maintain our spirits, we must become politically aware and active. Awareness by itself can lead to cynicism and a sense of futility, so activism is essential.

Perhaps moments of despair are inevitable. But if we can remind ourselves daily of the mutual importance of student and teacher, and that as guardians of public education we are essential to U.S. democracy, we can find the strength to be great teachers, even in the face of the "reform" movement. As the "reformers" work to make us and our best work invisible under the glare of test scores and school ratings, we need to find the courage to resist domestication and fight for our students and our democracy. As teachers, we owe our students and the future of democracy nothing less.

TEACHING AND FIGHTING BACK

Although many times unrecognized by them, teachers have the power to change the lives of their students, their schools, and even policies in their cities and the nation, and this is evident in the chapters in Part VI. Heather Brooke Robertson is a teacher of English as a Second Language in Madison, Wisconsin, and has also been a bilingual teacher. The daughter of educators, she was nurtured on union activism and teaching as social justice. Describing in vivid detail the actions surrounding the elimination of teachers' unions in Wisconsin, she remains an activist with a love of bilingualism, multilingualism, and her students. The child of immigrant farmworkers, Jorge López learned the value of education early on. In Chapter 17, he illuminates what it means to teach for social and economic justice and community empowerment. One of Jorge's fervent goals is to instill this value in his students while at the same time helping them discover their own potential and activism.

Mary Cowhey, well known for her book *Black Ants and Buddhists* (2006) and other writings, continues to teach in the same school in which she has taught for over a dozen years, although in quite a different context. In her essay, Mary makes the case that social justice teaching is chiefly about helping students become successful learners. She now achieves this as a math teacher and tutor, bringing her activist and social justice background to bear on fractions, decimals, and long division. Her essay is a compelling example of how social justice work can, and must be done anywhere. In Chapter 19, "Teaching on the Frontline," María Rosario documents how her own painful school experiences brought her to the teaching profession. By using a critical pedagogy approach with her young students, she describes the ways in which her commitment to them is giving them a far different experience from the one she had as a child.

In the final essay in Part VI, Jesse Hagopian writes about his life as an education activist, including the struggle against the MAP standardized test at Garfield High School in Seattle that made his name a household word for teachers and others in many places around the nation. In his essay, Jesse describes his entry to teaching through the Teach for America Program, and how this experience of inappropriate preparation, as well as a shattering experience in Haiti after the 2010 earthquake, the passage of NCLB, and other events, reaffirmed his work as an activist for students and for public education both in and outside of his classroom.

CHAPTER 16

The Activist Teacher

Heather Brooke Robertson

I teach in spite of . . .

- continually being required to measure students' deficits rather than their assets
- the increase of standardized testing
- the misappropriation of school funding
- the decisions regarding education that support politicians, not students
- the one-size-fits all approach to curriculum
- the adoption of mega-corporate curricula, and
- the dismantling of Wisconsin's teacher unions

Early in 2011, Wisconsin's newly elected legislature introduced some devastating legislation. I was working as a District Professional Development Teacher Leader. It had been a difficult move for me to make for many reasons, but mostly because I believe the classroom teacher plays the most important role in education. Before taking the position, I sat through many disconnected and disengaging professional development sessions. In the fall of 2010, when I had the opportunity to be a teacher leader at the district level, I was hopeful that I could bring the voice of the classroom to the district office and make real change. After only 3 months, my optimism had faded and was quickly crushed when Wisconsin's legislature proposed Act 10, a law that would eliminate teacher unions in the state.

My parents were both lifelong educators. My father was a high school social studies teacher for 32 years and my mother was a high school biology teacher and guidance counselor for 27 years. My father was also very active in their teacher union, serving as a negotiator for many years, and also holding terms as president and vice president. It was not until Act 10 was proposed that I really understood what it meant to be in a union. My father shared with me that when he started working for the school district, teachers' contracts were only a page long. Some people—my close family members included—think union contracts are all about padding teachers' pockets. And although it is true that I have really straight and healthy teeth because my parents had good dental insurance, it is also true that my parents have master's degrees and many credits beyond their master's degrees. They are dedicated professional learners, and if we value their role in our society, then we need to compensate them. My father also shared with me that he was commonly frustrated negotiating contracts alongside elementary school teachers because they continually shortchanged themselves and didn't want to rock the boat or ask for too much. As a woman and an elementary school teacher, I recognize that wage negotiation is our greatest weakness. Sure, we get pregnant and many don't work as many years as males do, but that doesn't mean we deserve less financial compensation. I am further perplexed by women's unwillingness to fiercely negotiate in order to protect children while we continually shortchange our wages and working environment.

As an educator and the child of educators, I believe Act 10 was a blatant attack on my profession and our teaching culture. After a few weeks of educating the public and protesting after work, my union decided to have a "sick out." It was a painful decision because we knew it would adversely affect the children we were ultimately trying to protect. The first day we called in sick to school, I anxiously waited for the news to see what would happen. Because my principal was also my best friend, I agonized over her having to manage all our students with limited help. Fortunately, the teachers' united efforts were so successful that schools were forced to close. This was what we wanted. We wanted people to feel the blow of schools not functioning because we knew that the impact of Act 10 would have harsh consequences on schools, students, and ultimately our society.

We continued to call in sick for the next 2 days. I did not stay home and eat chips and watch daytime TV. Instead, I walked around the Wisconsin State Capitol, sometimes with my sign and sometimes without my sign. I sang solidarity songs. I chanted with my union brothers and sisters. I cried as firefighters with their bagpipes walked through the Capitol building with signs that said "We Support Teachers' Right to Organize." Moments like those, as well as marching with Reverend Jesse Jackson, reminded me that our protests were not just about Wisconsin teachers, but about workers' rights throughout our country. The intensity of these days was similar to the World Trade Organization Protests in Seattle I had participated in 10 years earlier. But that was only for 1 day and this was so much more personal. I felt support from people around the world. I remember reading on the chalkboard outside of Ian's Pizza Restaurant the many different countries people had called from to donate money for pizzas to nourish the protestors. Tom Morello of Rage Against the Machine as well as many other musicians played live shows to show their support. A writer friend in Los Angeles messaged me, "Fight on, Heather! Your union brothers in LA are behind you!" Those things encouraged me.

However, the pressure for us to return to work from the community increased. People were tired of rearranging their lives to care for their kids (I found this ironic), and we were feeling that the passage of Act 10 was imminent. I was willing to make monetary sacrifices but I did not want to give up my right to organize. We returned to work, and one evening a few weeks later I received a text from a friend that Act 10 was going to be voted on within the hour. At this time security was heightened so we had to wait in line to go through metal detectors. It felt like an eternity. Once I finally passed security, I ran up the stairs of the capitol to the congressional chambers as the chants of protesters became increasingly louder. When I reached the mass of people outside the chambers, it was too late: The legislators were being booed as they exited. Tears streamed down my face. I couldn't boo; I couldn't speak. I was devastated.

It has been just over 3 years since the passage of Act 10. Our public schools are still standing and on the surface things are not very different from 3 years ago except for the one-page contract I signed this year when I moved to a new school district—similar to the one my dad signed more than 40 years earlier when he started teaching.

I TEACH BECAUSE I'M AN ACTIVIST

My first experience with activism was as a freshman in high school. It was in the early 1990s, the height of the AIDS epidemic in the United States. As a member of the county youth group, I met a young heterosexual couple infected with AIDS. Their story was very moving and nonthreatening to the White, homophobic community I grew up in. So when my high school student council wanted to organize some speakers to talk to our school about AIDS, I volunteered this couple and took the lead on bringing them to our high school. Their presentation to the 1,200 students in the school gym was extremely successful. It was this experience that first exposed me to the power of activism.

During the rest of my time in high school, I continued to organize dances and events as a student council member and eventually as president, but it was never as rewarding as the work I did as a member of the HIT (HIV Intervention for Teens) Squad. As a HIT Squad member, we educated our peers about HIV transmission and prevention. The rewarding work of educating my peers about HIV/AIDS and addressing their fears around the transmission was the kick-start of my many years as an activist.

After high school, I attended the University of Wisconsin–Madison. There, I was involved in environmental and social justice groups. As part of my involvement, I helped organize rallies and protests around mining in Wisconsin and social justice procurement issues. I was most passionate about anti-sweatshop apparel and fair-trade products. To educate students about these issues, we set up informational tables at community events, had sit-ins in the chancellor's office, infiltrated a Disney employment recruiting session, and had a "Disparage Bucky (Badger)" intramural soccer team.

Yet of all of my activist activities, I am most proud of the work I did in 1997 with a fair-trade coffee company, Equal Exchange. Equal Exchange is a worker-owned cooperative in Boston, Massachusetts, some of whose members came to Madison, Wisconsin, to organize a fair-trade coffee movement. I worked with two of Equal Exchange's community organizers to educate the Madison community about the benefits of fair-trade coffee. We set up samples and information tables at community events like the farmers' market. We met with local leaders of what we would now call the "slow food" movement. Our culminating activity was sponsoring a female Nicaraguan coffee farmer to come to Madison to share her story with the university and local community at the Great Hall of our Student Union. The farmer's story of how fair-trade coffee has improved her quality of life was moving and deepened my understanding of the interconnectedness of our actions.

The result of the fair-trade organizing campaign led by the forward-thinking people of Equal Exchange and my passionate yet immature efforts as an organizer contributed to creating more informed consumers. As a result of our efforts, local coffee roasters began to carry fair-trade coffee and the local large grocery chain started to carry—and still carries—Equal Exchange coffee.

Equal Exchange's organizing efforts evolved into other forms of consumer activism. A few years later, I led another fair-trade coffee organizing effort for Equal Exchange in Portland, Oregon. It was during that time I realized how invaluable a connection to community was for deep learning to occur. I realized that a classroom teacher has the opportunity to create community in his or her classroom in an ongoing and systematic way, so I hung up (didn't put away, just hung up) my community activist sneakers and enrolled in a teacher licensure program in Milwaukee, Wisconsin.

I TEACH FOR EQUITY

I'm White and bilingual. I speak English and Spanish. Spanish speakers don't think I'm a native speaker, but they always comment on how well I speak Spanish. And English speakers often comment on how amazing it is that I speak Spanish. Yet, in spite of speaking Spanish, my Latino/a students are labeled as "limited English proficient," "English as a Second Language learners," "English language learners," and, most recently, "emergent bilinguals." This infuriates me. Even as I type this I can't spell *infuriates* in English, but my school did not consider me an "English language learner" or "emergent English speaker." I'm 36 and I still can't master the insane rules of English (as if there are any! How can you call it a rule if there are a million exceptions!). The labels placed on our students are racist social constructions that I work to eliminate every day.

I am White because that's how everyone else sees me. I learned what WASP (White-Anglo-Saxon-Protestants) meant at a very young age. My grandmother was a member of the Daughters of the American Revolution. Most recently, my dad had a genetic test done and confirmed his Whiteness. It is possible that my mom carries some non-White genes, but regardless, I need to start coming to terms with the fact that I'm more than half White.

I just don't feel super-White because, as I mentioned, I am also fluent in Spanish. In the U.S. and White culture, it is unusual to be bilingual. Contrary to my high school Spanish teacher's assumption, I am not bilingual because of the outstanding foreign language instruction I received. I found my foreign language classes horribly boring, extremely decontextualized, and irrelevant in the monolingual, homogenous small town in which I grew up. However, I have always been interested in other cultures. It was books that introduced me to a world beyond myself. My favorite book as a kid— which I still look at often—was *People* by Peter Spier. Then, when I was in middle school I read *Kaffir Boy* by Marc Mathabane. Mathabane's life story of growing up in Johannesburg, South Africa under Apartheid was earth-shattering. I was 12 years old, and I didn't yet have an understanding of privilege and dominant culture, but I knew I never wanted to contribute to, or be part of, a system that caused so much pain to another human.

When it came time to study abroad in college (because that's what White privileged girls do when they are in college), I decided to go to Chile. I really wanted to go to Africa to answer many questions I had from long ago, but I was still taking Spanish and Chile seemed a logical choice. There I fell in love—no, not with a man as most *gringas* do, but with a culture and a family. I became *la hija del norte* (daughter of the North) and *chilena de corazón* (Chilean in my heart), as their anthem states. I became *hermanita* (little sister) not because I am the youngest, but because my Chilean brother said I was the last to join the family. I did not realize how lucky I was to have another family until I really needed them. My first marriage was very challenging, so challenging that my own family could no longer support me being in it. However, instead of being alone when I most needed love and support, my Chilean parents and brother were there for me. My Chilean brother helped me find myself again and helped me leave the relationship without completely losing myself. I realize that many people who learn another language are not as fortunate as I have been to have another incredibly supportive family. Learning another language increases the number of people you can fit into your community. When you are multilingual, not only does your brain become more elastic (as brain researchers have proven), but I would also argue that your arms learn to stretch around more than just the community you live in.

My Chilean family has not only helped me in my personal life, but they have also helped me acquire equitable resources for my students. Six years after teaching in two middle schools, I moved to an elementary school in Madison, Wisconsin. I felt strong in my classroom management, but weak in content knowledge. I was ready to dig deeper into literacy and math pedagogy. It was a good thing I was ready because the intellectuals I worked with challenged me daily! They taught me how to implement guided reading groups in my split 3rd- and 4th-grade bilingual classroom. The literacy coach at the school was African American and had acquired an amazing collection of multicultural books. However, our Spanish children's book collection was limited. I was very excited to read *Ramona Quimby, Age 8*, my favorite book when I was my students' age, and even more excited that it was translated into Spanish. Nevertheless, the read-aloud every day was painfully boring. The translation was poor and, even worse, the content was for White girls growing up in the suburbs, not immigrants growing up in the city. I was very frustrated. When I stepped out of the classroom and started working with teachers throughout our school district, I realized the book selection for students reading in Spanish at a 3rd-grade level and beyond was extremely limited. Bilingual students in the United States already face many barriers, but books seemed like something I could do something about.

I was determined to find resources for our students, so I applied for a Fulbright scholarship to study children's literature in Chile. I was hoping I would find resources and looking forward to seeing my Chilean family, but I was designated the "alternate" and couldn't go on the trip. Fortunately, I knew some of the teachers who went and I consulted with them upon their return. I got their list of books and tried to purchase them at both the big and small book distributors, but these books were not available for purchase in the United States.

I decided to contact my Chilean brother in Santiago, Chile, and I explained our situation to him. We agreed that I would travel to Chile that summer, and he would set up some meetings. Our meetings with South American publishers and authors were very encouraging but we soon realized the only way to get these books to bilingual students in the United States would be to form a company. We met with a close friend to design our logo. I told him I wanted the company to be called Books del Sur (books from the South) because our mission is to bring books from the South to children in the North. I wanted the name to get people thinking about my favorite verse from the song "Prisioneros": *"Latino America es un pueblo al Sur de los Estados Unidos"* (Latin America is a town south of the United States). He created a logo in the shape of South America flying north. It is beautiful, and it inspires me each time I see it.

With books in tow and a logo to match our mission, I came home to the United States, filled out paperwork, and Books del Sur was born. With the support of teachers from my school, we selected books from a large sample and we filled the bookroom at the elementary school so that it is more equitably stocked with English and Spanish books. No surprise to us, the students are enjoying the chapter books more than the translated version of *Ramona Quimby, Age 8*.

In addition to advocating for resources for my students, I promote equity through my teaching lessons. For example, in my 4th- and 5th-grade Spanish as a foreign language classroom, I recognize those who speak Spanish at home and call on them as "experts." They often engage in conversations about words with me in front of their peers. They are models for reading in my small guided Spanish reading groups. I incorporate cultural lessons that evoke critical thinking about holidays. For example, this January, instead of making New Year's resolutions, we studied the Mayan calendar. We discussed that the January New Year is based on the Roman Gregorian calendar, and the Mayan calendar measures time differently than we do.

I also teach for equity by pushing English as a Second Language services into the classroom. This means that I work with small groups of students who speak a language other than English at home. My lessons support vocabulary and concepts in their classroom instruction through oral language groups, additional reading, and writing. This year is the first time I have ever been an English as a Second Language teacher. Previously, I was a Spanish as a foreign language teacher, 6th-grade language arts and social studies teacher, and I have also been a 3rd- through 6th-grade bilingual teacher. As an advocate for equity, I believe in inclusion, even though it is challenging. At the start of the school year, I knew that I needed to "push in" services. I started by "pushing in" to five different classes and five different grade levels. I now "push in" to four classes and pull out one. Admittedly, I'm exhausted because pushing into classrooms increases the number of relationships I manage fourfold and I have to give up a lot of control. However, I am fortunate to collaborate with amazing educators, and that keeps me motivated. One example of collaboration is with a kindergarten teacher whom I convinced, because of the large numbers of Latinos in her class, that we should be teaching all the students Spanish. So we decided to start off with a daily mini-lesson. It has been very successful for both the teacher and students. The confidence of Latino students has increased, and relationships between the Latino and non-Latino students have improved. Furthermore, literacy instruction has risen to a new level because every day the teacher gains a new understanding of how Spanish can increase the literacy of all students. For example, when I was previewing a read-aloud book, I shared with the class a word family in Spanish. The teacher's face lit up and she launched into her own mini-lesson about word families in English, and then she had the students compare them. The students discussed that in Spanish word families are at the beginning of words, whereas in English they are at the end. Gratefully, she is a masterful teacher and she will continue to incorporate this understanding into her reading lessons like she has many other connections between English and Spanish.

I also teach for equity for my students' families. Most recently, a mother of one of my bilingual students started to volunteer in my Spanish class. She had never volunteered in school before because of *vergüenza* (shame) of her English. When I asked her if she would be interested in working in my Spanish class she said that she only attended 1st grade in Mexico, but can read and write in Spanish. After the first day in class, the students kept asking for her and have even said "I can't wait until next class when I get to play the game with Esperanza." She is a gift to us. She asks the kids in her small group "*¿Cómo estas?*" (How are you?) at the beginning of each session, and unlike when they are with me, they feel obligated to answer her in Spanish. She is also an amazing resource for me. For example, when I couldn't pronounce *hippopotamus* in Spanish last week she did it for me. Her work in my classroom has helped my students form a relationship with an adult who speaks Spanish, and they see her as a person who speaks Spanish rather than how she is often seen, a Mexican who doesn't speak English.

I am very interested in economic disparities in society, and it was the focus of my undergraduate studies in international relations. While studying economic theories that explain why economic disparities exist and economic development theories that would lessen or eliminate them, I quickly understood that humans and their interactions lead to the perpetuation of the theory, or to its demise. I know that I am a part of the economic system and my labor can contribute to maintaining the gap between the haves and have-nots, or to lessening it.

My students' families remind me of my mother's family. Her life story is an example of how education leads to economic opportunities or economic equity. She grew up in a large family. My mother's mother did not work outside the home; therefore her father was the sole income provider for a family of 10 (8 kids and 2 adults). My mom was the second child and at the time her father was working as a farmhand and they lived in a house on the farm property that was a converted chicken coop. Their homes became larger as their family grew, but money was always a struggle. My mom was the only one in her family to graduate from a 4-year college. When I ask her what she thinks made the difference, she credits her father's belief in her, but most of all she credits books. She reminisces about the times she would go to a corner of the house and escape into the world of a book. Books opened her eyes to the world beyond her own. She saw school as a means to reach those worlds, and despite economic struggles and holey shoes, she completed her undergraduate degree in biology and ecology education and a master's degree in school counseling. Although she did not enter a lucrative field, she entered a profession that was financially secure and in which she continued to learn. She and my dad have retired and they have been able to travel to many parts of the world. Most recently they spent 3 weeks with my Chilean family and they experienced many new worlds. Her favorite was seeing an iceberg in Patagonia. I cannot help but think that their life was largely possible because of books and education. It is my goal to expose my students to the possibilities for their lives and I can do this best through quality literature just like my mom experienced.

I TEACH FOR A MULTILINGUAL UNITED STATES

Research that supports multilingualism is a powerful tool to help administrators, politicians, and our communities recognize the benefits of knowing
more than one language. However, the data I have been collecting over the
years are anecdotal. I do not believe the following interaction would have
happened if the nurse I interacted with had learned another language. It
happened during the polar vortex of the Midwest. I was at the doctor's
office and per my usual talkative self, I mentioned that I was an English
as a Second Language teacher. Her response was disappointing and, sadly,
typical. At first, she stated that I should be teaching the adults instead of the
kids because "they are the ones who need it." Yup, that's when the "they"
talk began. Next, she told me about an Italian woman she knows who has
lived in a small town in northern Illinois for 50 years and STILL DOESN'T
SPEAK ENGLISH! "How can that happen?!" she wondered.

The teacher I am, I thought this would be a good teachable moment.
So I responded to her comment with, "Well, some people work in their
homes and prefer to stay close to their communities. And producing language is much more difficult than understanding it." Then I was hit with,
"You teachers have an excuse for everything." And she walked away.

Stung by her comment, I decided to stop talking and started reading
my Twitter feed for comfort. It comforts me because it is full of like-minded
people who are working toward equality and don't say crappy things like
the nurse had just said. One of my tweets that day was from the Dali Lama,
and serendipitously he had tweeted, "We can only transform humanity and
create a happier more compassionate world through education."

If I could relive that moment, is there something else I could have said
that might have transformed the nurse's thinking? I don't know. What I do
know is this: I feel hopeful that "the immigrant" mentioned by the nurse has
maintained her language despite our culture's monolinguistic perspective.
However, if you are more of a science person and like "hard facts," brain
research overwhelmingly supports multilingualism. Research also reminds
us that speaking a language other than the one you were born hearing is
really, really challenging.

I would like to think that if the nurse had an experience learning another
language (and when I say that I'm not talking about the classic foreign language class in the United States where you memorize a list of vocabulary
and learn to conjugate verbs), only then would she understand how challenging it is to learn another language, and she would not have called my
explanation an excuse. Instead, she might have been able to relate to how

challenging and enriching it is to speak, listen, read, and write in more than one language.

Multilingualism not only holds possibilities for a deeper understanding of others, but it also matters for families. Prior to this year, I worked in a bilingual school. I have always been an advocate of bilingual education because of its many benefits; however, this year has opened my eyes to the consequences of not having bilingual education. The mother who works in my classroom told her friend, a mother of another of my students, that she was helping me in Spanish class. The other mother approached me about also working in my classroom. She said how glad she was to know her daughter was learning Spanish because her daughter does not speak Spanish at home to her or to her husband. I was a bit confused because she just told me that she speaks very little English. Now take a minute to digest this: The child's mother does not speak English and her daughter does not speak Spanish. Can you imagine not being able to have a conversation with your child? Even worse, this is not the only parent who has shared the same thing with me this year. I find this criminal, heartbreaking, and even worse, avoidable.

As a Spanish as a foreign language teacher and an English as a Second Language teacher, I am doing my best to use students' knowledge of their first language to strengthen their understanding of a second language. I try to collaborate with their classroom teachers' lessons, especially with big ideas, and I bring them into the small guided reading groups in Spanish class. We analyze text and words and make connections between Spanish and English. I have found that this is not only powerful for my bilingual Latino students, but also my English-speaking students. I also find it *so* much fun! I love talking to kids about how a word can change meaning by changing one letter or leaving out an accent mark. It is fun and funny, and it sticks. They remember these things. It is through our conversations that I hope my students begin to value more than English and gain an understanding of the benefits of speaking, listening, reading, and writing in another language.

I TEACH BECAUSE I LIKE TO PLAY

My first teaching partner taught me that kids learn best when they are happy, and in order for them to be happy, they must have fun learning. Later, I learned that teacher jargon and theory identify this as "engagement" and "motivation." I spent my first 7 years teaching, thinking, and planning lessons near students' what Lev Vygotsky (1978) called the "zone of proximal development" so that they could learn new things easily and joyfully. Then

I would engage with them and try to use questioning and new application of vocabulary to heighten their knowledge. I was very successful at this, and so were my students.

I also knew that the best way to engage my students was to get to know them and what their interests were so I could incorporate or connect this knowledge into my classroom curriculum and pedagogy. More and more my students were talking about video games. But it was no longer just boys talking about video games, it was both boys and girls. Video games were familiar to me because my brother played them all the time. I did not, but at the same time I knew learning was changing because it was changing for me. I was learning more from tweets and Facebook posts, and less from books. Fortunately, I was able to enroll in a course about games and learning at the University of Wisconsin, Madison, where the Games + Learning + Society Lab is, and . . . well, now I get it and it's amazing.

What I now understand from university research and my own experiences about games and learning is:

1. games are very engaging for students;
2. games are opportunities for students to have concrete experiences with ideas and worlds that are very abstract; and
3. games are fun

As a result, if games are used thoughtfully with curriculum there are opportunities to greatly increase students' language and understanding of abstract concepts threaded throughout our curricula. For example, the electoral college is an abstract and somewhat illogical system that is nevertheless essential to the U.S. federal political system. The game "Win the White House" by iCivics, Sandra Day O'Connor's nonprofit organization, was an extremely powerful tool for my students. It gave all of us a common experience to discuss. I could name events with academic vocabulary and, furthermore, it was accessible to all my students, those who were children of professors as well as recent Nepalese immigrants. And did I mention that it's fun? It was fun when my students would shout out during class, "Ms. Heather, I won! I won the White House!" And at that time, all you think as a teacher, is "Yes! I cannot wait for you to really win the White House because it is time the United States had a female Latina president!"

CHAPTER 17

Teaching for Social Justice and Community Empowerment

Jorge López

MY EARLY JOURNEY

It has been 12 years since I stepped into the class-room and today I am just as passionate about being a teacher as I was then. Being in the classroom fills me with life, as if I am manifesting the purpose of my life's journey beyond my generation and myself. I am blessed to have the opportunity to make change as a participant in the movement for social and economic justice.

As a college undergraduate I was an activist and organizer for Latino (also called *Raza*) communities and youth of color. My purpose was to get more kids of color to attend college, politicize youth, and be an advocate for farm workers toiling in oppressive conditions in the fields of America. My parents were immigrant farm workers who taught their children the value of struggle, unity, resilience, and education. These values are interwoven in what I have built in my classroom, in the community that I serve, and in my life. Growing up in poverty in the fields of the Imperial Valley, I always saw my parents physically struggle to earn a living for our family. What kept us strong, given the limited economic resources, was *familia*. Loving parents and a caring extended family surrounded us. I can still recall the words of my grandfather Chalio, who stressed during our weekly family gatherings that we must remain "unidos," united, a true pedagogy of love.

My grandparents descended from the mountains of Michoacán, Mexico, and were also farm workers in California. I believe what has kept our family resilient is our unity, and the recognition that struggle is a part of life.

A Frederick Douglass quote that hangs on my classroom wall—"If there is no struggle, there is no progress" (1985, p. 204)—reminds me of this value, one that my family taught me. Although my parents could not help me academically while in grade school, or much less afford educational resources for us, my three siblings and I all worked very hard in school. My father always reminded us, "*si no estudian, se van a fregar en el trabajo del fil como yo*" (if you don't study, you will be broken by the work in the fields like me).

My parents' mission was to provide their children and generations to come with a better life. My parents would take my siblings and me to work in the fields and pick tomatoes during the summer. With temperatures above 100 degrees, we experienced the same physical labor and struggle as our parents, and we learned to value literacy and education. Our parents' approach and teachings worked: We all graduated from college and did not end up toiling in the fields of the Imperial Valley.

While in college, I began taking courses in ethnic studies. I got involved in student organizing with *Movimiento Estudiantil Chicano de Aztlán* (MEChA) and began a United Farm Workers (UFW) Support Committee of college students guided by the UFW national organization. I started to develop a critical lens and a language to understand my family history and oppression in America. As I embraced my Mexican and indigenous culture, and as my identity took shape, my responsibility to serve my people and all oppressed people to whom I felt connected grew. My family instilled in me the value of relentless struggle, unity, and education. My father gave his life for us through his struggle and illness, and today, as an educator I pay tribute to my parents' mission. In continuing the work of social justice movements, I am working to improve the lives of my students and their families and create a more just world for future generations.

EDUCATION IS POLITICAL

I began teaching in 2002 when No Child Left Behind was signed into law, the era when testing and school accountability took off, and today, more than a decade later, hundreds of public schools are closed down and thousands of teachers displaced in what has become an all-out neoliberal corporate attack on public schools, teachers, and unions. It is crucial for educators to be resilient, and involved in movements of resistance against school corporatization. I went into teaching as a means to continue the social justice work I began as a college student organizer. In college I grew knowledgeable of my history and culture as well as of politics, and philosophy, and the empowerment that this knowledge generated drew me to want to share it with other young people. Majoring in social studies and Chicana/o studies politicized me. My worldview built on the past and gave me a critical lens to the present and what is possible for the future. I draw inspiration and purpose as an educator from social justice movements of the past, and I feel compelled to continue the struggles that civil rights Black, Brown, and Native leaders began. Teaching is a political act.

Now more than ever, I believe that teachers, and educators displaced from public schools, need to work to organize together, resist the take-over of our schools, and protect teacher autonomy in creating culturally relevant and empowering curriculum. I always find inspiration in teach-ers from Latin America who are at the forefront of organizing efforts and direct action when their schools and jobs are threatened by government cuts and privatization. Being a teacher activist and being involved in organizing youth and educators connects me to a larger global movement and builds in me a spirit of solidarity and hope. At our school site, we created a collective of educators and student activists. Our collective, Politics and Pedagogy, is guided by the words of Paulo Freire that "All education is with a purpose and that purpose can only be political, for we either educate to liberate or we educate to dominate" (cited in Ladson-Billings, 2005, p. 54). Our col-lective is dedicated to challenging injustices such as inequitable access to educational resources facing students and communities of color. Our goal is to create spaces of empowerment where educators, youth, and community members can converge to engage in critical dialogue for community libera-tion and educational transformation.

Our collective organizes students and teachers around a yearly con-ference that gathers parents, organizers, youth, and educators throughout Los Angeles to come together to identify problems, find solutions, and take action around issues in education and in the community. The conference, East Side Stories, has become the pinnacle of the school year, dedicated to youth empowerment and social justice in our schools and community. It takes place at the end of the school year, and many students who have become leaders, politically involved, and intellectually eager to share their knowledge have an opportunity to facilitate workshops. Hundreds of stu-dents, community leaders, and progressive educators gather on a Saturday to learn, connect, and plan how to continue to do good social justice work. At our last conference, Tucson, Arizona teacher Curtis Acosta was a keynote speaker. He talked about the dismantling of their Chicano/a studies pro-gram, and he inspired students and teachers with the message that it's time to "stop asking, and begin taking!" His message resonated with our cause, and spoke to the need for a deep commitment to action for our communities' educational needs. Patrick Camangian, the morning keynote speaker, took our audience through a presentation on colonization through education, and the need to create decolonized curriculum that teaches students how to liberate themselves. We are currently working with other educator groups in Los Angeles that collaborate in sharing curriculum and organizing to create a more progressive teachers' union that can effectively challenge school takeovers and school charterization. We are joining a campaign for a citywide effort that creates the socially just schools that students deserve.

Collaborating with politically minded educators and students creates a family environment and a strong solidarity for a common purpose at our work site. Having such a strong support network makes coming to work at my school meaningful. It is not only a social support network, but also a professional and political "backup." We look out for one another and advocate for each other as allies and friends. I encourage all social justice educators to work in community rather than in isolation; the very nature of being a social justice educator is one of solidarity with others. Our mission is to transform minds, youth, communities, and education in America. This work cannot happen in isolation behind a teacher's classroom door. It is always a huge loss to youth and communities to see social justice educators leave the profession because of lack of support. Urban communities are full of good people, organizations, and networks, as well as numerous opportunities to link with like-minded support groups.

TEACHING AGENTS OF CHANGE

I teach to empower young people to become agents of change with the skills, the passion, and the tools to engage civically to make their communities just and the institutions in those communities democratic. John Dewey talks about schools as sites that prepare young people how to be citizens in a democracy through civic engagement. One of his quotes that resonates with me is "Only in this connection of knowledge and social action can education generate the understanding . . . necessary for the continued existence of democracy" (1987, p. 184). This quote stood out to me in my early development as an educator at UCLA's Institute for Democracy, Education and Access (IDEA). At the center of my curriculum are themes, lessons, and skill sets that become building blocks for educating well-rounded young citizens. I believe schools in America have failed to educate young people to become true citizens of a participatory democracy. Far too many Americans are uninterested in politics, unaware of their rights, and unaware of the power to create and change laws and policies through social action. Market capitalism, consumerism, and corporate-ruled mass media have swayed the public from civic engagement and politically minded citizenry. Noam Chomsky points to mass media as a corporate tool that entertains and distorts the reality of citizens, and covers up the assault of our democracy by corporations. I find it crucial for educators to unveil this tragic occurrence in our society through critical media pedagogy.

American schools have a long history of inequality, and they continue to play a role in the reproduction of social inequality, particularly for communities of color. Social justice educators and schools can play a role in creating school communities that build social equality. If we want a society and American future that will be equitable and just to its citizens, and to people of color in particular, we need to turn to the curriculum in our classrooms. Is the pedagogy liberatory? Are the lessons being taught critical of societal institutions? Are students learning to question oppressive elements of their reality and community conditions? Are students learning the skills to deconstruct media and the skills to produce their own media? Are students given the confidence and communication skills to advocate for themselves and their communities? Are classrooms and schools investing in giving students the social capital they need? If the curriculum is not giving students the tools to navigate through various institutions and the tools to influence change, then educators need to rethink their lessons.

I teach not only for my students to learn their social studies content, which actually informs their worldview, but I also teach them critical literacies to become agents of change. In the process, change also begins within. Every revolution begins in the mind, and every manifestation was first conceived in the minds of the people. In my classroom, students read the thoughts of the greatest leaders and revolutionaries through their writings. My students learn about the actions of these leaders, and they study the incredible social changes they achieved. Throughout the course of the year, I create projects, lessons, and opportunities for students to model themselves after great agents of change, while progressively shifting their identity as poets, artists, writers, philosophers, organizers, leaders, and activists.

When I began teaching 12 years ago, I immediately began to sponsor and support student clubs with a social justice purpose. This work can be done in partnership with other interested teachers, or by connecting with community organizers to help run meetings and workshops. I have supported clubs such as MEChA (Movimiento Estudiantil Chicano de Aztlán, a student organization on many campuses that supports education, culture, and history), United Students, Taking Action, Environmental Justice Club, and an ART Club, which is an acronym for "art of revolutionary teens." Some clubs I have helped students start, and for others, I have offered my support and classroom to community organizers to run the student organization. Teaching is a time-intensive craft, but I feel it is necessary to be involved with youth and educators outside of teaching. This involvement has been very rewarding and has kept me energized as an educator. Student clubs and organizations also provide young people with a real-world experience to what many social justice educators teach in their curriculum. It provides a space for the passion and fervor that begins to grow outside classroom learning. When students learn about injustices throughout history and study movements of resistance, many of them will want to get involved and do something about the many existing injustices and conditions. Learning and civic skill building can become most powerful when young people have a space, an outlet, a purpose, and a way to contribute in the fight for justice. These spaces provide a unique, meaningful, and powerful learning opportunity for youth.

Educators can play a significant role in merging the community and school into a single force that can offer students, parents, and community members resources, skills, services, and networks to build community power. In the book *Learning Power* (2006) Jeannie Oakes and John Rogers write about the need for "learning" and "power" to go together, and point to the process of organizing and community building around change and reform as a process of learning as well as power building. Los Angeles, similar to many communities throughout the country, has existing grassroots movements working to improve communities and schools that educators can leverage for their students and families. I have found that students who have gotten involved in justice-focused clubs and organizations go on to become lifelong leaders and continue their leadership and activism in postsecondary educational settings and organizations. In my years of supporting young people in leadership and organizing I have helped form bridges and support networks, and I have assisted young people in building their social capital.

TEACHING FOR COMMUNITY CULTURAL WEALTH

The shaping of my identity as a young adult in college was one of my most powerful and transformative life experiences and it served as a catalyst for academic achievement, resiliency, and advocacy for a lifelong dedication to the service of young people and communities of color. The pillars to my transformation were ethnic studies, cultural knowledge, activism, and critical theory. In my years as an educator, I have attempted to replicate this framework through my teaching in hopes of raising academic achievement, self-empowerment, and leadership in my students. While teaching at Theodore Roosevelt High School in Boyle Heights, I have had the opportunity to teach numerous electives with a focus on ethnic and cultural studies courses. In core courses such as world history, U.S. history, and government/economics, I make certain to teach them through an ethnic studies lens, addressing the culture and experience of people of color and oppressed communities throughout the world.

Culturally relevant curriculum engages the voices and experiences of students in communities of color. I have found it critically important to address urban youth cultures in my curriculum, specifically the experience and interests of Latino youth in the Los Angeles Eastside community. In my elective and core courses students read critical theory from many intellectuals and educators such as Noam Chomsky, Paulo Freire, and Danny Solórzano. Students in my world history class read Franz Fanon to make sense of colonialism, or analyze lyrics from conscious hip-hop rappers such as Mos Def or Immortal Technique to learn about resistance to oppression. I want my students to feel like young intellectuals. I believe in their capability to make sense of complicated texts that are key to developing a critical lens and theoretical foundation. I believe it is crucial for young people to be given frameworks and a language with concepts to assist them in making sense of global systems of oppression that influence their lives. Freire teaches us that critical literacy is reading both the "word" and the "world." Students, and humans in general, have the capacity to solve problems and create better living conditions; critical literacy facilitates that process.

As courses progress, students begin to develop a spirit of resistance to oppression, or what Tara J. Yosso (2005) refers to as *resistant capital,* a form of cultural wealth that includes the knowledge and skills that challenge structures of inequality such as racism, patriarchy, and capitalism, as well as a motivation to work toward justice. I believe that if students develop *resistant capital* they will increase their resiliency, academic motivation, and civic engagement. As a result, they will gain more skills in academics, communication, and community leadership. I make sure to encourage all my students to get involved in youth clubs, service projects, organizations, internships, and community events. Participation is key not only for students' college applications, but also for the development of their voice, advocacy, and understanding of institutions. Through the engagement process, students increase their networks, which is important for the development of their *navigational capital to acquire the skills to maneuver through social institutions* (Yosso, 2005). Having a strong understanding of race, politics, and a people's history developed in the classroom, along with real-world hands-on experience through community work and social interactions, gives students the capability and skills to maneuver through the social institutions they will face through their educational, professional, and life journeys.

Many teachers get locked into their content as isolated class work, and they fail to ask themselves how curriculum and the student school experience can assist and empower youth beyond the classroom walls. I see it as part of my teaching responsibility to provide young people with a real-world experience that will elevate them not only intellectually, but also holistically. Teachers can work with their school administration and local leaders to begin to create and nurture a *community school* environment, a model where the school serves as a community hub that leverages social capital by opening the doors to service providers, employers, organizations, and after-school programs. For example, community members, parents, and elders can hold mentoring programs or classes on community gardening and medicinal plants, or local attorneys and elected officials can provide students with internships. Local artists and musicians can offer lessons. In this model, the school day can be extended to open opportunities where teachers can provide academic support, engage in youth organizing, or run a program in the arts. The community school model can tap into *community cultural wealth*, whose benefits are monumental for community and student holistic support.

TEACHING FOR HUMANIZATION

Paulo Freire teaches us about the pedagogy of liberation, the struggle to become free from oppression and begin the restoration of our humanity. The conditions that young people of color live and experience—such as poverty, hunger, malnourishment, physical and emotional abuse, trauma, violence, racism, discrimination, hopelessness, fear, and all forms of oppression that are a consequence of social and economic inequality—have deeply dehumanized youth. As an educator who believes in the pedagogy of liberation and love, when they first enroll in my courses, I feel it is in my duty as a teacher to begin to understand the lived experiences that have dehumanized many of my students. Connecting with young people, and having an open mind and heart, is a foundation for creating a caring classroom community.

When the school year begins, I find many students to be guarded, and rightfully so. They are on the defensive because their experience with U.S. institutions, particularly schools, has been negative and dehumanizing. The school system and other institutions such as the courts, police, media, and dominant society view young people of color through a deficit lens. Young men of color especially continue to be demonized by mainstream media, consequently shaping negative views, even among educators. Our mission as educators should be to counter these views through liberatory curriculum and by healing the damage that has been done to young men. Teachers can design curriculum that teaches students how to challenge dominant ideologies, such as creating their own media and knowledge and learning how to best disseminate it to the general public.

Another effective approach I use in my classroom to support and heal young people is restorative justice circles, a process used for facilitating dialogue for peacemaking, building relationships and community, and healing trauma done to a young person. Schools in Oakland and Los Angeles are beginning to use this approach as a response to the dehumanizing and punitive school environments that have been pushing young people on the school-to-jail track. Educators and youth can organize and learn true civic education while working to change the school-to-prison pipeline that thrives on unjust laws and policies that target youth. In Los Angeles, I collaborated with local organizations, youth, and other educators to change a daytime curfew law that ticketed over 47,000 mostly students of color from poor communities for being late or truant to school. Putting young people face to face with police contributes to a school environment of fear, intimidation, and abuse.

What drove me as an educator to be involved in the struggle to interrupt the school-to-prison pipeline is what Duncan-Andrade and Morrell (2008) call *revolutionary love*, "the love that is strong enough to bring about radical change in individual students, classrooms, school systems, and the larger society that controls them" (p. 187). They teach us that it is only this kind of love that is going to change our schools and our "morally bankrupt society" that has traditionally not shown enough love to our children to give them what they need (Duncan-Andrade & Morrell, 2008, pp. 187–188).

Doing all that I can in my power, as my students' teacher, is revolutionary. Freire (1985) asserts that "Being revolutionary implies struggling against oppression and exploitation, for the liberation and freedom of the oppressed, concretely and not idealistically . . . to help them experience what it means to be *persons*" (p. 128, emphasis in original). While in college I found educators and leaders who helped me learn my history and understand my family experience in a historical and political context. They demonstrated love and guided my self-reflection to help me make sense of harsh life experiences with racism, exploitation, poverty, shame, and identity issues. During this transformation, I felt the power of liberation, and I felt restored as a human being. This process was necessary before I could enter the classroom as an educator and begin to assist my students' transformation and humanization. To be humanized, liberated, and empowered as a young person is radical.

I teach because I want young people to experience freedom from oppression, and to help build a community of young people who continue to dream and believe that they can achieve and that they can change the world.

CHAPTER 18

Doing Social Justice Work Through Math

Mary Cowhey

Things change. We change. If we refuse to change, to adapt, we won't survive for long. When teachers who've read *Black Ants and Buddhists* ask me expectantly, "You're still teaching 2nd grade?" and I answer, "I'm a Title 1 math teacher and a math coach now," I can sometimes read confusion and disappointment on their faces, as though I've gone over to the dark side. I am as critical and reflective a teacher as ever, building on the principles of rigor, relevance, and relationships, engaging and empowering students and their families. I just do it through math now.

Have my reasons for teaching changed? In 2005, I wrote that I teach to make a positive change in the world, so that I can live and work fully as the whole person that I am, because I can think critically and keep learning, so that I can be there for a child who needs me to notice, to listen, to care, because I would be foolish to think I am done learning or that I could learn more by myself than with others, because I would be selfish to not share what I've learned, because I am part of a community, a country, and a world that could be better, and because I agree with Gandhi, "If we are to have real peace in this world, we shall have to begin with the children." (Cowhey, 2005).

Of course, in the last 10 years, the national landscape has changed and is littered with ever more educational acronyms: joining NCLB, AYP, and MCAS we have the new Common Core standards (CCSS), the PARCC assessment, a new teacher evaluation system, replete with SMART goals, SMARTer goals, and DDMs. Even in a school that doesn't pressure teachers to teach to the test, test pressure is in the air. Test scores of two other elementary schools in our district have caused the whole district to be designated as "Level 3," a kind of "you'd better get your act together" warning zone. Decisions made at a district level in hopes of improving the schools with lower scores could affect all of us, in the name of "consistency," that is, conformity.

TEACHING JASMINE TO SUCCEED

After teaching 1st and 2nd grade for a dozen years, in 2009 I took a year's leave to take care of my mother, who has Alzheimer's disease, at home. The following year, I wanted to return to the classroom half time, sharing a 2nd-grade classroom position, but the superintendent at the time wouldn't allow it. Instead, she offered me a part-time job teaching Title 1 math. I'd always enjoyed teaching math, but I didn't like the way Title 1 math services had been provided when I was a classroom teacher. I thought of it as a "helping hands" model: A Title1 math teacher would drift in during my math lesson, observe, circulate a little, suggesting a student use cubes or a hundred chart, and drift out again. Each spring, there was a standardized math test, and the students whose scores were in the lowest 10% in each grade were designated "Title 1." The Title 1 math teacher didn't individually assess students, set learning goals, plan or teach any lessons in small groups or whole class, or consult with the classroom teacher. At some point, due to budget cuts, the position was eliminated, and only Title 1 reading remained. Then I was offered that job. I negotiated with my principal, saying I would do it if a chunk of my job could be parent engagement and if she'd let me figure out an effective way to do it.

That first year as Title 1 math teacher I was part time, but I threw myself into the job, taking graduate courses in math, attending seminars, researching different models for Title 1 math. I asked classroom teachers what they felt would be useful and within the constraints of my half-time schedule, I tried to provide support for their struggling students.

By then, the last 2nd-graders I had taught were 4th-graders. We had a new teacher in 4th grade and she asked me to come in during her math period to support some of her students. Because we had no universal screening assessment, I modified an assessment I'd designed for my 2nd-graders. I was surprised to learn that one of my former 2nd-graders, Jasmine, now in 4th grade, could not double or find half of a number and couldn't explain the meaning of even and odd numbers. She added by counting on ones. The 4th-graders' first math unit was about factoring, and she was completely lost. She was not the only 4th grader in that boat, but she had been *my* student in 2nd grade. This troubled me deeply. How had this happened?

She was an English language learner, and she had some social and behavioral issues in 2nd grade. Those were factors, but not reasons to fail.

In 2004 I wrote that I teach because I want to be there for students who need me to notice, to listen, to care (Cowhey, 2005). Those are still reasons I teach now, but there's something additional: I teach to help my students succeed. To me, that means developing grade-level skills and conceptual understanding, as well as the vocabulary and confidence for every student to actively participate in rich mathematical discussions. Years ago, I would have thought, "Jasmine's trying hard, and she's making progress." True, but she didn't have solid understandings of important mathematical ideas that 2nd-graders need, such as that $7 + 7$ is 14 because $5 + 5$ is 10 and $2 + 2$ is 4, so $10 + 4 = 14$, and that 36 is an even number even though 3 is odd, and that *because* 36 is even, we can start to find its factors by considering that half of it is 18, that half of that is 9, and that although you can't split 9 into two equal whole numbers, you can divide it evenly because $3 \times 3 = 9$. Surely, we'd talked about things like that in Jasmine's class, but I hadn't checked or noticed that Jasmine didn't understand those ideas and, more important, I didn't ascertain what Jasmine *did* understand and work in her zone of proximal development to bring her the distance. I see this very much as a social justice issue, an equity issue. It's not fair to Jasmine for us to plunge ahead into the next math unit or to dive into yet another rich mathematical discussion that she can't access.

Our math curriculum was rich and constructivist. I'd been trained in the math curriculum and had taught it for a dozen years. I had high expectations for all of my students and was passionate about the subject. I integrated math into our morning meeting, did 10-Minute Math, and taught an hour-long math lesson every day. Every day we had math workshop, and students solved problems and played math games. Every day we had rich mathematical discussions about strategies that students used.

As a 2nd-grade classroom teacher, sometimes I had new students arrive who could not read numerals or count to 20 in any language, who had to count the 4 dots on a die to know it was 4, who didn't have one-to-one correspondence. With a class of 25 2nd-graders, many of whom were English language learners, some of whom had individualized education programs (IEPs), some of whom had posttraumatic stress disorder (PTSD) and attention-deficit hyperactivity disorder (ADHD), it had been daunting to figure out how to catch up children like this. I told myself I had a "developmental perspective" and believed that creating an environment where children felt safe taking risks, where they were engaged in solving problems and sharing strategies, where math was integrated and authentic—I believed that they would develop the skills and understanding they needed. For some students, perhaps it had worked and had been enough. But this one student, Jasmine, shook that belief. I didn't need to look at her MCAS scores. We had one mathematical conversation, and I realized that if I'd failed with her, I had probably failed with others. I was determined to figure out how this happened and to learn how to teach math better. Jasmine wasn't the only 4th-grader struggling in math. I could see the problem and the solution were bigger than me.

SEEKING ANSWERS

That first year in Title 1 math, I was trying to learn the math curriculum in all of the grades, from 1st through 5th. I was trying to identify the categories of things students typically struggled with. I tried to increase my repertoire of ways to help children learn, understand, and practice the skills where they'd been lagging. Along the way, I kept learning. I learned about Response to Intervention (RTI) and proposed to our director of academic effectiveness that we develop an RTI model for math in the district. He wasn't interested. The district had gotten a grant for RTI in behavior, so we weren't going to "do math." I thought about how our school secretary said she could tell you when each class taught math, because the discipline referrals always increased during math. Really, if you were in 4th grade and couldn't find half of a number, or in 5th grade and had to figure out 24 + 10 on your fingers, wouldn't misbehaving in order to get sent to the office seem like a reasonable plan?

I'd learned from talking with math interventionists and Title 1 math teachers from other districts and states that they used a "universal screening tool" as a pre- and posttest each year. I proposed this to the district administrator, who said, "You can download something like that for free." I was skeptical. The district had to invest thousands of dollars to buy the materials and get the professional development for us to use the Benchmark Assessment System (BAS) in reading. It was hard to imagine that something just as good in math would be available for free. I asked what website he suggested. He gave me one, dismissively. I went there and found a math fact worksheet generator. He didn't have a clue what I was talking about. No one was telling me how to do this job. I had to "make the road by walking."

I went to another district to get training in Math Recovery, for diagnostic math assessment and targeted instruction. I developed a series of trainings for my colleagues, so they could understand the language and rubrics used in Math Recovery and so we could improve the transfer between the skill and concept development I do with my students in small groups and how students apply those in their classroom math lessons. Other schools in our district focused their Title 1 math resources in the 4th and 5th grades, where they take standardized math tests. I looked critically at my data, shared it with my principal, and said I saw more impact, in terms of student growth, with my younger students and less with 4th- and 5th-graders. We reasoned that if students who have been struggling with mathematics haven't had effective intervention before 4th grade, it is harder to go back at that point, to untangle everything that's gotten tangled, to undo the habit of guessing rather than persevering in problem solving and the misconception that mathematics doesn't make sense. These kids, for whom mathematics stopped making sense in 1st grade, have internalized the view of math as a collection of facts and tricks to memorize. Many kindergarteners and 1st-graders who struggle with math just haven't had the same level of exposure to and practice with numbers, problem solving, and vocabulary as their classmates. With effective intervention, these kids can get in the game instead of being left on the sidelines. Because there is only one of me, we decided to shift my Math Recovery focus to early intervention (K–3). At the request of 4th- and 5th-grade teachers, I am piloting a tutoring model this year with their students. I continue to look critically at the effectiveness of my teaching, soliciting feedback from students and colleagues about how to improve what I do. I haven't yet found the perfect balance; it is a work in progress.

Being a mathematician, I did a face-to-face survey with every teacher in my school to find out who needed training in implementing our math curriculum, got them all registered, and scratched up some funds from the district to pay for it. Last year, another math coach and I organized a Professional Learning Community to develop a culture of public teaching, recruiting our most experienced teachers to learn alongside our newest about how to increase the press for mathematical reasoning. We paired up with "critical math buddies" to observe each other.

I collaborated with teachers in 2nd through 5th grades last year to pilot what we call Mix It Up Math, weekly math periods when we mix students between all the classes in a grade level, based on formative assessments, to provide intervention, practice, and extension. We bring in every available adult we can muster, from the principal and visiting district administrators to the speech therapist and student teachers, so that we can give students the most personal attention possible. Now in its second year, including kindergarten and 1st grade, I am heartened to see students taking more ownership and responsibility for their own learning. Two weeks ago, a 5th-grader told me she thought she should be in Mrs. G.'s group. I asked why and she said, "She's doing double-digit multiplication and I really don't get that yet." Last week, another 5th-grader came up to me the day before our Mix It Up Math session and said, "Can I please be in the group on fractions? I really don't understand what we're doing with fractions." I asked her what she didn't understand about fractions and she said, "The thing with equivalent percents. I don't know what they're talking about, how that connects to fractions." We have a long way to go to help all of our students to become more active learners, more self-aware of their progress in learning mathematical ideas and more responsible about getting the help they need to reach the goals. But we're on our way, not because someone from the state told us we had to make a plan with yet another acronym, but because our principal gives us the autonomy as professionals to collaborate, research, design, innovate, reflect, and fine tune with each other.

TEACHING MATH CRITICALLY

In 2005, I wrote that I teach because I can think critically and keep learning, because I would be foolish to think I am done learning or that I could learn more by myself than with others, because I would be selfish to not share what I've learned, because I am part of a community, a country, and a world that could be better (Cowhey, 2005). That's still true, although my learning is less broadly academic about science, history, philosophy, and so forth, like when I was a classroom teacher. In the academic content realm, I have delved much more deeply into math, through taking lots of courses like Developing Mathematical Ideas and Mathematical Knowledge for Teachers. I am always looking for authentic ways to connect math to the world: a data unit that gathers, represents, and analyzes data about where our shirts were made, collaborating with a local farmer/photographer and parents to make a bilingual counting book featuring my students at a local farmers' market, asking an arborist/parent of one of my students to bring in dozens of small stumps for my young students to step/count on to develop one-to-one correspondence.

The bulk of my self-directed learning has been pedagogical, largely focused on how we can teach better and help all students succeed (note: not "how we can raise standardized test scores"). I think critically about things like assessment, most important, *what it's for*. I think critically about *what type of assessment* it is and what we plan to *do with the data*, and *how quickly and easily we can process and access that data*, and even *what getting that data costs us*. I hear administrators who feel pressured to raise standardized test scores say, "We need more data." I am critical of some decisions that seem wasteful and aren't thought through, like spending thousands of dollars to set up online "student accounts" for every student in the district for an assessment program that teachers haven't been trained in using, without a vision for how this tsunami of additional data will be used to improve instruction. We don't need more data that continues to compare students to each other. We don't need more standardized test data to keep telling the kids in the 95th percentile how superior they are (really?!) and the kids who score below average that they still (surprise!) "need improvement."

Right now I am organizing a Professional Learning Community (PLC) of teachers so that we can educate ourselves proactively about assessment, think critically about assessment together, and engage in a collegial conversation with administrators about assessment for learning. I believe that our route out of the corporate-dominated high-stakes testing frenzy that currently defines our educational landscape is through teacher leadership and teacher activism. I am heartened by the teacher leadership I experience when I visit and work with Canadian teachers. I recently attended an Early Childhood Education Council Conference organized by teachers in the Alberta Teachers Association that focused on the importance of play in children's social development and infusing play into their learning. Teachers in the United States are currently exhausted just trying to keep up with ever-changing standards and expectations. My husband and I are both teachers and have spent half of the last 2 weeks of "winter vacation" doing schoolwork and education-related reading and research. That constant "dancing as fast as I can" exhaustion deprives teachers of the time and energy needed to learn deeply about things like assessment for ourselves, the space to discuss it critically with our colleagues, to collaborate on action research and reflect on our progress together so that we can articulate our critique and organize with our allies: teachers in other schools, districts, states, and countries; our students, their families, and communities.

In 2005, I wrote that I teach to make a positive change in the world, so that I can live and work fully as the whole person that I am (Cowhey, 2005). When I was a classroom teacher, it was easier to bring in many more parts of who I am: poet/writer, peace activist, scientist, sustainable gardener. I still write poems, but they are less a part of my teaching these days. My interest in gardening has been channeled into collaborating with colleagues and families to develop our school garden, which functions as an outdoor classroom for our entire school. I am able to frequently bring my students out into the garden and draw on the garden for many authentic applications of mathematics, such as finding the areas and perimeters of garden beds; writing story problems about combining or comparing groups as we pick different kinds of flowers or tomatoes; or removal problems as we cook, eat, or give away those things; fractions and doubling as we cook and bake things from the garden; and multiplication and division scenarios as students generate story problems to illustrate multiplication and division. As someone who raises backyard/community garden chickens, I've used chicks, chickens, and eggs to help my students learn everything from counting and operations to fractions and data. In the last 10 years, as I have gotten more involved with sustainable agriculture, I've been able to engage in activism with families to increase access to farmers' markets for low-income families, with all local markets and community supported agriculture (CSA) farm shares now accepting food stamps and some farmers' markets doubling them. I've gotten involved with the agriculture-in-the-classroom movement statewide and farm-to-school activism in my community.

ORGANIZING COMMUNITIES THROUGH AND FOR MATH

I've been a teacher for 17 years and a community organizer for 35 years. Organizing is an important part of who I am and it is a still a driving reason for why I teach *now*. I suppose it seems counterintuitive that I do more organizing than ever as a math teacher. In 2007, some parents and a colleague and I started Families with Power/*Familias con Poder*, a community organization of low-income families with children, dedicated to cultivating grassroots leadership among parents and youth and helping our children succeed. We were inspired by Miles Horton and the popular education model of the Highlander Folk School. For the first few years, all of our activities were in the community, mostly in living rooms and community rooms in apartment complexes around the city. In 2010, when I started back to part-time teaching and negotiated that part of my job include family engagement, Families With Power started using the math room for monthly "Cafés," referring to it as "our room."

I had invited one of the parents from Families with Power, Esmeralda, to volunteer one afternoon. She helped me play some games with a group of 2nd-graders and then helped with putting together some booklets I wanted to send home to parents. Esmeralda said she liked the games and would play them with her kids. I asked if she thought the parents would find these booklets helpful. Esmeralda said, "Oh, my sister-in-law, Vivian, wouldn't read that." I asked, "Why not? It's in Spanish."

She looked surprised, "It's in Spanish?" I showed her how some were in Spanish and some were in English. "Well she wouldn't read it anyway."

"Why not?" I asked.

"Cause it's too . . . ." she sighed, then opened a booklet and gestured toward the pages, " . . . 'mathy.' See all these boxes and numbers and arrows? She'd never read it."

I was disappointed. I'd been making these booklets precisely for Esmeralda, Vivian, and other parents like them. I considered myself lucky that Esmeralda was honest enough to tell me the truth. I looked at the pile of booklets we'd just stapled. "What do you think we should do with all these?" I asked. Esmeralda looked from me, to the pile, and back to me. "Recycle?" she said, smiling, and dumped them in the bin.

I asked her how we could teach these games to the families, if she thought they were helpful. She thought a moment, then shrugged and said, "I could teach them." I asked how she'd do that. "Well, you know how I do those Families with Power Reading Parties in my living room? We could do that, but with math games."

At the Café that afternoon, Esmeralda told this story to the other parents, who all started talking about how they figured out their math facts such as 8 plus 8. Vivian said, "I show my kid, 'Do it like this. Put the 8 in your head.'" She smacked her forehead for emphasis. She continued, "Then you go 9, 10, 11, 12, 13, 14, 15, 16!" counting on her fingers. Other parents agreed, demonstrating how they figure out $9 + 9$ or $7 + 7$, in the same manner. I had been worried that some of our 2nd- and 3rd-graders hadn't memorized these addition facts and had been hoping the parents would help them practice at home. Then I realized their parents were also figuring these out on their fingers. Esmeralda explained her idea about doing Math Parties in her living room. Tony Garcia, the father of a 1st-grader, objected to the proposal. "Wait, I work nights, so I can't go when you do a Reading Party or a Math Party at night. And I *need* this, because I don't understand the math my daughter is bringing home. Why can't we do it in the morning before school, when the kids are eating breakfast? We could do it here, in our room. I could make the *café con leche*."

So our Morning Math Club was born, staffed by parents who were all English language learners, most of whom had not graduated from high school. A group of students at Math Club recently designed a multiplication with money board game called "Jackson Street Tag Sale Times" based on a familiar tag sale that runs at the housing project near our school. Our Morning Math Club is in its third year, with an average of 25 (K–4) students and 7 parent volunteers coming early two mornings a week for an hour, to have fun learning and playing with math together, while affirming their families' funds of knowledge and cultivating leadership.

In 2005, I wrote that I teach because I agree with Gandhi, "If we are to have real peace in this world, we shall have to begin with the children" (Cowhey, 2005, p. 200). I still agree with Gandhi, and I still want to have real peace in this world, but this aspect of my work looks different now. For many people, when they imagine what multicultural, peace, or social justice education or critical pedagogy might look like in elementary school, they think about social studies or literacy. Surely, when I was a classroom teacher, you could easily find those in social studies or literacy; they were in math and science too but less easily and less obviously. Just because it is less easy or less obvious doesn't mean it stops.

As a classroom teacher, I often saw how students with difficulties in self-regulation struggled with settling into math lessons. I had one student, Aníbal, who was gifted in math, but when something set him off at recess (as it often did) just before math, he often was so upset that he was simply unavailable for the lesson. Because I've always had a fair number of students with PTSD and/or ADHD, struggles with self-regulation presented a challenge in my teaching. I also observed how some of my students who struggled most with math were most afraid to take risks, or quit trying when their first attempt didn't work. For the last few years, I have gotten more and more involved with bringing mindfulness (Mindfulness Based Stress Reduction, MBSR) into our school. As someone gifted and challenged with a busy brain, I enjoy the practice of meditation. I take comfort in the practice of noticing without judgment whatever thought distracted me, letting go, and returning to the breath, to begin again. Those are touchstones for me: to notice, to let go, to begin again.

Two years ago, many of our staff members took an 8-week introductory course in mindfulness, and many continue a mindfulness practice on their own. Last year, we brought an 8-week mindfulness program into our classrooms. During this same period of time, we've been introducing mindfulness in Families with Power, where many parents, especially those whose families are stressed with poverty, poor health, and depression, have become interested in mindfulness as a way to reduce stress. This month, through Families with Power, we are starting a 6-week mindfulness program for families.

MATH, SOCIAL JUSTICE, AND MINDFULNESS

These days, my teaching for peace is more likely co-facilitating a mindfulness course with parents from Families with Power. My teaching for social justice is more likely engaging in a culture circle at a Families with Power Café to understand the last round of food stamp cuts and the potential for more food stamp cuts in the near future, and brainstorming possible actions, from meeting with our local congressman, to supporting families in starting plots at the community garden, to meeting with local farmers about mobile farmers' markets that accept food stamps and come to each of the housing projects in the city. I have the same values, but my teaching/organizing practice continues to evolve.

I still teach for the reasons I reflected on in 2005, but I am more conscious now that while my students need me to really see them, really listen, really care, they also need me to help them succeed. In 2005, I would have been thinking about that as a classroom teacher, with just my 2nd-graders. Jasmine, as a 4th-grader, helped me realize I wasn't as effective for all students as I hoped to be. Now, as a Title 1 math teacher and math coach, I reflect much more critically about what success looks like for every student in every class in every grade in our school through Mix It Up Math. I offer programs not just for the parents of students in my class, but for all of the parents in the school. As a math coach, I work with my colleagues to organize PLCs and professional development to improve our teaching with a focus on practices like raising the level of mathematical discourse and assessment for learning—practices that will have a direct impact on students and reinforce the work of weekly Mix It Up Math sessions back in the classrooms every day.

My lifelong learning is now focused more specifically on math, sustainable agriculture, mindfulness, and pedagogical areas like assessment for learning, increasing the push for mathematical reasoning, in addition to culturally responsive teaching. The "peace education" I do is more about mindfulness and equitable access to sustainable agriculture than peace demonstrations and deconstructing the Columbus story. So yes, I've changed and my teaching has changed, although my core values and reasons for teaching remain.

CHAPTER 19

Teaching on the Frontline

Maria Rosario

Ours was one of the first Puerto Rican families to attend the local parish elementary school during the 1970s. I entered school knowing only Spanish and, because of that, my kindergarten year was one of isolation and silence. I vividly remember being separated from the class, and kept in the back because the teacher did not know what to do with me. If it weren't for a very kind elderly lady who knew me from the block and came to the school to volunteer, I would not have had contact with anyone during my first few months of schooling.

It was during a free and unstructured art period that I finally connected with a classmate. I remember not being able to communicate with my partner verbally; instead, it was through painting and a shared experience that I felt I was able to finally connect with someone. These experiences are very vivid because they are the foundation for my understanding of what school is like for students with a similar background as mine.

SOCIAL JUSTICE IGNORED AND OVERLOOKED

It was a couple of years later, in a 2nd-grade classroom, that I started to question the fairness of my education. From a very early age, even though I wasn't able to name my feelings, I felt unable to connect with anything going on at school because nothing that we studied or learned reflected me, told the story of my history, or was about my lived experiences. I developed a sense of justice very early on during that Catholic school upbringing, but not because social justice was taught. On the contrary, it was because it was ignored and overlooked.

It was in this same 2nd-grade classroom that I witnessed another student, also Puerto Rican, suffer one of the worst injustices of all. Not sitting perfectly still on the rug during read-aloud time, he was threatened by the teacher, who said she'd "slap his face" if he didn't shut up. A day or two later the principal lined us up in the classroom and one by one took us outside into the hallway to question us. She wanted to verify if we had heard anything in particular that had been said by the teacher to our classmate. Being last in line, I was the only person to repeat the teacher's exact words. Later that afternoon, to my surprise as well as my mother's surprise, my classmate's mother appeared at our front door to thank me for telling the truth. She gave me a cross, which I still hold onto today.

At that moment as I was being questioned, I clearly remember thinking that I had to be honest and take a stand about an injustice against my classmate. I also know now that I would have repeated the teacher's words no matter to whom they might have been directed. A part of me also knew that I was finally standing up for a greater injustice inflicted on the minority students at that school, students who looked like me and felt like me and were disconnected from those responsible for providing us with a quality education.

After this incident, the teacher was very cold and indifferent toward me. She didn't act very different from before, but now she really kept her distance from me and made no effort to gain my trust. It could have been that she realized that little people were watching and could defend themselves by giving voice to the abuses. I like to think that was why. I also was very confused for a long time because my mother was upset with me. I had not kept out of "other people's business."

That school gave my siblings and me little except the will to overcome obstacles such as racism, discrimination, and worse at such a young age. They took pleasure in disciplining us, shaming us because our first language was Spanish, and using us as examples for how not to be. I struggled during grammar school to catch up to my peers, struggling to learn how to read and write in English because I was so behind my peers, even in conversational English. For this reason, I withdrew into myself, with no interest in excelling.

It wasn't until the 5th grade that I finally met a terrific teacher. She was new that year. I was so happy to meet someone free from any kind of negative reputation. I literally remember the feeling of hope for a different kind of experience. She easily became the best teacher of my grammar school years. I think it was because she was kind. That's it; that's all it took. She was also the type of teacher who did a lot of group activities, pairing up students to help them navigate in an English-only setting. She incorporated art into as many subjects as possible. She saw the potential in me and affirmed my talents. She drew all of us into the center of the classroom because she honored us all. She gave of herself by sharing her stories and experiences with us. She made me feel like I was part of a community and that I had something to contribute. My 5th-grade teacher provided me with a different way of learning that was transmitted, co-constructed, and co-authored (Nakkula & Toshalis, 2006) with each individual student, both subliminally and directly, that said all kids deserved to feel they belonged and that each person enriched the setting; they did not take away from it and no one was a burden to the community. Because she honored her profession, 5th grade became the one and only year where I was happy at school.

I teach today because of those early, sometimes unintentional, lessons I received in school. I know that the parish school didn't intentionally exclude children different from the majority population. I'm sure that if they had known what it was like for students like me, they would have made an effort to provide a more inclusive setting. Yet, they made me believe I had to behave like them, and even look like them, in order to feel like part of the community.

Schooling did get better as I progressed through the years. A more diverse population began attending, so the school had to adjust and respond appropriately. But in a way, I am grateful to have had those painful experiences because they formed my sense of justice early in life. They taught me to be aware and to listen to my inner dialogue, correcting it whenever it said I was not good enough, especially when those negative messages came from the adults responsible for my education. I learned to trust myself and I also learned that education is a personal responsibility.

THE POWER OF TEACHERS

Teachers have the power to mold a child's inner dialogue. Teachers shape the messages students receive and how they interpret themselves in the world. Teachers can help students imagine, and then achieve, a more positive internal script for themselves and of their culture within the school system and not in opposition to it, by creating an identity-safe environment. By creating such an environment, one where students of color view school and achievement as synonymous with their identity and their culture, they may be able to achieve academic standing comparable to their White peers. Effective teachers from different backgrounds of their students, such as my 5th-grade teacher, often make an effort to help the development of the adolescents they teach by choosing topics of study or literature that reflect a holistic worldview. A teacher doesn't necessarily have to share the same cultural background as her students when co-authoring a pro-academic script with them. Teachers can share their experiences with students, which can be encouraging for adolescents in developing the "theoretical imagination" (Nakkula & Toshalis, 2006) of what success in academia looks like. Educators are in a position where they are active contributors to the co-construction of adolescents' development and what adolescents are able to imagine for their futures. Teachers, as mentors, are able to help youths see themselves through new modes of thinking. Nakkula and Toshalis describe this process as "coauthoring." In the process of imagining who they'll become, what they stand for, and what they're against, students are assisted in this self-determining, theoretical imagination of their lives.

Through this process, a partnership is created between the student and the teacher in the day-to-day building of the theoretical imagination, the development of thinking skills necessary to facilitate a positive life outlook, and to counteract damaging negative outlooks. Adults in the educational field must do all they can to make school a safe and nurturing environment by setting up a space free from dominance from one social group so that everyone feels included, honored, and respected (Garner, 2006). Academic achievement does not belong to one race or social group, and teachers need to be aware and vigilant of the messages they send to their students by closely selecting topics, people, and themes that reflect positive messages about who students are and who they can expect to become in the future.

Nakkula and Toshalis (2006) argue that as adolescents experience life, they develop a life story that allows them to interpret and rationalize their lived experiences. This self-authoring of one's life happens within a larger space. People closest to adolescents play an important role in how adolescents interpret experiences, which leads to identity development. The commitment and partnership through which teachers connect with students to engage in authentic ways of learning and interpreting the world is part and parcel of how a student develops.

Young people are aware, even at a very early age, of injustice in the world; they can tell you what's fair and what's not fair. They come to school with a curiosity and willingness to learn and participate. They are eager to do their share for a cause and can commit to others on behalf of justice. Students are inspiring to me in this sense. I am in awe of their dedication to their passions and sense of justice. They expect teachers to meet them at this point and they make it clear when they aren't being welcomed. This is why all students, and especially students of color, need to learn their history and control their own narrative. They need to participate in the events that become the history of tomorrow. All students must be exposed to many versions of the stories told about history because history is not always rooted in fact. History, many times, is told because of the effect it has on a people. As a young student, I studied all about the forefathers of our country because it instilled a sense of national pride for the teachers presenting the material. It was traditional textbook history that was taught. I later learned, and not through schooling, just how that traditional style of teaching history blurs the understanding of true accounts. The blurring and imperialistic view of history alienated me as a student. Students need to be able to access the different sides of the story to form a more accurate account of history and gain a better sense of self.

CURRICULUM AND PEDAGOGY TO CHANGE CHILDREN'S WORLDS

One unit I always begin the year with is titled "Discovering Our Roots: History in Self." This unit has developed into a 10-week study, although critical pedagogy is always at the forefront of how I teach. My students know I care not only about them but I also care that they know about themselves. It is the kind of teaching and learning about history that goes against the grain and in the tradition of pedagogues like Paulo Freire and Howard Zinn. As Paulo Freire has written, students must learn to read both the "word" and the "world."

In language arts, we begin with a combination of shared reading and book club, where we read many novels that relate to the cultural background of the students. As they read about the fictional and nonfictional lives of characters who may look like them and have the same point of reference as them, the students start to research the countries of their ancestors. Many of them have never been to their country of origin, but they begin to develop a more detailed picture of where their parents and grandparents came from.

In a Socratic seminar setting, they learn about the history of the United States alongside the history of their country of origin so that they begin to develop an understanding of history in a more global sense. They question, compare, and contrast the influence of Great Britain on other governments and countries, and can trace a more direct route from one country to another as the so-called "New World" developed. This is the experience for the students of Mexico, who make up the majority at my current school population. Working side by side, students whose ancestors come from the West Antilles and Africa also have similar experiences in learning about multiple histories. Students of European descent compare and learn about the development of the "New World" through a different lens. When our 5th-grade class learns about the Revolutionary War, they also learn about the Mexican Revolutions and are encouraged to ask questions and research the similarities between the wars. The classroom becomes a community of learners and teachers, with me learning right along with them.

Critical pedagogy has moved me to become very transparent with my students about our school system. I have come to accept that a testing unit has to be interwoven into the other units we study. Testing is the currency of today, and students need to have access to the knowledge of the inner workings of that system. My students need to understand that because the system is designed to give a pass to those who can attain a certain score, they need to work with that purpose in mind. It is as Vygotsky wrote with regard to interpsychological development: Students develop an interpsychological connectedness with me to help them see themselves as capable of success in testing and schooling. I believe that it is justifiable to teach and prepare our students of color about testing. To let students go all year without exposing them to this information is detrimental to their future possibilities. But along with the test prep is material that will motivate my students to read critically.

When students are active participants in their own learning because they ask questions and actively investigate a topic or theme based on personal experiences, references, or interests, they learn to read critically and their level of academic success grows because the learning is relevant to them. This approach motivates a child to learn; test prep becomes secondary. There is no need to stop learning when standardized tests are around the corner. Students are ready to take on that challenge because the material they study and rely on for research motivates and prepares them for testing. Allowing for action research within my classroom has been one of the greatest reasons for the gains my students have made when it comes to standardized test scores.

For 3 years I invited an educational researcher into my classroom, and for each of those years the students' learning took new directions because the students were the center of the community. Even though we were intentional with the units we were covering, it was the students who drove the learning and research based on their passions and sense of justice. One year the learning was very local: Students dove into investigating more about their own neighborhood; the changes happening there became their platform for action and social justice. The very next year, students were more inclined to raise money for a cause that took their learning and action across the world to a different country. The one constant is that students rise to the occasion. Learning through action and social justice is a purpose for why I still teach.

Partnering with educators to advance my own professional development has also benefited my students greatly and has kept test prep in its proper place. To my delight and surprise, the students' work took them on a trip to Texas to present their learning at a conference. The work I did with my students also took me to New Orleans to present our research and it resulted in a publication. I tell teachers to accept the many opportunities that arise. The opportunities and challenges have made me a better educator. I am co-creating what is possible for my students with the help of other educators, something that I could never have envisioned as a 2nd-grader more than 30 years ago.

LESSONS LEARNED

I teach today because I believe that as I continue to pay attention to the climate surrounding my profession, I am aware of the obstacles facing my students and me. Because schooling has always existed to indoctrinate young people into a system where the vote might be better controlled or their minds might be better molded to serve as members of the working class, I am able to be there to help my students dream of other possibilities for themselves, regardless of the original purpose of compulsory schooling (Gatto, 2000). As a teacher, I am the person with whom students share their aspirations, dreams, and even heartaches. Students come to trust me and throughout the years they have confided in me their many hopes and tragedies.

Young people deserve to see people who look like them, have had the same experiences as they have, and who can be their advocates when no one else is willing to do the exceptionally hard work that must be done when a child is suffering. Teachers need to be willing to be that advocate when all other people have failed them. I have made the comment to other teachers that if a teacher isn't willing to listen and hear a child when he or she is being hurt, then they should step aside and do something else with their lives. I know many teachers do not agree with me on this, but we are sometimes the last line of defense for a child and we must be willing to speak up on behalf of students when all other adults fail to do so. A space created within the walls of a school can help students come to understand the harshness of their realities, and if a teacher is willing to let students dwell in the center of that space, they often turn to teachers to help them when no one else is listening.

These are lessons I received early in life and they have been tested and reaffirmed after 18 years of teaching. I teach today, sometimes despite the harsh climate, for that exact reason. I rededicate myself every year. Through reflection and error, I acknowledge my limitations and I push on to help my students achieve success no matter what circumstances may be altering their true human potential. I teach because I am a humanist and the classroom is the frontline.

We Can Win

Social Justice Advocacy
Inside and Out of the Classroom

Jesse Hagopian

My life has long been animated by the belief that public education should belong to the public and be in service of the needs of the public. Yet I have taken a circuitous route to becoming aware of my role as an educator in a society of such vast inequality. Successive transformative experiences since the first time I stood in front of a class and solicited their attention have altered my understanding of the teaching profession, my role in it, and the very nature of teaching and learning.

FROM TFA TO REAL SOCIAL JUSTICE EDUCATION ACTIVISM

My entrance into the education profession began when a representative from Teach for America (TFA) came to the Macalester College campus in my senior year and described—with glossy brochures and persuasive slide show presentations—that I could be part of the "modern-day civil rights movement" for equitable education. After an interview and a lesson-plan demonstration, I was selected to participate in the program and I signed up enthusiastically, believing the program was amassing our generation's Freedom Riders for an epic struggle to empower students to transform their world. Never having been "good" at school—to which my test scores attested—I was now terrified by the prospect of being the person in the classroom responsible for something as important as a child's education. Yet I felt compelled by the severity of the problems in the world to overcome my fear and attempt to make a difference.

After graduating from college, I headed for the Bronx, New York, where I underwent TFA's "teacher boot camp." My first hint that TFA was not going to be a Stokely Carmichael training camp for direct action that would take on the education establishment occurred when my next-door roommate, an outspoken Black teacher candidate, was put on a probation plan, ostensibly because he refused to stop insisting that TFA include more anti-racist components to its trainings. This was deeply troubling to me, but we had no time to stop and think. With just five sleepless weeks of on-the-job training in which we taught summer school to 4th-graders, plus team meetings and night classes, I was given the stamp of approval and shipped off to Washington, D.C. From 2001 through 2004, I taught at Hendley Elementary School in South East Washington, D.C., an area sectioned off from the city both geographically by the Anacostia River and socially by its dearth of everything from jobs to grocery stores. To borrow from the great educator and author Jonathan Kozol, the schools there are "savagely unequal" (Kozol, 1991).

The elementary school at which I taught was completely segregated, serving 100% African American students until my third year, when one White student entered kindergarten. Directly across from the entrance of the school was a decrepit building with vegetation growing through the windows. Around the corner lay a pile of cars that had been stripped and incinerated. Our school offered neither a grass field nor a basketball hoop for kids to use at recess. The library's book collection was more appropriate for an archeological study than a source for topical information. Our textbooks were woefully out of date and we seldom had enough for every student. Police roamed the halls of our elementary school looking for mouthy kids to jack up against the wall.

But to fully capture the ambience, you would have to enter my classroom. I had one hole in the middle of the chalkboard—the kids called it the "bullet hole in the lesson"—and another hole in the ceiling. The first time I noticed the opening in the ceiling near the bank of opaque windows was a Monday morning when I came back to school after a rainy weekend and found standing water on the floor and all of my students' U.S. history poster-board projects waterlogged. After the second flooding of my room, I got smart and put an industrial-sized garbage can underneath the hole.

One lasting memory of my teaching experience in D.C. came on the third day that I stood before these 6th-graders. I had asked the students to bring a meaningful object from home for a show-and-tell activity. We gathered in a circle in the back of the room that Friday morning and the kids sat eagerly with paper bags on their laps that concealed their autobiographical mementos. One after another, each and every hand came out of those crumpled brown lunch sacks clutching a photo of a close family member—usually a dad or an uncle—that was either dead or in jail. By the time it got to me, all I could do was stare stupidly at the baseball I had pulled out and pick nervously at the red stitches as I mumbled something about how I had played in college.

Only a few days after this lesson, the tragic attacks of 9/11 changed the nation forever and were closely followed by the government's launching of the war on Afghanistan. I received a higher degree in education theory then as I witnessed the cynicism of our nation's ability to bomb children halfway around the world but refuse to find the money to fix the hole in my ceiling or properly care for these children in the shadow of the White House. This too was the year the No Child Left Behind Act (NCLB) was implemented, a law that called for more standardized testing to hold teachers accountable. It became apparent in all of the NCLB rhetoric about accountability that I was being asked, from inside the classroom, to correct all the mistaken priorities of politicians.

As much as my youthful energy, naiveté, and ambition helped me reach many of my students that year, it became soberingly obvious that many factors shaping my students' lives and educations were beyond my control: homelessness, a prison industrial complex that had torn many of their families apart, the lack of jobs for even the better-educated parents, and a war budget that necessarily left so many students behind. Working in the "other America" was a formative experience that inspired me to dedicate my life to finding solutions that could transform public education, as well as the broader society that chose to allow such neglect. Although TFA allowed me this window into the problems of our country, it didn't prepare me to address any of these challenges. With only 5 weeks of training, it wasn't just that I was not equipped to differentiate instruction to meet the needs of students with a wide range of ability levels, create portfolios that accurately assessed student progress, or cultivate qualities of civic courage—it was that I had no idea that these things were indispensable components of an effective education.

My lack of proper training as an educator, coupled with the relentless toll of poverty and institutional racism were taking on my students, made me decide—consciously or not—to focus my energy not on developing a liberatory pedagogy, but instead on transforming social structures and educational policy. I had entered the teaching profession to help empower students so they could fix the problems they encountered in the world, but those 3 years I spent at Hendley Elementary led me to believe this approach was a cop-out, a dead end, ultimately a waste of my time, and also of my students' time. Because of my experience teaching in the Anacostia ghetto, I came to understand why I *had* to act in the world outside of my classroom—had to struggle for the changes I wanted to see occur in the economic and political world—if my classroom was ever going to have the resources my students would need to overcome conditions that disadvantaged them. When other teachers spoke to me about how their activism was in the classroom, I can remember being polite but thinking to myself that they were making an excuse to evade "real" activism themselves.

While in D.C. I participated in as many major national demonstrations as I could. I marched on the World Bank to demand an end to structural adjustment programs in the developing world that undermined their economies. I rallied at the "March for Women's Lives," to demand that women have the basic right to control their own bodies; I traveled to New York City to participate in the February 15, 2003, antiwar demonstration that became the biggest global protest in history, and I participated in our union's victorious struggle for dignity for educators and the reinstatement of our promised 9% wage increase.

BECOMING A PROFESSIONAL, LOSING MY PROFESSION

After three intense and emotionally draining years in Washington, D.C., I realized that if I was going to be an educator in the long term—something only 33% of TFA teachers accomplish according to TFA's own study—I would have to return to school and get my master's degree. I returned to Seattle, my hometown, and earned my Masters in Education while student teaching at Madison Middle School, later taking a full-time humanities position there.

Then in 2008 the Great Recession hit. I watched in disbelief as the very banks that had sabotaged the global economy were rewarded with unfathomable amounts of public money at the very time our school district decided to close five schools. This contradiction was intolerable for me and I co-founded an organization called Educators, Students and Parents for a Better Vision of the Public Schools (ESP Vision) to unite all of the schools slated for closure and fight against the decision. Although we lost that struggle, we were able to forge a new education-activist community in Seattle that has proven critical to many subsequent struggles. Then the Great Recession hit me in a more personal way. Only a few months after the birth of my first son, I was laid off due to budget cuts. This year away from the classroom would transform my understanding of my place in the world in ways I could never have imagined.

SHAKEN: SHOCK DOCTRINE SCHOOLING

My wife Sarah worked in global public health, focusing on HIV in Haiti. Just after our son Miles celebrated his first birthday, Sarah was sent to Port-au-Prince to oversee training for nurses and doctors. Because I was out of the classroom, I was free to travel with her. Our whole family arrived in Port-au-Prince on January 10, 2010. Two days later our lives would be forever changed as we survived, uninjured, one of the most deadly earthquakes in human history.

We had one emergency medical technician (EMT) at our hotel, and when word got out that there was a trained medical professional present, people began flocking to what became a makeshift medical clinic for hundreds of badly injured Haitians. The EMT quickly deputized my wife and me as orderlies in his driveway "emergency room," where we assisted in whatever way we could—ripping sheets to use as bandages, setting splints, tying tourniquets—despite our lack of training.

It was during the second day after the quake that I witnessed, for the first time, someone die. This beautiful boy was about 8 years old and I remember he was wearing a bright yellow shirt with a graphic of the sun rising over mountains. His father had worked all night, a translator relayed to us, digging him out of the concrete debris that had been their home. His son's screams, which had served to guide rescuers to his location, had turned to irregular intervals of low moans by the time he reached us. The boy was laid out on a cream-colored polyester blanket with part of his brain exposed where a brick had crushed his skull. His father knelt at his side blowing frantically into his mouth. The father was not administering cardiopulmonary resuscitation (CPR)—I doubt he had formal medical training; rather, it was a devoted attempt to animate his son's listless body with his own life force. Yet even as we began dressing his abrasion, the boy took his final breath. The father, with a look of anguish that made me avert my eyes, quickly fled the area to grieve in seclusion. The child's motionless body lay on the blanket for some time before anyone could bring themselves to remove him.

On the third day after the earthquake, we drove through the streets of downtown Port-au-Prince and witnessed hundreds of dead bodies lining the streets and people still desperately trying to dig loved ones out of the rubble, while the UN and U.S. soldiers were deployed to security details to protect against what worried them more than rescuing people: possible civil strife, which could threaten U.S. interests.

At one point we passed a school that had completely collapsed. I remember successfully convincing myself as we drove by that not one student or teacher was struck by the chunks of drab-gray cinderblock that lay scattered in the courtyard. I could not allow the image of being trapped with my students under the debris of the school to enter my thoughts, and I managed to become certain that no one had been in the building when it collapsed. After spending the prior 2 days wrapping countless children's bloodied appendages with bed sheets, I needed the peace of mind that these students lived. But teachers too sometimes get the answers wrong. After I returned to Seattle and reviewed the statistics, it seems increasingly likely that my confidence in the well-being of that school community was more coping mechanism than fact.

The Haitian government estimates that at least 38,000 students and more than 1,300 teachers and other education personnel died in the earthquake. As UNICEF reported, "80 percent of schools west of Port-au-Prince were destroyed or severely damaged in the earthquake, and 35 to 40 percent were destroyed in the southeast. This means that as many as 5,000 schools were destroyed and up to 2.9 million children here are being deprived of the right to education." In the earthquake's aftermath, Haiti's Education Minister Joel Jean-Pierre declared "the total collapse of the Haitian education system."

Then I watched in horror as the corporate education reform program of NCLB and Race to the Top that was threatening the public schools in our country was exported as the solution to the devastation of the Haitian school system. For most people, Haiti's broken school system—literally buried under tons of rubble—was an incomprehensible horror. But for a few, the earthquake created a big break.

"There's a real opportunity here, I can taste it. That is why I've flown [to Haiti] so many times" Chang (2010). Meet Paul Vallas. Vallas is the former chief executive officer (CEO) of the Chicago and Philadelphia public school systems and was hired in the aftermath of Hurricane Katrina as superintendent of the Recovery School District of Louisiana that oversaw the privatization of the New Orleans school system. With no background as an educator, a Connecticut judge ruled on June 28, 2013, that Vallas did not have the credentials under Connecticut law to be in charge of the Bridgeport schools. And yet his lack of education experience and his privatization disposition made him overqualified to oversee the remaking of the Haitian school system in a bid to funnel government money to a largely private school system.

Already suffering from posttraumatic stress disorder (PTSD) as a result of my experiences in Haiti, seeing the United States seek to undermine the desperate education system in Haiti was nothing less than tormenting as I tried to reintegrate into society. Pushing back against the corporate education reform agenda was inextricably linked to my own recovery from the mental trauma of my experience in Haiti.

SOCIAL JUSTICE PEDAGOGY: INSIDE AND OUT OF THE CLASSROOM

Soon after my return from Haiti, I attended an activist conference in San Francisco where a much less dramatic, yet nonetheless impactful, moment again retooled my sense of myself as an educator. Sarah Knopp, a teacher from Los Angeles, made the simple yet brilliant proposal that being a social justice educator had to mean two things: *both* a focus on pedagogy in the classroom that would empower students to understand the challenges they faced and help them develop their own strategies for resistance, *as well as* organizing one's coworkers and union brothers and sisters to actively resist the corporate education reform agenda and social policies that were undermining our ability to address the needs of our students.

When I was rehired by the Seattle schools to teach at my alma mater, Garfield High School, I decided to consciously approach my role as educator with this two-pronged approach. I began focusing not only on the next protest, but also on how protest would be integrated into my next lesson plan. *Rethinking Schools* magazine and the Zinn Education Project website became critical to the development of my pedagogy. I soon became hooked on the new energy that was created in my classroom by students who "traveled back in time" to reenact the debates during the Seneca Falls women's rights convention, or the 1860 presidential election, or the origins of standardized testing in the public schools.

Then in November of 2012, I achieved the greatest moment in my teaching career (up until that point, anyway). Although billionaire education reformers may fall out of their brass-studded leather chairs when they hear it, I did not celebrate this moment of euphoria by running a bubble test through a Scantron machine and reading the red-inked percentages it spit back out. It occurred, in fact, as hundreds upon hundreds of students—some from my classes—streamed past me in the hallway, leaving school in the middle of the day carrying hand-made signs that read, "Fund Our Future!" and "No More Cuts." I was simply overwhelmed with emotion.

This moment was precipitated by Washington State's announcement that it would hold a special legislative session to decide how to further slash the education and health-care budgets. An organization I had helped form, the Social Equality Educators (SEE), headed to Olympia, the state capital, to issue citizen's arrest warrants to any legislators who failed to adhere to the Washington State Constitution, which declares education is the state's "Paramount Duty." In the course of delivering arrest warrants to the House Ways and Means Committee, I was arrested.

While I was in jail, and unbeknownst to me, my students at Garfield set up a Facebook page titled "Free Mr. Hagopian." Hundreds of student Bulldogs joined the page in my support. After I was released that night and appeared at school the next day, the students changed the Facebook page to "Seattle Student Walkout for Education." I had often hoped my students would one day learn the lessons of history I had taught—from the struggles of the abolitionists, to student movements against the Vietnam War, to the Freedom Riders of the civil rights movement—and use them to start their own revolution. The moment my students lost their contentedness with studying history and started making their own—that was one of the most gratifying days of my career.

Only weeks after the student mass walkout, the Washington State Supreme Court declared the state legislature in violation of the Washington State Constitution and said they would need to increase funding to education, which resulted in a billion extra dollars added to the K–12 budget in 2013.

The momentum from that struggle to fund our schools no doubt helped to shape the much-better-known eruption of activism at Garfield the following year, the MAP test boycott. When our entire staff voted without a single "no" vote to refuse to administer the district-mandated standardized test, our collective act of resistance helped to transform the national debate about public education. The Garfield Parent Teacher Student Association (PTSA) voted unanimously to support us, as did the student body government. The Seattle Public Schools threatened MAP-boycotting teachers with a 10-day suspension without pay, and then had to retreat from the threat when none of the teachers backed down and thousands of parents, students, and teachers from around the country wrote letters, signed petitions, and made phone calls in support of our movement. In the wake of our public refusal to waste our students' time on another standardized test—one not even aligned to our curriculum—test protests erupted in what became known as the "education spring."

In Portland, students initiated their own boycott of the OAKS tests. Kindergartners and their parents staged a "play-in" at the Chicago School District headquarters against the replacement of the arts with norm-referenced exams. The National Union of Teachers in Great Britain sent Garfield High School a letter of solidarity—and then they launched their own boycott of a standardized test.

After a couple of months, when the school district attempted to circumnavigate our MAP boycott by forcing our school administration to pull kids from class and march them off to the computer lab to take the test, parents began opting their children out of the test by the hundreds, while hundreds of other students refused to get out of their seats to take the test or simply hit the "A" key over and over until the test was invalidated because it was completed in only a few seconds.

At the end of the year the superintendent of the Seattle Public Schools made a stunning announcement: the MAP test would no longer be required at the high school level. This was a vindication of our belief that the destination of a quality education was not on the MAP. The struggle seems to have irreversibly charted the course of my life as a high school history teacher.

WE CAN WIN

Education currently plays a contradictory role in our society. On the one hand, there are amazing moments in school where intellectual curiosity is ignited and where students make vital insights about who they are, what they believe in, and how to collectively solve the problems our society faces. On the other hand, many of the structures and policies of the school system—high-stakes testing, tracking, zero-tolerance discipline policies, culturally biased curriculum, large class sizes, funding shortages, and beyond—work to reproduce the vast inequality in our society.

We know we face a desperate situation in the world today: Endless wars, mass incarceration, worldwide economic implosion, and climate change threaten the very future of humanity. If politicians and billionaires use public education to further the aims of the privatizers, to rank and sort students into a hierarchy of jobs and into the class strata in our vastly unequal society, and scapegoat teachers and their unions for the problems that have been created by the 1%, then our future truly is in peril.

My life as an activist teacher has put me in face-to-face opposition against some of the most powerful people in the education establishment.

When U.S. Secretary of Education Arne Duncan came to a Seattle-area high school in July 2010, he agreed to meet with a small group of teachers who were protesting his appearance, and I had the opportunity to debate him on his advocacy for teacher "merit pay." When filmmaker David Guggenheim held a special screening of *Waiting for Superman* in Seattle, I was on the list of those invited to attend. When the film was over, I gave his privatization-pushing propaganda "two thumbs down," and engaged him in a rigorous debate about how charter schools were undermining public education. I joined the Occupy Education "policy throwdown" with the Gates Foundation and confronted the Foundation's public relations spokesperson on its advocacy of using students' standardized test scores in evaluating teachers. After helping to lead a successful boycott of the Measures of Academic Progress (MAP) test at Seattle's Garfield High School, I had a chance to confront one of the makers of that test at a Town Hall panel discussion.

I teach because I want to empower my students with pedagogy that doesn't reduce them to a test score, respects their intellect, and is designed to facilitate dialogue about how to solve the problems they face in their communities, in their country, and in their world. I teach because I know it is possible to organize students, parents, teachers, and administrators to fight for an education system that is democratically run by the people who make up that system, rather than the whims of philanthro-capitalists. I teach because I have seen the beauty of education in pursuit of the fulfillment of human potential and I have witnessed the horror of education used to reproduce inequality and oppression. And I am still teaching because of what I've been taught by the remarkable students, families, and colleagues from Hendley Elementary to Garfield High: We can struggle and we can win.

LOOKING FORWARD

Part VII, the final section of the teachers' essays, is about the future, and how teachers forge their paths, sometimes within the profession and sometimes outside of it. In her essay, Amanda VandeHei retraces her steps from adolescence to the present to understand how she became the social justice teacher she is today. She also describes how standardization and high-stakes testing have both changed her teaching life and how, through her mentors and colleagues in graduate school, she has learned to negotiate difficult conversations while remaining true to her principles. Criselda Guerra, a veteran science teacher of Mexican American immigrant children in the Rio Grande Valley, Texas, even at the age of 65, cannot think of a life without teaching. Despite the fact that she was once summarily removed from her junior high school science teaching position and assigned to teach art at the high school level—because, as she later found out, there were some complaints that she was too "hard" on the students— Criselda found a way to combine her love of science with her love of the arts. Her essay describes some of the ways in which she makes science comprehensible and even exciting for her high school students.

In Chapter 23, teacher Michael Silverstone writes about the joys of and, increasingly, the obstacles to being the kind of teacher he wanted to be. Documenting his extraordinary journey when beginning his essay to shortly after completing it, Michael decided to leave his position and take time off to think about the future. His essay ends with a newfound resolution to find meaning in teaching in a different context.

CHAPTER 21

Becoming the Teacher
I Am Today

Amanda VandeHei

I have always enjoyed the company of young children. My sister blessed me as an aunt when I was 8 years old and my writing samples from elementary school are proof that my precious nephew was constantly on my mind. As my siblings' families grew, I longed for holiday get-togethers to be in the company of my young nieces and nephew.

As I grew older, I began to realize that experiences with my young family members had given me a unique familiarity and comfort when working with and teaching young children. As a middle and high school student I spent countless hours babysitting, mentoring, and coaching elementary students during summer youth basketball camps and teaching elementary religious education courses. The summer before my freshman year of college I was a camp counselor and had my first real experience with middle school girls. Their attitudes and drama always had me on my toes, but the tears they shed when they left the last day of camp reminded me why I agreed to be part of this leadership team.

When registering for college, there was no hesitation: I knew I would become an elementary school teacher. I distinctly remember declaring my major before I had my first class in college; I never wavered from this decision. I started as an elementary education major, and 4½ years later, that is the degree I received. As I reflect on my choice of career, I realize there have been many experiences throughout my life influencing me to become the type of teacher I am today. A few incidents in particular have shaped my definition of what it means to be a teacher and why it's important that I teach *now*.

THE PE CLASS

In my last year of high school I had a hectic academic schedule and refused to quit band or advanced Spanish in order to make room for my last physical education (PE) course. Although all of these courses were considered electives, PE was the only one necessary to meet the graduation requirements. With few options of when to fit these three electives into my schedule, I had no alternative but to take the PE course during a different class period than my senior classmates. Anticipating a type of independent study with a PE teacher who was a friend of my basketball coach, I was surprised to walk into the gymnasium and see other students standing and chatting. I quickly became aware that the school's English language learners (ELLs) took this physical education elective together. It was the late 1990s and these students were learning English while taking classes as a cohort, including this PE elective. Although I didn't know any of them and I would like to think it was because they were often not part of the mainstream classes, I believe my selfish high school attitude kept me in a different social circle. Until this point in my high school career, I was concerned only with the peers in my immediate circle, which didn't include students from the ELL cohort. Having a locker near the ELL classroom, I would smile at individual students from time to time and say hello but it was always while surrounded by my own group of friends. It wasn't until the first day of physical education in my senior year of high school that I realized my group of friends was not surrounding me and I was the only White student among the ELL cohort. I was also the only one not speaking Spanish. For a second I was relieved to see the teacher—someone I had known—hoping this situation would get better.

As it turned out, the situation only worsened. The teacher was glad to see me too but took advantage of the time to mock the way the other students were dressed and the language they were speaking. I was offended by his derogatory comments and, even more disconcerting, I felt I had to choose to be on "his" team or to quickly try to fit in with my classmates. Knowing I had more to lose by befriending the teacher, I tried to join a group of girls who were in a corner nearby. Thankfully, they accepted me and in a good-natured manner began teasing me about my broken Spanish.

While separating me from the rest of the class, the teacher would make small talk with me about my basketball games and explain to me that he was working with the guidance office to get me out of this class because he knew it was not where I belonged. When I asked why he thought I should be removed from the class, he told me I shouldn't have to take a class with a bunch of people who don't even speak my language. I tried to explain to him that I actually enjoyed being in the class, I had won the trust of the original group of girls I had joined on the first day, and even a few of the boys had started to practice English with me while we would shoot hoops, but the teacher remained adamant that I should be removed from the class. In fact, he would often tell me I didn't have to participate in the events with the other students and told me I could shoot around or lift weights. Needless to say, I always did what the other students were doing. As a result, the teacher and I stopped talking. In fact, one day he told me not to ask him for any favors because I didn't deserve any if I was going to disrespect him the way I had. Although to some these acts of discrimination by my physical education teacher may seem small and insignificant, to me, they are part of the reason I teach now. Examples of marginalization and discrimination have happened and continue to happen far too often in the public school where I was a student as well as those in which I have taught, and although these acts are sometimes fairly covert, they have become blatantly obvious and troublesome to me. Whether it is a teacher speaking from a deficit perspective regarding a particular family or student, national test scores delineated by students' racial background, or charter schools that are segregating students even further, I feel responsible to provide a voice to those who are not a part of the conversation.

BECOMING A PARKEE

During my college career, I always looked for opportunities to work with young children, and when I would return to my hometown to earn money for the following school year, one of my many jobs was what we called a "parkee." Essentially, my job was to create some kind of organizational playtime at a local park. In the numerous public parks throughout the city, "parkees" were paired and stationed at the same park for the entire summer. From kickball tournaments to arts and crafts contests, our creativity and leadership were tested every day.

The long days of outdoor fun and themed events in one of the many local parks were hard work. What I didn't realize, though, was how the relationships I was building with the young students who attended the park, who came from different backgrounds from me racially, ethnically, and socioeconomically, were defining me as a future teacher. The 30 or so local children who visited our park daily almost all spoke English as their second language. On the occasions that we would hang out on the picnic tables,

I was constantly asking questions and learning about their cultures, families, languages, and, most interesting to me, the food they brought to the park. They would laugh when I asked them to repeat words over and over in their first language, be it Spanish or Hmong, and I would try to repeat them with incorrect intonation. They would bring new games and cultural toys to the park and teach me how to play with them. Although I didn't have the understanding to name what was happening while I was a "parkee," I knew that although these children didn't have a lot to say about their successes or desires to be in school, it became obvious that they knew a great deal about things I didn't know about. Different from the traditional culture of school, the park provided a safe place for students to share information and stories about their families' languages and traditions as well as an opportunity for the students to be the experts.

The culminating event of this summer job was a parade in the downtown area of our small town, which entailed every park making a float and the children riding and walking with the "parkees" representing their park. I will never forget when my older brother came to the park to hook his large truck to our float. The children were so excited and thankful that he had a new, big truck and that he was willing to pull the float we had worked on for weeks. Our float was pretty amazing given the fact that all the supplies had been donated and our most powerful tools were a staple gun and paintbrush. Feeling confident and proud of our work, we hooked up the float and made our way to the meeting area. On the way to our place in line we passed many floats and it suddenly became obvious, at least to me, that our float wasn't of quite the same quality as many of the others. The other floats were bigger and more colorful and the children were in fairly elaborate costumes. I started to feel slightly deflated but decided to put on my best face and pump up our children for the parade that was about to begin.

Although our float was far from the best and our costumes were limited compared to those of the children from many of the other parks, our students had a great time. They had never been part of a parade before and it clearly was only me who had noticed the drastic difference between our productions and those of the other parks. Not one student from our park was embarrassed or even mentioned feeling inferior to the other parks. I thought I was doing a good job hiding my slight embarrassment, but I should have known that my brother would notice my disappointment. I'll never forget when he came up to me, put his arm around me, and said he was proud of me. He was happy to pull our float and in his big brother way told me he wouldn't want to drive any of the floats from a park in the suburbs. And then he stated the truth: "You know the parents built those floats, Amanda. You actually let your students design and build yours. You let them be in charge."

Many years have passed since then. At the time, I was not able to define or explain the feelings of unfairness that consumed me that day at the parade; now, however, I understand this experience as an instance of institutional discrimination. Although I was extremely proud of what my students and our park had produced, the realization that we were not given a fair playing ground was disheartening. The parents of my students didn't have money or time to donate to our float and costumes. In fact, most of them didn't have automobiles to provide transportation to and from the parade, which partly explains the children's reactions to my brother's fancy truck. Little did I know how my college summers as a "parkee" were preparing me for other situations to come in my teaching career.

BECOMING A TEACHER: HARD LESSONS LEARNED

These memories shaped the kind of teacher I knew I wanted to become or, in the case of the PE class, what I knew I wanted to avoid. My preparation to become an elementary school teacher at the University of Wisconsin Eau Claire was extraordinary, and although I didn't realize how phenomenal it was at the time, it became quite obvious in my first few years in the classroom that I had been much better prepared than many of my fellow novice teachers. Although my preparation program did not include social justice curricula, I received some of this content in a few of my undergraduate courses. Furthermore, I left college feeling fairly certain how to use current methodologies to teach reading, writing, and math in the elementary setting.

As a novice teacher, my first academic year, 2003–2004, was a rollercoaster. I remember starting the day feeling extremely prepared and ending the day wondering if the students had learned *anything*. Luckily for me, my 2nd-graders returned every day and I know my teaching got better each day. Although I received a great deal of professional development in math my first year of teaching because of a particular grant my school had received, there was little professional development in the area of literacy.

Taking matters into my own hands, I began a master's in literacy my first year of teaching. A couple of years later, the final project for my master's program was to conduct research in the field of literacy and home visitation. With the help of my assistant principal, I was able to carry over the work I had done for my master's thesis to a grant in the school district where I was working. In the grant we were able to include my salary as an additional literacy specialist responsible for the implementation of our new home visitation program. The assistant principal and I designed the program and were able to pay teachers to visit the homes of students in our school. The teachers traveled in pairs and would visit each household three times. The first time they would get to know the family; the second visit would include delivering over $100 of bilingual books to the family and modeling how to read with and to young children as well as how to respond to literature. The last visit was to follow up with the strategies that had been taught. Naturally, I thought the plan was brilliant and the support of my assistant principal made me feel like we had created a great program for the teachers and students in our school. You can imagine the sense of accomplishment we felt, especially when we were awarded the grant and given the opportunity to pay our teachers to visit students' homes and provide their families with literacy materials.

This grant went into effect midway through my third year of teaching, and I accepted the new position as the home visitation coordinator with the responsibility of creating and implementing the new program. Although the program seemed to be well received at first, I quickly became aware that someone on staff was sabotaging both my efforts and the mission of the program. In fact, she was rallying a group of teachers to leave the home visitation program because it was encouraging parents to speak their first language at home.

One of the goals of the home visitation program was to educate parents about the importance of strong acquisition of one's first language, and as I would practice and model the procedures of the home visits during teacher orientation, I would mention to the teachers the importance of providing parents and families with reasons why using their first language at home is essential to the development of their literacy skills in their second language, usually English. In retrospect, I should have known this philosophy would cause a bit of controversy, but at the same time, I didn't understand why language development had been a part of my undergraduate and graduate studies but clearly had not "shown up" in other teachers' preparation courses.

The leader of the opposition was a veteran teacher well respected in the school, so her cruelty toward me, and toward the progressive nature of the home visitation program, quickly spread throughout the building. I couldn't believe that elementary school staff members working in a school where more than half the students were learning English as their second language were opposed to encouraging parents to speak Spanish in their homes. I tried to remain firm to my beliefs, but I quickly realized that even in the eyes of my once-supportive administration, I was no longer a voice of reason, but a voice of annoyance. This was solidified when I was asked into the administrator's office to not only discuss the literacy home visitation program but also the questions I was raising regarding the basal text our school was being forced to adopt. This was one of my first instances of resistance to the wave of the standardization and accountability measures and practices that are now commonplace.

As it turned out, it felt as if there was limited appreciation for my efforts to encourage the parent community to read and write in their first language, and others in my teaching community were becoming even more annoyed with the questions I was asking regarding the lack of teacher autonomy when using basal readers and scripted programs. Later, in a meeting with my grade-level colleagues, I was rattling on about feeling that my teaching degree had no significance and asking why I had wasted time learning how to be a good teacher if a scripted program was going to tell me how to teach and ensure that I did it poorly. Another 2nd-grade teacher, who was not traditionally certified through an elementary education degree program, looked at me and said, "Maybe you should have gotten your degree in something else. That's what I did." It was then that I became aware of the differences in my teacher preparation program compared to others. I also became even more aware of the differences between a great majority of the people I worked with on a daily basis.

Don't get me wrong: There were a few teachers who supported my ideas and concerns, but their encouragement was usually offered behind closed doors where they were sure the principal, and any other teacher for that matter, wouldn't be able to hear them. It became very obvious to me that while trying to improve the lives of the children at our school, I had somehow ostracized myself by becoming "the outspoken one." Only a year after initiating the home visitation program, I left the school to return to a classroom and open a new school. I told myself it would be better if I remained quiet. Ultimately, I should have known better; there's no way I could be quiet.

Opening a brand new school was a once-in-a-lifetime opportunity. I was returning to the classroom and ready for yet another change in my teaching career. I learned quickly after arriving that one of the many benefits of opening a new school was that testing data were not used to assess the school for the first 2 years. It was sort of a grace period to allow staff in the new facility to work out any problems. What this meant to me was teacher autonomy. There was no state involvement yet and as long as you were using texts adopted by the district, which was pretty much anything under the sun, you were able to teach how you pleased. I decided then that

I was going to become a "new school chaser," going from one new school to another throughout my career to in order to be able to continue to teach how I believed was best and without scripted and mandated curriculum. Soon after my brilliant discovery, funding for new schools was discontinued.

The first couple of years at my new school were delightful and then standardization began to ensue—scripted texts, matching assessments for the entire grade level, identical-looking grade books for the entire K–5 staff, mandated time using specified computer software. The most disheartening part of all of these confining mandates was the silence on the part of the teachers. They rarely spoke up and, in my experience, they almost never asked questions. Rather, they voiced their concerns among small groups of comrades, but never in the arenas where these concerns needed to be heard. Some even appreciated the constraints: They would tell me they thought it would be easier to write lesson plans with the new mandates and scripted materials. So, here I was again, alone, wondering why my ideas of teaching were so different from those of the majority of the people with whom I worked. Once again, I returned to graduate school looking for answers.

ASKING QUESTIONS, SEEKING NEW ANSWERS

Six years later, I am still in graduate school and I am still teaching. After being on my best behavior for 2 years at my new school, I decided that asking questions in the interest of my profession and the students I teach is part of who I am and part of why I teach *now*. I believe in teachers and, in particular, I believe in the notion of teachers as intellectuals. I believe in our profession and our ability to meet the needs of our students without standardization. I believe in schools of education and teacher education programs that prepare teachers to adapt their teaching based on differing contexts throughout the world. And with almost all of my beliefs under constant scrutiny at the local and regional levels, without hesitation I have decided not to be the teacher who simply does as she is told.

My graduate education has helped me understand the market-driven systems and corporate pedagogy fueling educational debates and policy. I have been able to read about and name the injustices inside and outside of the educational world. Specifically, I have devoted a great deal of my studies to Whiteness and the institutional racism that is still evident today. I have created relationships with researchers and scholars in the field of education who continue to encourage me to speak up against the notion of "teachers as technicians," in other words, teachers who unquestioningly follow prescribed and scripted curriculum. It is because of these relationships that I am empowered to walk a sometimes lonely path.

Perhaps most important to my development in this process has been learning the discourse to address these sometimes delicate subjects. I can admit that when dealing with injustices in the past, I sometimes came across as angry—because I was—but I have realized that this attitude did not make my already controversial ideas appealing to others. In the past I knew I was fighting something, or as my graduate school advisor would say, "pushing back" against something, but I couldn't negotiate the tension between my "push back" against the standardization of schools and maintaining a level of respect for those I may be "pushing back" against. Luckily for me, my advisor in the doctoral program is a senior scholar in the field of multi-cultural education who constantly models how to engage in and negotiate these kinds of dialogical conversations effectively. It is with her modeling that I now feel more comfortable engaging in conversations that can be uncomfortable.

Immersing myself in research regarding cultural capital and culturally relevant pedagogy empowers me to have faith that I am meeting my students' needs. My graduate friends and mentors are my critical peers and they encourage my continued dialogue. Although I sometimes don't find the support I need from my colleagues at the school where I teach, it is through the fellowship and continued research and discussions I have with my graduate school colleagues and friends that I make sense of what teaching means to me.

I teach *now* because, more than ever, we need teachers who are asking critical questions concerning educational policy and the standardization of schooling. I know that sometimes I will not be the most popular person in my school; I will sometimes make principals and teachers a bit uncomfortable, just as I did my PE teacher years ago. Nevertheless, I know I will be doing it for the students, giving them a voice, and to me, that is all that matters.

CHAPTER 22

Indispensable Me
(Wouldn't That Be Nice?)

Criselda J. Guerra

"What are you doing here?" an administrator exclaimed with irritation in her voice. "I'm getting my room ready for Monday," I replied. "Well, this is *not* your room anymore!" she bellowed as she walked away.

I stood there, totally baffled. What's this all about? I had been the junior high school science teacher in this small school district for over 3 decades, and now I'm wondering, *What happened? What did I do wrong?* No explanation, nor reason given, *nada!*

I walked over to the school office and asked to speak to the superintendent. After a short wait, I was allowed into his office. I stated my concern and asked, "Where am I going to teach?" The reply floored me!

"Oh, you are no longer the science teacher," he announced. He didn't say I was fired, so I braved to ask, "*What* am I going to teach?"

"High school art," he replied. A major pause occurred as my mind rushed through a variety of thoughts. Biology major with a geology minor, to art? *Really?* I had volunteered to help with a mainstreaming art class for the Special Education Department for years, but high school art? "Will I be able to contribute successfully to this?" I wondered.

He then tactlessly announced that he could change any teacher's assignment whenever he needed to and, thus, that was that. So once again, I asked, "*Where* am I going to teach?" He paused and then told me to use the Band Hall temporarily, and with that, I was dismissed.

I felt derailed, depressed, and demoralized. I took the rest of that day off and then a couple more days off. I fell into a deep mourning, as if my self-esteem and identity had died. I felt unappreciated, kind of like an old shoe that is discarded. I couldn't eat, sleep, or think rationally. My husband thought I was overreacting. Now after all these years, I tend to agree. At the time, however, I felt totally justified in my feelings.

I finally got a grip on myself and prepared for the first day of school and a new quest in my teaching career. "I can do this!" I decided. I quickly adjusted to my new situation, and set out to do my very best, just as I had done as the junior high science teacher. Previously, I had obtained 12 college credits in art from Texas A&I University, and with the art classes I took during the summers taught by artists who specialized in different disciplines, I had found the confidence I needed. With painting, sculpture, charcoal, pastels, and even tooling leather, I had found a new niche in teaching. Gradually, I added to my teaching curriculum by incorporating geology and anatomy and physiology courses into my schedule. I couldn't help myself; I still needed science in my life. So life is good, I'm happy, and that's why I teach *now*!

BY WAY OF AN INTRODUCTION

I am the third daughter of Benito Juarez and Laurentina Ramos. I was born in Delmita, Texas, at a ranch that is about 10 miles southwest of San Isidro, Texas. I started school at San Isidro Independent School District (ISD) back in 1956. As a youngster, I could understand everything and answered any question asked orally, but I had trouble with most aspects of reading and writing. As I had dyslexia, I wrote some of my letters backwards and reversed some of my numbers. The other students would groan every time it was my turn to read. I was called lazy, as if I wasn't trying hard enough to grasp what the teacher was trying to teach. I was often kept in during recess to finish copying work from the chalkboard. Because I was usually one of the few students left in the classroom during that time, I was allowed to get up and get closer to the chalkboard to see more clearly. I was in the 5th grade before my teacher noticed I was having problems with my vision. The nurse checked my vision and concluded that I was extremely near-sighted. Thank goodness that back then the school purchased glasses for all students whose parents couldn't afford to buy them. The students in need of glasses were bused to town for our yearly check-up and our trademark identical frames. Now I could see what was written on the chalkboard. What a world of difference that made! (I am legally blind without my glasses.) During my junior high years, my grades continued to improve.

For years, my parents, siblings, and I worked the land and picked cotton to buy living essentials and to pay off our grocery bill every summer at Hilario's store. Thank goodness that he gave our father credit, for my dad was a proud man who wanted no government assistance, relief, for his family. *Para él era una vergüenza!* For him, it was a source of shame. We had chickens and pigs, and dad hunted for a few jackrabbits to provide for the family. By the summer of my junior year in high school, the fields were so mined of the minerals that the cotton crop was dwindling. So I decided to join my aunt and her family to go up north, *para los trabajos* for the jobs, to become a farm worker. After 2 months of labor, I came back home with enough money to buy and select my own glasses and stylish frames, plus more.

I graduated salutatorian in 1968 from that small rural school district in deep South Texas. Although my parents were very hardworking, we were poor. They did, however, instill in my siblings and me the value of getting a college education, and we did not disappoint them. I attended Texas A&I University in Kingsville, Texas. There I met and married my husband, Dario. Because we could not afford for both of us to go to college, I had to drop out so he could finish his studies. We started our family and, within a few years, moved back to my hometown of San Isidro, where Dario was hired to teach industrial arts.

Within 3 months of living on campus, in school housing, we experienced the tragic death of our second son, Javier Benito. He had just been diagnosed with a congenital heart disorder. Needless to say, this left us entirely devastated. I can't even remember who took care of my 3-year-old son, Ditto. Me? Months went by, our sorrow multiplied and our marriage suffered. My husband became very concerned about my detached behavior, and after consulting with his parents, they decided to send me back to college.

Their hypothesis was correct. I became so involved in my studies that I didn't have time to feel sorry for myself. I graduated from Pan America University in 1974 with a major in elementary education. However, after teaching 2nd grade for one semester in Alton, Texas, I decided to go back to college. Within a few months, I received a second degree in biology.

I applied and was later hired as the first female science teacher at San Isidro ISD. This was considered a man's position in those years. Time passed, and my family grew to a total of five sons and, by the way, my own sons were also my students. Teaching at a small rural school can be a very nurturing, yet isolated affair. There wasn't another junior high science teacher to ask for advice or to compare myself with. I was the whole science department! There is only one teacher per grade level in elementary school and one teacher per subject area in both junior high school and high school. Luckily, everyone in this community is involved with and concerned about our students' welfare and education, as if we are all part of the same family. Everyone around here knows everything about *everyone*, if you know what I mean!

TEACHING SCIENCE

Like many new teachers, I wanted to be a model teacher. So I tried to impress my students with all the wonders in every aspect of science. Within a few weeks, I discovered that it was the quality of teaching that was more important than the quantity of information given. Whatever subject area I taught, I would try to ensure that each student was immersed in the learning process. I once overheard a teacher from another school brag that he had "covered" the entire biology book in one semester. That, to me, sounded ridiculous! I learned to expand, and not be in such a rush to "cover" the whole book. I experimented with different approaches to develop my own style.

Teaching science provided the opportunity for a lot of experimentation, which in turn helped students understand the lessons better. The 6th-graders had to study physical science, so experiments about the laws of motion, levers, and so on were not only educational, but also fun. The students built rockets powered with engines, or with pressured water. Some of their rockets carried a payload of small animals that actually survived their trip. The students needed to measure wind direction and calculate the angle of the flight in order to land their rockets within the desired "landing pad." They also had to use an altitude calculator to determine the height reached by their rockets. Once a rocket landed on the Band Hall's roof. Oops!

A few years ago a professor from the University of Texas-Pan American asked his students if any of their high school teachers had developed an easy way for them to remember the sequence of the electromagnetic spectrum. No one raised his or her hand to respond. One of my former junior high students, Rolando, quietly whispered to his friend, "*Grandma X usually visits in my room.*" This was a technique I had developed to help my 6th-grade students remember the waves of the electromagnetic spectrum (gamma rays, x-rays, ultraviolet radiation, visible light, infrared light, microwaves, radio waves). His friend abruptly waved his hand and declared, "This guy knows one!" The professor then asked Rolando to stand up and share this easy way to remember with everyone. He then instructed his class to write it down. (*NICE! I hope the saying goes viral!*)

As for the elements chart, there were thieves and victims elements that created or destroyed molecules. There were also bachelor elements that preferred to be left alone. Homemade flash cards of the elements provided the students with a variety of games to help them learn the symbols, atomic numbers, and their valance electrons. Teams were chosen and challenged to see who knew the elements chart best. Also, by drawing concentric circles on paper and gluing hole-puncher dots of colored construction paper, the students could create a variety of molecules. The students were having fun as they learned their science. I would often overhear a passerby comment, "What are they doing in there?" Or, "What's that smell?"

The 7th-graders had to study life science. The first semester, cells were introduced and studied in great detail. Later, edible models of the cells with all their organelles were created and eaten *only if* the students could identify the organelle and its function. Team competition was fast and furious! Next, plant and animal characteristics were studied and then classified into their proper taxonomy. During the second semester, I taught one human body system at a time, and the students dissected lab-prepared cats for comparison and labeling. After reviewing and testing, the cats were stored and I would introduce the next body system. By the end of the year, those cats were. . . . Well, anyway, one very industrious student took one of the discarded cats home. Over the summer, she removed all the muscles and organs and cleaned it. When school started the following year, she wired and glued the skeleton together, placed it on a stand, and submitted it to the Science Project Fair. She got disqualified because the judges ruled that it was inhumane to kill a cat!

Learning about the human skeleton was fun and soon developed into a speed contest. Team members would tutor each other to ensure a win. The students were allowed only 5 minutes to tell me all the bones on Rafael the skeleton. They would get excited as they tried to beat each other's time. If they were successful, they would not only make a good grade, they would also be given a tiny plastic skeleton pin to wear with pride. When they learned the muscular system, I had to pull out the stopwatch again at their request. They were having fun!

The 8th-graders studied earth science. Rock and mineral samples were not only collected, but also analyzed. Some rocks floated, others smelled earthy, and others split into sheets as thin as paper. Some of my students became rock hounds. They could even identify the chemical formulas and the crystal systems of the minerals. Plate tectonics, meteorology, and so on were subjects that the students learned and could use for their science projects.

One year, I invited Tim Smith, meteorologist from the Rio Grande Valley Channel 5 News, to visit my classes. He explained how hurricanes develop and many other weather topics. My students were so impressed with his knowledge, and with the fact that he had actually traveled all the way up to San Isidro! Astronomy, however, was probably their favorite subject. Finding the different constellations and locating the planets and even possible UFOs were exciting activities and generated very interesting classroom discussions.

UIL/TMSCA

My students participated in the University Interscholastic League (UIL), which was created by the University of Texas at Austin. UIL provided extracurricular leadership events and guidance to public school debate and athletic teachers. Eventually, the league incorporated impromptu, current issues and events, math, science, calculator applications, one-act plays, and writing events. I'd coach the junior high science team and we would more often than not win against other school districts in our category at the district level.

In 1991, I joined the Texas Math and Science Coach's Association (TMSCA). We participated at the state level for over 10 years and we came home with some pretty awesome first-, second-, and third-place trophies. One year, however, my science team won Top 8th-Grader, Top 7th-Grader, and Top-6th Grader for Class 1A statewide. This resulted in my team receiving the largest first-place trophy we had ever won as well as the Coach of the Year award for myself.

When I was assigned to teach at the high school level, I was asked to coach UIL Current Issues and Events. This is a contest in which the student participants must be able to keep up with the daily news. They must be aware of science in the news, world politics and leaders, sports, national catastrophes, the Middle East, wars, terrorism, atrocities against citizens worldwide, art, religion, celebrities, and just about everything. It is my job to keep the students as informed as I can so that they become aware of what's newsworthy. I prepare PowerPoint presentations on all of the above-mentioned categories and other incidentals to make sure my students have an edge for competition. Students use their flash drives to access all my information and transfer it to their own computers so that they can study at home. We meet after school once a week to take sample tests to prepare for the bi-monthly contests.

I still teach *now* because I see how the students improve in this event as the year goes by. That is very satisfying not only for myself, but also for the students. When my students do well at contests, I feel that sense of accomplishment that fuels my desire to continue to work. We have done well in district competitions in Current Issues and Events, and a few of my team members have advanced to the regional level. I encourage my team members to study, watch the news, and opine/debate issues against each other. My goal is that soon my students may qualify and participate at the state level.

LEARNING THROUGH SEEING AND DOING

Teachers can and do make a difference in their students' lives. As the years pass, I have tried to provide learning experiences to my students that are not only educational, but also memorable. I strived to become a role model whose example of proper behavior and job dedication would make a lasting positive impression to my students. It worked for me!

Science trips were an incentive that became a yearly quest. NASA, Moody Gardens, mountain climbing, river tubing, visiting caves, South Padre Island, and other such places made excellent destinations for my students. Good grades and behavior ensured a student's pass to go on the trip. Needless to say, all the students would work hard to make the grade, which is a 70 and above, and their efforts at having good behavior were impressive. Parents would also encourage their children to study so that they could accompany us on the trips. There would be a caravan of vehicles following the school bus on what had become the famous yearly science trip. The school nurse and our lifeguards were also included on our trips. Parent and student participation with money-raising activities to fund our trips was very successful.

It's good to teach at a rural area school because both teachers and parents are united in that we want the best for our children. We want to ensure that they will eventually become productive members of society and continue to develop morally and educationally and thus pass on what they were taught to their own children. I believe this sentiment is universal for most teachers, but the smaller the school district is, the easier it seems to be to accomplish.

I still teach *now* because I know that I can still inspire my students to get excited and motivated with their learning process. I feel that their academic success is one of the driving factors that inspires me to continue to not only teach, but also to improve as a teacher.

Every day holds new learning experiences for both the students and the teacher, whether it is a well-planned activity like the science trip, or when something spontaneous or funny occurs during class. Often I would (and still) use personal experiences to teach a science concept. For instance, once while working in the fields, a small rattlesnake crawled over my foot while I was leaning on my hoe daydreaming. I froze in fear! Adrenaline from my adrenal glands that sit on top of my kidneys flowed through my system in a "fight-or-flight" response, which resulted in a violent and untimely death for the snake. Another incident was generated by the appearance of a figure at a distance from the cotton field. Was the genotype of that figure a cow or a human? And if it was a human, was the phenotype that of my aunt, Tía Isabel? (For more personal experiences, call 1-800-RU-Kidding! LOL.)

One personal experience that I shared with my students is about how my dyslexia made me work harder to succeed in school. I was determined to prove that a disability such as dyslexia did not hinder nor have anything to do with intelligence, and that people with disabilities too can overcome and succeed in life. I feel that because of my own disability, I am a more compassionate and patient teacher with not only my special needs students, but with all my students. Two of my own sons also have difficulties with dyslexia and, like many others, they have adjusted. I will always have problems with dyslexia, but my students are quick to let me know that I have once again asked them to open their books to the wrong page!

Students' needs drive us to give more of our time and effort to ensure that they can focus on their studies. My staying after school daily provides my students an opportunity to get extra time to finish a project or test, or just to hang out until it is time for them to go to a school sporting event. If they miss the school bus, they stay in my classroom for safety and then call their parents to pick them up. There were countless times when I would have to take a student home.

I loved teaching science then as much as I love it now, so that is why I still teach. I feel that I can still guide students academically and thus help improve their educational achievements. This in turn motivates me to try to make a positive impact in their lives. I try to provide learning experiences that will give them a roadmap to success. One such experience occurred when I attended the Fort Worth Museum of Science and History's Lone Star Dinosaurs Field Institute dig one summer. We were the first group of 19 rural educators from across the state of Texas to participate in this venture. We found the fossilized bones of a 111-million-year-old dinosaur called Pleurocoelus. That experience provided me with a wealth of knowledge that I shared with students. There were several other science-related summer institutes, such as at NASA, that I attended that gave me more such hands-on experiences. During one of those institutes, I met my first famous scientist, Sylvia Earle! I still treasure that group picture with her at the center.

Another reason I still teach *now* is because some of my former students have become teachers, doctors, college professors, and other professionals. I want to continue to contribute to today's youth so that more students from San Isidro can also become successful. I also think it's just so gratifying to be teaching the children of my former students. It is amazing how much they remind me of their parents. Our superintendent and principal are not only my former students, but are now my bosses! Seven more of my former students are now teaching in our school district. Is that *cool* or what?

TEACHING AND TECHNOLOGY

Technology was minimal back when I started teaching, and few families could afford to purchase whatever device was available. Students had few places to go, so school was not only educational, but it was also the only place for social events such as sports, school dances, and so on. Therefore, coming to school was more interesting than staying at home. I would allow them access to my classroom computers so that after school, they could do research for their homework and/or just play games. In this community, there are no places to really "hang out."

Today's students are so involved with the latest technology that it is hard to retain their attention for an extended period of time. So, I try to show as much enthusiasm as possible for whatever subject I teach. Sometimes my teaching "performance" can be entertaining, yet prudent, and that keeps the students' attention span intact. (Carol Burnett, beware!) I try, for instance, to get students to participate by role-playing the part of organelles in cells or the path of blood cells in the circulatory system. I do whatever reasonable thing I can to keep the students interested and engaged in the learning process.

Most teachers are now using computers, tablets, and so on to enhance their lessons. Because our textbooks are often outdated, we must keep up with the latest information to enrich our knowledge. Computers provide us with an almost instantaneous source of information. PowerPoint presentations, student research activities, and more elevate the computer as an important resource to educate not only our students, but also ourselves. So by combining both computers and other teaching methods, students will become more actively involved in the learning process. Computer images, maps, pictures, and videos can help students who are visual learners absorb and retain knowledge more effectively. This can also motivate the teacher to a more effective teaching experience that replaces the lecture-based techniques of old. In spite of the significance of technology, I don't believe that teachers will become obsolete. We will still be needed as facilitators to guide the students in their selection of proper websites. We would also be needed to make sure that the students stay within the subject area and time limits.

I once asked a student to hand me a piece of typewriter paper and he asked, "What's a typewriter?" "Sorry," I replied, "Would you please hand me a piece of computer paper?" OMG! Am I dated or what!

WHY DO I STILL TEACH *NOW*?

I still teach *now* because I want to remain actively involved with the latest trends in teaching. Yes, even a young 65-year-old spry whippersnapper no bigger than a flea (like me) can still be part of the latest innovations and inspire youth. I teach because I feel I can still inspire my students to get excited and motivated with their learning process. The students, however, inspire me as well. They often say or write the funniest things, and that is another reason I still teach. They bring excitement into the classroom and brighten my day. When I retire, I fear that without my students, I will become totally "classless," and extremely bored. I will probably become a couch potato or, worse, a tourist in checkered Bermuda shorts with a camera hanging around my neck!

Teachers are *not* perfect, and that we easily acknowledge. I have learned from my mistakes and I have tried to improve my teaching techniques to meet today's new school requirements and challenges. I also developed a good working relationship with the high school science teacher so we could exchange ideas and experiences and apply that knowledge with the students. We were able to contribute a gradual scope and sequence in science to ease the students' progress into high school and thus help them become confident in their transition. Attending teacher workshops helps us keep pace with new learning trends in education and thus we can support each other in a mutual quest to educate. Those of us who love our profession continue to teach to a ripe old age (like me), while those who don't eventually move on to other professions.

Teaching is not just my job; it's my life and passion. It's the only thing that I really feel competent in doing. I can't sing, dance, or cook! (Mr. G. wants me to learn how to cook when I retire—*no way Jose*! It's like trying to teach an old dog new tricks; it's not gonna happen!) So why retire? I'd go stir-crazy! Anyway, as long as I am healthy and can continue to have the same enthusiastic love for teaching and still perform all my duties, why shouldn't I continue to work? If not, I need to step aside and allow another teacher the chance to influence the next generation of students. In the meantime, I'm still teaching geology, anatomy and physiology, art, and leather tooling. I continue to keep up with the latest worldwide news and updating my UIL Current Issues and Events PowerPoint presentations. I am looking forward to having a teaching position for next year.

EPILOGUE

For 5 years I wondered about the real reason why my teaching assignment was so abruptly changed. There were rumors circulating, so a couple of years ago I finally asked a very reliable school-related person to tell me. It seems that a couple of very affluent parents were concerned that I was "too hard" to teach their upcoming 6th-graders. *Really!* I had taught their older siblings and hundreds of other students in my classes for years, and yet they somehow survived and thrived. The high school science teacher told me he really appreciated that my students were very well prepared to meet his expectations for high school. Their transition to high school science was a smooth and progressive adjustment.

Throughout all this time, there have been five different teachers assigned to teach junior high science in my stead. Most of them were neither biology nor geology majors in college. I am glad to say, however, that one of my former students has taken and passed the science certification test and now is becoming a great science teacher.

As a retired-rehired teacher, my salary was reduced to that of a beginning teacher, but that's okay. I still have the joy of teaching! So, the last reason why I still teach *now* is evidently not about the money, but because I still feel I can contribute to and prepare students for their future.

CHAPTER 23

Jumping Off Cliffs and Touching the Ground with Wings

Michael Silverstone

At the core of every committed and passionate teacher is a driven teacher. What drives us is something so essential that you couldn't pay someone who wasn't born with it to have it, and you can't scare it out of them. Despite all current efforts to place obstacles in the path of students and teachers who do not conform to the test or the rubric, the drive to standardization will never prevail.

[I am tempted to either write this essay under a pseudonym or else to leave instructions that it be published 10 minutes after my separation from the teaching profession, but I will live as a free man and risk the sinking vulnerable feeling I got once when an evaluator with a rubric asked me a series of open-ended questions about the attitudes I have about my teaching practice and said to me, "Thank you for being candid," much like an executioner thanking me for rope.]

MY MANIFESTO

I came to teaching late, in my 40s. Something happened in 3rd grade that started me in that direction. My parents were divorcing. Up to that point, my relatives have told me, I was joyful, innocent, and happy by nature. "After that something happened. You stopped looking people in the eye," my uncle once told me. He is probably right. I've seen my "before" and "after" photographs captured by Polaroid and Kodak Instamatic cameras.

I remember feeling that my parents' splitting up was big trouble and that we were all in big trouble. And in the logic of children, I felt I had a part in causing this big trouble and that there was something I could do that would undo it. I remember thinking that my child-like efforts and wishing would bring them back together the way I believed that putting on a certain Cleveland baseball hat in the 7th inning of a radio broadcast would cause my usually losing team to suddenly start scoring runs to come from behind and win—the kind of irrational passionate belief that afflicts those who otherwise feel utterly powerless.

I also felt I was in big trouble when I was in school. My 3rd-grade teacher was 24 years old; my parents were also in their 20s. When my parents or my teacher wanted me to do something, I didn't just trust that it was for a good reason the way an untroubled child might. I usually wanted to know why. Neither would tell me. Sometimes it was because they didn't know. They hadn't thought it out. Sometimes it was because it made them feel vulnerable to be questioned and their responses were forceful—some version of, "Because I said so."

I don't believe I was trying to undermine their authority, but rather that I was looking for authority I could believe in. This impulse is often misinterpreted as insubordination. Once you know, especially in childhood, how truly illegitimate the claims of moral authority are by empires, by institutional managers, and in my particular case by confused, young parents, it eventually feels dangerous to follow authority without questioning it. A special brand of hostility and ridicule has long been reserved for those who question authority, but as I came of age, there was a brief time that honest questioning of authority and moral opposition to injustice were in fashion.

I used to ride my bicycle to Heights Pharmacy in the Cleveland suburbs with money I'd earned from my paper route. I'd buy copies of the *New York Times* and *Mad* magazine. The United States was at war with Vietnam. Even now this idea seems insane. Protests were widespread. I couldn't figure it out. Why was the United States at war with Vietnam? For most children at the time, it was sufficient to know that our country was in a war, that our country is a good place where we are safe, and if we were in a war, it was for a good reason, like in most World War II movies: to beat the bad guys.

There were people in the *New York Times* who questioned why the United States was bombing Vietnam. There were even more of them in *Mad Magazine*. The more I read about bombing and death counts, the more I wanted it to stop, to not continue for another week. There was nothing to win and people were dying. Why did it have to go on? Planes and bombs cost a lot, but food is cheap. If there were poor people, wasn't it easier to help poor people instead of hurting them with war?

Even when I was 9 years old, my parents, my teacher, and President Johnson seemed to be three prominent examples to me of adults who were in over their heads and quick to bluster when challenged. They were in roles where they had to be in charge and were merely perpetuating their authority through force and will whether it was deserved or not.

However, my family valued education. To them it was better than money, because with education you could enter a professional field and replicate and continue the fortunes of the family. My father was an attorney, and so were his brother, both of his parents, and several of my cousins. My grandmother was one of the first women to practice law in Wisconsin in spite of formidable discouragement. She was told not to go to law school. Then when she finished at the top of her class, she was advised not to take cases. After she married my grandfather they developed a joint practice. She had grown up poor and with obstacles, but she never cooperated with those who said that women were not suited for the field. She practiced for 60 years. To this day, I see my grandparents as examples of people who were wise and had good reasons for what they did in a world that wasn't always right or fair.

BECOMING A TEACHER

So many things seemed out of my hands as a child. The one thing I felt I had was the space of my own mind. I could read and question and get my brain smarter so I could understand things and know what was right. By the time I went to college, I didn't want to be a lawyer, though. The idea of working in my father's field felt too limiting to me at a time I wanted to be independent. I wanted to be a writer because I relished the feeling that comes with coming to your own conclusions independently and sincerely out of curiosity and the desire to test and explore what is worth believing in, rather than simply adopting the unchallenged opinions of others out of expediency or laziness. When I was a boy, my mother sometimes called me "a little old man," and I knew that she was lamenting that I wasn't otherwise, but I knew there was something worth holding onto in my refusal to get completely onboard with the program.

My first teaching experiences were as a college intern with Teachers and Writers Collaborative, an organization that sent writers into New York

City public schools to work on imaginative writing with teachers in class-rooms. I instantly enjoyed how teaching let me be a conduit of curiosity, interest, and respect to children in their experiences and thoughts. I worked with students from kindergarten to 6th grade, and then with adults in a variety of settings from senior centers to Sing Sing Prison. Teaching made emotional sense to me. It was the one occupation where I felt I could treat people as I would want to be treated, and I could give them something I would want to have myself: the ability to enjoy and use the mind to envision and create and understand. And loving writing as I did, I wanted to teach it.

I didn't plan to become an elementary school teacher. In fact, when I was studying for my master's degree in education to teach college English, I could have had elementary licensure if I'd taken one additional course. I thought, "Why would I ever want to do that?"

What changed was having my own family. Our son was approaching an age when he would be in school. I saw early childhood educators close up and I was grateful to them and intrigued by school and what it could be. A classroom could be a place where life was fair, where children had a voice, and where people learned to live and imagine and think and learn together. It seemed to be a commercial- and violence-free zone, a place where a child's voice mattered and could be heard. When I entered class-room teaching in 1998, it was incredibly hard work but I turned myself over to it gladly.

During the 15 years I have been in a 2nd-grade classroom, something has gradually changed in the profession for reasons that probably have to do with the decline of U.S. economic status, the growth of computer data, and the rightward drift of the country's politics as wealth and politi-cal power get concentrated in fewer hands. Public education, like the rest of the commons, is being eroded and is under attack by those who have the cynicism to attempt to profit from it while simultaneously trying to weaken and starve it out of existence. Educators who would be champi-ons of public education as a haven of possibility for children to come into their potential as whole beings, educated, creative, and critical thinkers, able to find a path to pursuing the inner curiosity and interests as self-actualized adults and as citizens, now do this above and beyond their growing responsibilities documenting student- and self-improvement and their adherence to the state and national frameworks. They pursue what used to be their main calling in their spare time, or in disguise—rarely in the open.

The well-intentioned professionals in education are operating under a system of evaluations and accountability standards that pretty much guarantee that all schools and teachers will teach the same things in approximately the same way, or managerial sanctions will be imposed on those who do not. There is good news and bad news in this. The good news is that things are less sloppy than they have ever been. The bad news is that these standardized approaches are not suited to everyone and unless school communities and teachers decide to add something else to the equation, anxiety and the pressure to conform are the official and legally sanctioned elephants in every classroom. Everyone is in trouble, all the time.

In school districts where educated parents are affluent enough to afford quality time with their children, meeting accountability standards will be largely possible. In places where resources are scarce, where incomes are low, and the educational histories of parents do not include college, this will be an uphill battle for which the accountability for failure will rest squarely with teachers, with charter schools and educational publishing conglomerates and for-profits waiting in the wings to exploit the inevitable unfavorable "data" with quick solutions that will drag public education further down into a cycle of privatization, failure, and withdrawal of public funding support. Whether an activity or a reading program, or an "every child must know this by the end of the year" standard makes sense or is appropriate for a child or a group of children is no longer up for discussion. The procedures, as well as the standards and the measures of accountability, have all been determined by other people who may or may not have close relationships with actual children and who have a financial interest in their "solutions."

The day-to-day work of teachers has changed. In this context the routines must be invariant. Lessons must take a certain amount of time and this time is audited. Evaluations and assessments take place at certain dates, and the preparation for those assessments looks the same.

Work that I came to because of a personal drive to offer liberation and a bridge to sanity has become something else. It's still pretty much the only game in town as far as spending time using the mind and being with children is concerned, but it's a different game than the one I first joined.

For some of us in teaching, rule and schedule following and the suppression of spontaneous impulses are our gift. For others, whose brains operate in different ways and for different motives, this era is a little like when the tropical wetlands gave way to the ice age and killed the dinosaurs. It is possible to adapt, but the future promises to extract a heavy cost to those who do not.

BECOMING A PROFESSIONAL

The definition of a professional is someone who does his or her best work even when they may not want to. It's easy to teach when children love you and when you find that, through the inspiration you feel about a subject, you can open windows and doors for them. It's easy to teach when you feel students repay the kindness you feel and offer to them with a reflection of the spirit of cooperation and confidence and miraculous wonder that you want for them in your heart of hearts. It's as easy as it is rare, unfortunately.

Yes, it's easy to be nice when you're in a good mood. It's easy to be generous when you are not afraid. But perhaps the biggest stressor for those of us who are of a certain temperament is the stress of having to constantly manage children through things that you don't think they should be doing and that they don't think they should be doing either.

What is far more common is the daily, growing stress of being unable to imagine failing, unable to meet your own impossible expectations of time and organization and unflagging effort while facing the threat of professional and personal inadequacy and sanction directed toward you, your school, your administrators, your colleagues, your school community, your profession, and your society. Just enough stress may make us determined; too much impairs our ability to function. There's a narrow range of acceptable stress, and we have much less ability to change the circumstances that create it than we do in extending our own resilience in enduring it.

We're lucky when we find a useful and impossible challenge. Teaching is a fascinating challenge. It always has been, and it's just as fascinating and rewarding as it has ever been, but it also feels unnecessarily undermined by questionable authorities masquerading as friends of education and equity. When needing to do what feels impossible for our students, or even for ourselves creates a constant sense of stress, how do we learn to persist, and perhaps more crucially, sustain ourselves through a career?

What I'm about to say feels very unconfirmed by the world I live in, but I believe it to be true. Every single human being deserves a teacher who loves them, who thinks highly of the gift that they offer the world, and who sees a potential in them to generate abundant and unexpected miracles as they grow to become themselves. I will always believe this, whether it is confirmed or not. My students can count on me believing it as long as I am their teacher. They can count on it as long as I am alive, and they can count on it even when I am not alive.

To be a teacher is to live in a crucible. It forces evolution. When failure is unthinkable, but complete success is impossible, something has to change. Either you tip into failure and leave or are driven out of the field, or you develop a capacity you didn't have, or maybe more accurately, one that you had but hadn't yet learned how to use. For many of us, this means continuously jumping off cliffs and hoping we learn how to use wings by the time we hit the ground.

TWO POSTSCRIPTS

[A month later, Michael sent me this email message.]

Postscript 1

Quite abruptly, I found myself resigning from my Amherst teaching position. My last day was when December break began. Immediately I'm going to be co-writing a book about relationship-based learning and building personal connections among families, students, and colleagues (Zacarian and Silverstone, 2015). I feel very fortunate about that. Eventually I plan to go to a school or educational setting where I can give my best and it will be useful in ways that also help serve a model of alternative possibility.

The contradictions I felt between what I believed I was there for, and what I was being asked (told, compelled, evaluated) to do, just got to be unbridgeable. I see good intent in the idea of district standardization and accountability and assessment, even as it feels toxic to me personally. You could probably read this between the lines of the essay I sent you. At the time I thought I could continue to navigate the contradictions but the room for deviation from the master plan continues to shrink. My brain doesn't work like this, even when I want it to (even, and perhaps, especially, while trying as hard as I can). Many wonderful teachers—all my colleagues, for example—can flourish even in these conditions although they know this stress is insane, because they believe there's something redemptive according to their most cherished beliefs, in what they are doing. Obviously I don't take leaving the children and families lightly, but I also don't think there's any future in getting in the way of what the district is trying to do, even if it's a direction I don't happen to believe in. I'm not even saying that district reforms don't have merit. I just don't feel this way, and if I can't do something I can believe in to the bottom of my shoes, it's pretty hard to tap into the infinite source of determination and strength that makes the experience of teaching not only wonderful, but possible.

[A couple of months later, Michael sent the following update.]

Postscript 2

When I went to visit my former students and have lunch with them, one of them asked me, "Are you going to teach again?"

The answer came through me, before I knew what it would be. I felt such a wave of affection for my students, and for the questioner, that I melted and made a promise to fate. "Yes, of course, I love it too much to stay away."

I visited a good dozen schools to do observations and offer to do student teaching in the winter and spring after my resignation. I couldn't bear to go back to the same kind of classroom I had just left. The same allergy I had developed to being a teacher posting the lesson's objectives in adult language on the wall for the evaluator's clipboard kicked in when I saw children having to do what they didn't want to do, and distracting each other, falling off chairs, grinding pencils, going to the nurse's office. I wanted no part of it, although I wished I could, as it would have been easy.

I visited alternative schools. I went to a Reggio Emilia school where students from K–8 had lunch in mixed groups every day and 6th-graders created a theater and music spectacle based on the biological systems of the human body. I went to a private school based on the practices of the Responsive Classroom where a teacher summoned a class to a courteous discussion circle just by noodling on a wooden flute for 2 minutes. I went to a performing arts charter high school where students in the hallways had green hair and dressed like Charlie Chaplin.

But what amazed me the most were my visits to Montessori schools, where students of mixed ages chose work in apparent total absorption, and transitioned to the next one when purposeful impulse slowly gathered in them. I watched students ages 6 through 9 acting like students I'd only occasionally seen in 15 years of 2nd grade. They were content. They had a persistent, but relaxed drive to learn and cooperate, and they presumed kindness in their relations with peers and teachers. This was what teaching once had been for me back in the 20th century, before the testing and accountability mania. I visited several Montessori schools, and many classrooms. On several occasions, as I sat taking notes in the observer chair, tears formed in my eyes at the beauty of what I saw. These children were allowed to be themselves. These teachers were offering a very precise and useful kind of low-key and unobtrusive guidance while letting children have their own experience.

I felt some mechanism of locks and tumblers opening in my heart and the chamber opened wide. I knew this was what I had to do with my life. To make a long story shorter, I applied for a position at a Montessori school 70 miles from home. The school was looking for a teacher like me as eagerly as I wanted to be that teacher. I decided to trust this was the right thing, and obstacles fell away, melted away. I did a demonstration lesson with 10 children, witnessed by the head of the school. I researched my lesson for days, I watched YouTube videos of Montessori teachers demonstrating with children, I prepared my handmade materials, I created backup activities, I anticipated complications. I rehearsed in the mirror. I could feel the joy in the work of doing this to the bottom of my shoes. After the lesson, the head of school said, "Some people are natural Montessorians; I'd put you in that category."

I believe in the commons and public education and the right of every child to have something this good if they and their families want it. I've always thought you can change the world by fighting for change—advocating, standing up for, standing with.

I also believe you can change the world by being part of an alternative that stands up and exudes beauty. What I felt was as involuntary and politically unconsidered as falling in love. I am a Montessori teacher. I think I always was a Montessori teacher, before the culture in my school district made student-directed/teacher-supported learning on this scale more or less illegal. My allergy to my district's central office mandates I now realize was telling me, "Get out. This isn't what you want to do."

Without a deep belief in the values of my learning community, I felt myself agreeing to resort to training kids with promises and threats. (Call it positive behavioral intervention systems, or sending kids to the office—it all felt the same, and, to my way of thinking, untrustworthy.) By contrast, every encounter with Montessori education has made me happier and happier. I've felt it soothe my heart, as it had me glow from the inside with happiness and well-being I could feel spreading to my face. It makes me want to be a teacher forever and ever and ever. I thought I was metaphorically leaping off a cliff to leave my classroom at the peak of my career, and I was. But sometimes in a fall there is something that can hold and lift that you can't count on or anticipate. I'm grateful for what became unbearable because it drew me to what I instinctively always wanted, but couldn't know was there until I found myself instantly, astonishingly and mysteriously at home in a place I could finally see where a lifetime longing had always been leading me.

CHAPTER 24

Conclusion
Why on Earth Teach *Now*?

Sonia Nieto

I write this as yet another school year is beginning, teachers returning to their classrooms with renewed energy, new ideas, new lessons, and with enthusiasm to make a difference in the lives of their students. They are also returning with well-founded anxieties: They will confront new initiatives, new accountability measures, new tests for which to prepare students, new teacher assessments, and other examples of the standardization era. And yet, they return—but not all of them. The sorry state of public education is the reason many do not.

Researcher Richard Ingersoll has long studied the turnover of teachers. In his latest report with colleagues Lisa Merrill and Daniel Stuckey (Ingersoll, Merrill, & Stuckey, 2014), he found that although the teaching force is larger than ever (albeit leveling off since the economic downturn of 2008), it has become even more unstable in terms of teacher retention. From 1998–2009, attrition in the teaching force rose by an astonishing 41%, although it is not the same among all schools. Specifically, schools with a high enrollment of students of color, as well as high-poverty urban and rural schools, had among the highest levels of attrition. Most of those who left those schools, but chose to stay in the profession, went to very different schools, moving from high-poverty to low-poverty and from urban to suburban schools, as well as from schools with high concentrations of students of color to those with high concentrations of White students. Even more disturbing is the fact that teachers of color, especially those who have recently joined the profession, are leaving in higher rates than White teachers. Ingersoll and his colleagues explain the situation by asserting that hard-to-staff schools are the ones most likely to hire teachers of color; these schools also offer

"less-than-desirable working conditions," that "undermine efforts to diver-
sify the teaching force" (Ingersoll et al., p. 24).

A longstanding problem in staffing public schools has been the lack of
diversity of the teaching force. Although the situation has improved greatly
in the past decade or so—with teachers of color increasing from a low of 5%
or 6% to a current 17% or 18%—if the retention rate of teachers of color
doesn't improve, before long we'll be back where we started. Being a teacher
of color is often challenging, as these data show, and for many of them, so
was being a student of color. Several of the teachers wrote about this in their
essays. When Maria Rosario was a child, she experienced many of the same
problems of exclusion and lack of voice that teachers of color experience
later in their careers. Likewise, Jennifer Burgos-Carnes, although fluent in
Spanish, recounts being corrected for pronouncing Spanish words *correctly*,
and this experience influenced, years later, how she would view her own
work as a teacher. At the conclusion of their collective essay, Jennifer and
her sister Vanessa write, "A teacher can break you, or a teacher can help you
realize your potential."

African American teacher Mary Jade Haney also wrote about how education had disempowered her, including an incident with a guidance counselor
who informed her she was "not college material." And given her traumatic
experiences in the schools she attended, Sharim Hannegan-Martinez concludes that becoming a teacher was, "a way of saving, healing, and redeeming
myself." Fortunately for all these teachers, and for their students, they fought
back, refusing to accept classrooms as debilitating spaces, instead re-creating
them, in the words of Mary Jade Haney, as "spaces of hope," who insists on
reclaiming her education and her classroom. She writes, "I was born to teach
and I will give no one permission to discourage me from doing what is best
for children and their families." This is the kind of resilience called for in the
current climate, but not every teacher can summon this tenacity without support from others.

LESSONS TO BE RE-LEARNED

It should be obvious by now that teachers stay in the profession for many
different reasons. In the first iteration of *Why We Teach* (2005), I pondered
the lessons to be learned from the 21 teachers who wrote essays for the book
and I discussed five that were evident, in one way or another, for most of
the teachers. In this sequel, I expected to find some of the same values that
sustain teachers, although given the increasingly difficult context in which

teachers work, I also expected they would write about what makes it even more challenging now. Both turned out to be true. As in *Why We Teach*, all the teachers, for example, wrote about having *a sense of mission*. Criselda Guerra who, at the age of 65, refuses to think about retirement, wrote, "Teaching is not just my job; it's my life and passion." Some decided to become teachers when they were children: John Levasseur wrote that even as a child, "Great teachers were my heroes and interesting topics were to me more collectable than baseball cards." For Jesse Hagopian, life-changing experiences from Washington, D.C., to Haiti, to Seattle, rather than dissuade him from becoming a teacher, confirmed his social justice commitment to the profession. As he wrote about his first job in Washington, DC, "Working in the 'other America' was a formative experience that inspired me to dedicate my life to finding solutions that could transform public education as well as the broader society that chose to allow such neglect."

Other teachers, such as Pamelyn Williams and Michael Silverstone, tripped into teaching accidently and it has become their passion. Chuck Greanoff, starting out as a psychotherapist, switched to teaching where, even after 8 years, he says he has found his "piece of heaven." In whatever way they came into the profession, the teachers wrote about their work as being more than just a job. Jorge López wrote, "Being in the classroom fills me with life." And even after retirement and having spent 42 years in the classroom under increasingly rigid conditions, Mary Ginley wrote simply, "It's not a bad way to spend a life."

The answer to why teachers remain in the classroom in spite of difficult conditions is, according to Eileen Blanco Dougherty, "always quick and simple: it is for these kids." Mary Ginley, recalling the student who said he'd probably turn out to be a good father because she was his teacher, writes, "That's why I continued to teach even after the test became the *only* thing that mattered, because some little boy just might be a good dad because he had me in 5th grade." These sentiments are what I defined in the first *Why We Teach* as *solidarity with, and empathy for their students*. Just as in the teachers' essays 10 years ago, solidarity and empathy were evident in many of the teachers' essays in this volume as well. Nina Tepper's literacy activities with her students resulted in more than improving their writing. Marcus, for example, wrote about how while she taught him to write, more important, Nina taught him to love. The examples she writes about are also the reason for her persistence: "What started as idealism in my youth to make a contribution to the future by working with youth," Nina writes, "became a stubborn pursuit to create learning environments that support growth."

Rural teacher Missy Urbaniak describes her two great loves as her students and the land, saying, "These are *my* children," a sentiment that all parents would wish the teachers of their children to have. At the Boston Teachers Union School, Berta Berriz and her colleagues call the students "scholars," in this way making it clear their refusal to accept anything but the best from their urban students. Likewise, the BTU teachers' insistence on the significance of parents and other family members in the classroom and in their learning is another example of solidarity. And who knows where this kind of insistence will lead? As Jennifer Burgos-Carnes says, "I teach because I cannot think of anything more rewarding than to help nurture the mind of a child who may one day grow up to be the next Albert Einstein."

Just as in the first volume, another value exemplified by these teachers is *improvisation*. Philadelphia teacher Christina Puntel says she teaches in the *now*, a "stance rooted in presence, in being present to the moment, to myself, to my students, to the content in front of us." And, rather than rush to "cover the material," John Levasseur stops everything to connect with a disengaged student because he refuses to take "I don't know" for an answer. Instead, he re-groups and provides an impromptu lesson on "spurs."

Then as now, the teachers' essays embody *a passion for social justice*. Vanessa Burgos-Kelly wanted to change how she learned to view school by becoming a teacher herself. "High school," she writes, "left me with the impression that schools are factories whose job it is to maintain the status quo." For Matt Hicks, social justice emerged from a recognition of his White privilege, especially after developing deep relationships with his undocumented students. Realizing how unfair his students' lives were, he redefined his teaching to include helping students navigate the college admission process, and helping organize and attend rallies for undocumented students. Matt writes, "It was no longer an abstraction or intellectual pursuit. It was close to my heart each night as I prepared for school. It was what brought me there each day."

Amanda VandeHei became a social justice teacher because of her own experience as a student and, later, a "parkee." This incipient awareness was later fed by her experiences as a young teacher. For Sharim Hannegan-Martinez, it was the very process of becoming literate that made her a social justice educator. "Literacy," she writes, "saved my life." Mary Ginley, using her wealth of experience, knew that simply teaching a lesson about Ruby Bridges and desegregation wouldn't be very meaningful for her students. Instead, she put up a poster and said nothing about it until students started asking about it. Having her 5th-grade students engage in serious and self-initiated conversations about racism—asking, for example, if it still exists—was a far more provocative and, in the end, more productive strategy. And when one of her Black students told Mary that another teacher had discouraged her from thinking about attending Harvard, that really angered Mary. She writes, "And this I why I continued to teach . . . because someone has to make sure White kids realize that everyone isn't living happily ever after in a racism-free world and smart Black girls with accents know that they *can* go to Harvard if they set their minds to it."

Literacy and social justice are also linked in the work of Christina Puntel, whose poignant poem states, in part,

> when i say i teach now, i promise i will teach justice.
> Chile. El Salvador. Nicaragua.
> when i say i teach now, i promise i will teach truth.
> Sugar. Dominican Republic. Triangle Trade.

WHAT'S DIFFERENT?

As much as these teachers have in common with those from the first *Why We Teach,* there are also some stark differences. This is no surprise given the growing accountability and high-stakes testing mania in our public schools in the past decade. Luke Reynolds, a public school teacher and editor of a book of essays on imagining schooling differently, describes our national drift to a market-based orientation of schools by asking questions that get to the very heart of the purpose of education in a democratic society: "Is public education also built on the ideals of a market-industrial system, complete with economic justifications? Or are its intentions deeper, more complex, more fulfilling to both the self and to society?" (Reynolds, 2014, p. xii).

The teachers in *Why We Teach Now* make it clear that the intentions of public education should indeed differ from those of the marketplace. Education, they argue, should be about creating better futures for students individually and for our society as a whole. Teachers today are facing more prescriptive curricula and rigid standards than ever before, and rarely are they consulted on these. In their essays, all the teachers addressed this issue. Berta Berriz laments the "bureaucrats who render teachers' knowledge invisible in the policymaking process." Science teacher John Levasseur decries the "simplistic and quick-fix solutions" by those who know alarmingly little about teaching, schools, and education. These "reforms" and "solutions" not only have an impact on teachers' schedules but also, and more significantly, on teachers' psyches. Vanessa Burgos-Kelly describes the crisis of conscience she faced in her second year in the classroom. She writes, "I found myself intensifying the time spent on testing strategies and passing out more multiple-choice assessments for grades." By her fourth year in the classroom, the situation deteriorated even further:

> The vigor of data increased. The testing consumed more classroom time. The classroom environment was tense and the students were more aggressive. That was the year I truly questioned, "Why do I teach?" I am sure it is not for a passion to pass out #2 pencils and walk circles around students filling in bubbles.

While still being aware of dealing with the tests, Vanessa has redirected her efforts into creating more enriching and relevant experiences, and more often, for her students.

Berta Berriz, recently retired, wrote that most teachers do their best in good faith to conform to each new policy, "at least until compliance becomes complicity." Mary Ginley, also now retired, moved from a school district in Massachusetts where high-stakes testing was just beginning to take hold to one in Florida where it was in full swing and had, in fact, become the very purpose of teaching. She writes, "At a time when *everyone*—politicians, school officials, and maybe even mom and dad—are telling kids their worth can be summed up in a test score number we need to be there to tell them they are far more than that test score." For Mary and other teachers, the conditions in schools have led them to become subversive. And why wouldn't they? For example, when she wasn't even allowed to read real literature with her students—one of their favorite activities—Mary took to asking forgiveness rather than permission, saying, "So we *did* read novels and discuss them."

Greg Michie, returning to public school teaching after over a decade as a university professor, embodies the courage of teachers who want more for their students than just better test scores. He writes movingly about both the joys and the frustrations of returning. When he returned to the classroom, he found that accountability reigned supreme, even in the very first faculty meeting of the year. Greg's reaction? He writes, "This isn't what I came back to do, I thought to myself. I couldn't remember the word 'data' even being mentioned during my previous tenure as a teacher. Now, it was the centerpiece of discussion, the tail that wagged the dog." On the other hand, he recounts the pure joy of hearing one of his students say, "I love this book! It's *heartwarming*!," this from what some might think of as a jaded middle schooler not interested in reading.

Teachers today also have less power and less autonomy than a decade ago. A striking example of teachers' lack of power is related by Criselda Guerra, who was removed from the junior high school science position she had for many years and reassigned as a high school art teacher. From the stories she tells of her lessons, her motivations, her relationships with students and with the discipline of science itself, it is clear she was a gifted science teacher. Yet there was absolutely no explanation for this change. Criselda never got her junior high science teaching position back, but slowly she began asking for science classes to be added to her schedule at the high school. She started with geology, adding anatomy and physiology the following year. This year, she informs me, she is teaching those classes plus leather tooling and UIL Current Events. The resilience of teachers such as Criselda is nothing short of remarkable.

When I asked Michael Silverstone, who had been my granddaughter's teacher, to write an essay for this book, he readily agreed. With a calm demeanor that pervaded his classroom, Michael had been a favorite among 2nd-graders, often playing his guitar and leading them in song, and many times reading favorite stories to them. Within a few weeks of writing the essay, he decided quite suddenly to leave teaching, his chosen profession and passion. I was feeling a bit guilty about this because I thought that, in a way, writing the essay had spurred him to make this decision. Michael had become so disenchanted with what was happening in public education that he thought he might never be able to return even though he was resolutely certain that in the long run, "the drive to standardization will never prevail." Fortunately, he was able to rekindle his enthusiasm for authentic teaching by moving to a Montessori school. His passion for teaching is stronger than ever, but the question for us remains: What about all the other Michael Silverstones? Will their departure have to be the price we pay for rigid accountability and joyless schools?

How long will we be living with the destructive consequences of the No Child Left Behind era? In his blog, John Merrow, education reporter for PBS's *Newshour*, made a number of predictions about the beginning of the 2014 academic year (Merrow, 2014). His predictions included the following: that more school systems would begin weaning themselves from an overreliance on students' test scores to evaluate teachers because the results of such overzealous "test-based accountability" are often cheating, low morale, higher absenteeism/truancy, and other negative results (this retreat has already begun); that the tide may be turning in "the war against teachers," a war that had unfortunately taken too many good teachers from the profession; that the attack on teacher unions would remain strong, even though research suggests that there is a high correlation between educational outcomes and strong unions, and vice versa; and a continuing turmoil in the teaching force. Merrow ends his blog with the "big question": Can teaching become a well-respected profession? And how?

Although sometimes elusive, we also see signs of a changing tide in the teachers' essays. Greg Michie describes how teacher unions are adopting more social justice approaches to their work, and grassroots groups are challenging the corporate agenda with more vigor than ever. But much more needs to be done to keep him and other talented teachers in the classroom.

RENEWING THE COMMITMENT TO SOCIAL JUSTICE IN EDUCATION

Among the most powerful outcomes of the teachers' essays have been the reflections and questions they have left us with, questions that should be food for thought for all teachers, all teacher educators, and anyone who's concerned about the future of public education. These questions are critical, thoughtful, and necessary for all of us to consider. Berta Berriz, for example, asks, "Confronted by this sobering reality, where does a committed teacher find that last ounce of energy, the courage to take on one more—just one more—hopeful project for her students?" Concerned that we've lost sight of the true purpose of public education, John Levasseur asks rhetorically, "Isn't the origin and definition of social justice giving the tools of success to every student?" And after lamenting all the directives thrown at teachers, Jennifer Burgos-Carnes asks: "Confusing, right?" Yes, confusing indeed.

Even more devastating for teachers is the sense of despair articulated by some of them. Sharim Hannegan-Martinez asks questions that are no doubt on the minds of many teachers in today's educational context: "What's the point?" she asks. "Why teach now . . . in *these* schools, in these historically oppressive, rotten-to-the-core and unchanging, unrelenting institutions?" Chuck Greanoff, who views public education as "a bedrock principle of our democracy," asks, "Yet, if we give up the ship . . . if we don't fight with all we have, what message are we sending students?"

These questions have led me to the inescapable conclusion that we need more teachers committed to social justice than ever before, both in and out of the classroom. Chuck Greanoff combines his classroom teaching with outreach to the larger community, stating, "At the end of the day, political engagement not only strengthens my sense of agency in the classroom but also helps me sleep at night." Powerfully articulating the connection between public education and democracy, Chuck wrote: "I have always believed that teachers serve democracy in the broadest sense: We seek to cultivate informed citizenship and respect for diversity, as we also promote social justice."

The commitment to working both inside and outside the schools is evident also in Jesse Hagopian's essay. Jesse, one of the leaders of the Garfield High School push to boycott the MAP test and an associate editor of *Rethinking Schools*, writes,

> I teach because I want to empower my students with pedagogy that doesn't reduce them to a test score, respects their intellect, and is designed facilitate dialogue about how to solve the problems they face in their communities, in their country, and in their world.

There is no blueprint for social justice teaching, no one "best practice." In fact, in their essays, the teachers describe many different approaches, curricula, and lessons that promote social justice, from Restorative Justice Circles to organizing students to demand an equitable education, to starting a book company to bring Latino/a children the Spanish language literature missing in their schools. In other words, social justice education can happen in every context, every subject matter, every grade level. Some teachers, such as Heather Brooke Robertson and Jorge López, started out as political activists in their youth, whereas others came to it later because of the conditions in which they found themselves. Jorge López is very clear about what his role is, stating, "Teaching is a political act." He is explicit about what he means, explaining:

> I teach because I want young people to experience freedom from oppression, and to help build a community of young people who continue to dream and believe that they can achieve and change the world.

For Heather Brooke Robertson, social justice means finding resources for her bilingual students, supporting their parents and other community members, and celebrating the possibility of the first Latina president, hoping it will be one of her former students.

Mary Cowhey, now a Title I math teacher and coach, convincingly argues in her essay that helping students succeed academically is an indispensable social justice goal. After seeing a 4th grade student she had taught in 2nd grade struggling with math, Mary's social justice promise became doing all she can to help students succeed academically. And Maria Rosario sees social justice in her very decision to teach, saying, "I teach because I am a humanist and the classroom is the frontline."

The teachers in this book retain their hope and love in spite of it all. Pamelyn Williams's faith is renewed when, for example, she is treated like an intellectual when presenting her research at professional conferences. Sharim Hannegan-Martinez, in her powerful essay, describes a student "with more scars than birthdays," and comes to the conclusion that, "the young people I am blessed to stand in front of every day make me feel more human and more loved than I ever thought possible." But the context makes this kind of hope difficult. Even Mary Ginley, a more hopeful person than I've ever met—and although at the end of her essay coming to the conclusion that she would do it all again—writes, "there are days when I just can't see why creative, competent, imaginative, smart young people would choose a profession where they aren't allowed to make any decisions and have to follow scripted curriculums." If these are the reflections of a hopeful person, what about teachers who don't have such reserves of enthusiasm and energy? How are they to cope with the constant demands, the lack of power, the dictates thrown at them from every direction? These are unanswerable questions, yet they must be confronted if we are to retain teachers such as the ones whose essays have graced this book.

FINAL THOUGHTS: WHY TEACH *NOW?*

Judging by the essays in this book, many teachers today feel a sense of invisibility and powerlessness. Abandoned by the profession to which they have committed their time, energy, and passion, too often their ideas are dismissed, their professionalism doubted. At the same time, teachers are natural leaders with a great deal of power, even often unbeknownst to themselves. They not only manage all the goings-on of complex classrooms, but they also communicate with a multitude of those outside their classrooms, including colleagues and supervisors as well as families and community members. They influence the future, in some ways more profoundly than the most powerful corporate leaders or policymakers. Importantly, they continue their own process of learning in myriad ways, whether through graduate education, inquiry groups, by serving as professional developers in their own schools and beyond, or simply by conversations with colleagues (Bond, 2014). Teachers also take their concerns outside the classroom, whether through picket lines at the Wisconsin Statehouse, as Heather Brooke Robertson did, or through quieter although no less powerful means such as writing editorials for the local newspaper as Chuck Greanoff has done. In all these ways, teachers use their roles as instructors, consciousness-raisers, and moral guides not just to help raise the next generation, but also to help us ponder that age-old curriculum question, "What knowledge is of most worth?" And, I might add, "Why?" "Who says?" and, "How will this knowledge help students become better people?"

In this book, teachers present us with a portrait of public education as it is today, an unsustainable reality based on a corporate agenda, one that sees education as functionalism rather than as true learning, based on competition rather than collaboration, on rigid accountability rather than on authentic growth. Yet too many in the public, including many educators, have gone along with this damaging view of education. In a searing attack on the corporate takeover of our public schools and the accompanying silence of those who should be fighting back, John Kuhn, a courageous school superintendent, writes, "Speaking out (about anything, really) has little upside for educators and lots of potential downsides" (Kuhn, 2014, p. 2). The result, according to Kuhn is that "American educators have watched passively as a hit parade of ill-conceived education policies captured the attention of our nation's decisionmakers and were enshrined in our federal and state law books. We and our students were as meek as lambs led to a standardized slaughter" (Kuhn, p. 2).

Nevertheless, many teachers, including those in this book, are proposing alternatives to this portrait of public schools by sharing their hopes and dreams of what education might become, especially for our most vulnerable youths. These hopes include Greg Michie's stubborn insistence that terms such as "democratic education" and "social justice" are more significant than the latest fad words such as "text complexity," "accountable talk," and "close reading." Because of the emphasis on high-stakes tests and so-called "basic skills,' this concern was echoed in a conference report on the dearth of youth civic development in schools today (Malin, Ballard, Attai, Colby, & Damon, 2014), a situation that leads to questions that must be confronted, questions such as: What are we teaching our young people about their role in a democratic society? What do they learn from the humanities? Are they being prepared to have intelligent and nuanced conversations about significant issues that will affect them, their families, their communities, our nation, and the future? What are they learning about their responsibility to others? These concerns seem to be missing from most current conversations about public education.

In her book on what 4th-graders think about schooling in the United States, Inda Schaenen quotes children who recognize all the current faults, and the benefits, of education. Among other issues, the kids talk about the many tests they must take, the need for teachers to "cover the material," and the stress they and their teachers experience as a result. Through it all, Schaenen writes, "Still, people want to grow up and be teachers. They want to be good teachers, if not great teachers, like the very best teachers they remember from their own younger days" (Schaenen, 2014, p. 40). And these are precisely the teachers we need for our classrooms.

We return, then, to why teach *now*. Despite deep skepticism about the current "reform" era, teachers know that what they do every day matters. Mary Jade Haney put it beautifully when she wrote, "I teach because I am in a profession that balances the universe." From the youngest preschool toddlers to high school seniors walking across the stage on graduation day, every student has been touched by teachers, some in incredibly positive ways and others in very debilitating ways. If we continue to make teaching such an extraordinarily taxing profession, we risk losing the best among them. This has especially critical implications for students who've been marginalized by our society and public schools. Addressing our responsibility to these and all students, Greg Michie writes,

> All kids—especially kids our public schools have too often failed—deserve an education that honors and validates who they are, that makes room for their questions and concerns, that challenges them to think deeply, that helps them find meaning in a sometimes hostile and confusing world.

Mary Ginley ended her essay with a call to recognize the work good teachers do. In the end, she concludes, her work as a public school teacher for 42 years was worth the sacrifice, the sleepless nights, the crushing bureaucracy, the ever-increasing demands because "somehow, even today, even with all the insanity, all the rules, all the poorly designed textbooks, all the directives not to bother teaching anything that is not tested, in spite of everything, there are kids out there who need good teachers."

Our society would be poorer indeed—even unrecognizable—without good public school teachers. It's not only because they work so hard for so little recognition and public support, but also because without them, our nation's promise of a free, public, and quality education would be meaningless.

References

Allende, I. (1989). Writing as an act of hope. In W. Zinsser (Ed.), *Paths of resistance: The art and craft of the political novel* (pp. 41–45). Boston, MA: Houghton Mifflin.

Anyon, J. (2005). *Radical possibilities: Public policy, urban education, and a new social movement* (2nd ed.). New York, NY: Routledge.

Anzaldúa, G. (1981). Speaking in tongues: A letter to Third World women writers. In C. C. Moraga & G. Anzaldúa (Eds.), *This bridge called my back: Writing from radical women of color* (pp. 163–174). New York, NY: Kitchen Table Women of Color Press.

Apple, M. W. (2006). *Educating the right way: Markets, standards, God, and inequality*. New York, NY: Routledge.

Aristotle. (1984). *The complete works of Aristotle: The revised Oxford translation*. (J. Barnes, Trans.). Princeton, NJ: Princeton University Press.

Berliner, D. C., & Glass, G. V. (2014). *50 myths and lies that threaten America's public schools: The real crisis in education*. New York, NY: Teachers College Press.

Bond, N. (Ed.). (2014). *The power of teacher leaders: Their roles, influence, and impact*. Indianapolis, IN: Kappa Delta Pi International Honor Society in Education; New York, NY: Routledge.

Camangian, P. (2011). Making people our policy: Grounding literacy in lives. *Journal of Adolescent & Adult Literacy, 54*, 458–460.

Camarota, S. A. (2012). *Immigrants in the United States: A profile of America's foreign-born population*. Washington, DC: Center for Immigration Studies.

Cambourne, B. (1995). Towards an educationally relevant theory of literacy learning: Twenty years of inquiry. *The Reading Teacher, 49*(3), 183–190.

Cambourne, B., & Turbill, J. (1987). *Coping with chaos*. Newtown, Australia: Primary English Teacher Association, distributed by Heinemann Education Books.

Caref, C., Hainds, S., Hilgendorf, K., Jankov, P., & Russell, K. (2012). *The black and white of education in Chicago's public schools*. Chicago, IL: Chicago Teachers Union.

Carpenter, Z. (2013, November 20). Inequality is (literally) killing America. *The Nation*. Retrieved from www.thenation.com/blog/177304/inequality-literally-killing-america

Chang, C. (2010, October 4). Recovery school district's Vallas aided post-quake reform in Haiti. Retrieved from http://www.nola.com/education/index.ssf/2010/10recovery_school_districts_vall.html

Children's Defense Fund. (2014). *The state of America's children.* Washington, DC: Author.

Cody, A. (2013). Common Core Standards: Ten colossal errors. *Teacher blogs: Living in dialogue.* Retrieved from blogs.edweek.org/teachers/living-in-dialogue/2013/11/common_core_standards_ten_colo.html

Cowhey, M. (2003). A way to live in the world. In S. Nieto (Ed.), *What keeps teachers going?* (pp. 101–105). New York, NY: Teachers College Press.

Cowhey, M. (2006). *Black ants and Buddhists: Thinking critically and teaching differently in the primary grades.* Portland, ME: Stenhouse.

Darder, A. (1991). *Culture and power in the classroom.* Westport, CT: Bergin & Garvey.

Dawkins, R. (1989). *The selfish gene.* Oxford, England: Oxford University Press.

de los Reyes, E., & Gozemba, P. (2002). *Pockets of hope: How students and teachers change the world.* Westport, CT: Bergin & Garvey.

Delpit, L. (1988). The silenced dialogue: Power and pedagogy in educating other people's children. *Harvard Educational Review, 58,* 483–502.

Delpit, L. (1995). *Other people's children: Cultural conflict in the classroom.* New York, NY: New Press.

DeNavas-Walt, C., Proctor, B. C., & Smith, J. C. (2011). *Income, poverty, and health insurance coverage in the United States: 2010.* U. S. Bureau Current Population Reports, P60-239. Washington, DC: U.S. Government Printing Office.

Dewey, J. (1987). The challenge of democracy to education. In J. A. Boydston (Ed.), *The later works of John Dewey, volume 11, 1925–1953: 1935–1937 Essays, reviews, Trotsky inquiry, miscellany and liberalism and social action* (pp. 235–372). Carbondale, IL: Southern Illinois University. (Original work published 1937)

Douglass, F. (1985). The significance of emancipation in the West Indies. Speech, Canandaigua, New York, August 3, 1857. Collected in pamphlet by author. In John W. Blassingame (Ed.), *The Frederick Douglass papers. Series One: Speeches, debates, and interviews. Volume 3: 1855–63.* New Haven, CT: Yale University Press. (Original work published 1857)

Duncan-Andrade, J., & Morrell, E. (2008). *The art of critical pedagogy: Possibilities for moving from theory to practice in urban schools.* New York, NY: Peter Lang.

Dunn, B. (2005). Confessions of an underperforming teacher. In S. Nieto (Ed.), *Why we teach* (pp. 178–182). New York, NY: Teachers College Press.

Freire, P. (1970). *Pedagogy of the oppressed.* New York: Seabury.

Freire, P. (1985). *The politics of education: Culture, power and liberation.* Westport, CT: Bergin & Garvey.

Freire, P., & Macedo, D. (1987). *Literacy: Reading the word and the world.* Westport, CT: Bergin and Garvey.

Gatto, J. T. (2000). *Underground history of American education: A school teacher's intimate investigation into the problem of modern schooling.* New York, NY: Odysseus Group.

Ginwright, S. (2010). *Black youth rising: Activism and radical healing in urban America.* New York, NY: Teachers College Press.

Hughes, L. (1996). *The Dream Keeper and other poems.* (B. Pinkney, Illustrator). New York, NY: Knopf.

Ingersoll, R. M. (2012, May 16). Beginning teacher induction: What the data tell us. *Phi Delta Kappan International*. Retrieved from www.edweek.org/ew/articles/2012/05/16/kappan_ingersoll.h31.html

Ingersoll, R. M., Merrill, L., & Stuckey, D. (2014). *Seven trends: The transformation of the teaching force*. CPRE Report (#RR-80). Philadelphia, PA: Consortium for Policy Research in Education, University of Pennsylvania.

Kena, G., Aud, S., Johnson, F., Wang, X., Zhang, J., Rathbun, A., et al. (2014). *The condition of education 2014* (NCES 2014-083). Washington, DC: U.S. Department of Education, National Center for Education Statistics. Retrieved from nces.ed.gov/pubsearch

Kosterski, J. W. (1990). *The ethics of Aristotle*. Chantilly, VA: Teaching Company.

Kozol, J. (1967). *Death at an early age*. Boston, MA: Houghton Mifflin.

Kozol, J. (1991). Savage inequalities. Children in America's schools. New York: Crown.

Krashen, S. (2012, March 18). *New York Times* Sunday Dialogue: How to rate teachers. Retrieved from www.nytimes.com/2012/03/18/opinion/sunday/sunday-dialogue-how-to-rate-teachers.html?emc=eta1&_r=0

Kuhn, J. (2014). *Fear and learning in America: Bad data, good teachers, and the attack on public education*. New York, NY: Teachers College Press.

Ladson-Billings, G. (2005). *Beyond the big house: African-American educators on teacher education*. New York, NY: Teachers College Press.

Lopez, M. L. (2014). *In 2014, Latinos will surpass Whites as largest racial/ethnic group*. Washington, DC: Pew Research Council. Retrieved from www.pewresearch.org/fact-tank/2014/01/24/in-2014-latinos-will-surpass-whites-as-largest-racialethnic-group-in-california/

Malin, H., Ballard, P. J., Attai, M. L., Colby, A., & Damon, W. (2014). *Youth civic development and education: A conference consensus report*. Stanford, CA, and Seattle, WA: Center on Adolescence, and Center for Multicultural Education.

McAdoo, M. (2013, January 31). Teacher attrition up after recession-driven lull. *New York Times*. Retrieved from www.uft.org/insight/teacher-attrition-after-recession-driven-lull

Merrow, J. (2014). Some predictions as the new school year arrives. . . . Retrieved from takingnote.learningmatters.tv/?p=7151

Miller, E., & Carrlson-Paige, N. (2014). A tough critique of Common Core on early childhood education. In V. Strauss (2013, January 29), The Answer Sheet: *Washingtonpost.com*. Retrieved from www.washingtonpost.com/blogs/answer-sheet/wp/2013/01/29/a-tough-critique-of-common-core-on-early-childhood-education/

Miner, B. (2013). *Lessons from the heartland: A turbulent half-century of public education in an iconic American city*. New York, NY: The New Press.

Nakkula, M. J., & Toshalis, E. (2006). *Understanding youth: Adolescent development for educators*. Cambridge, MA: Harvard Education Press.

National Commission on Excellence in Education. (1983). *A nation at risk: The imperative for education reform*. Washington, DC: U.S. Government Printing Office.

National Governors Association Center for Best Practices & Council of Chief State School Officers. (2010). *Common Core State Standards*. Washington, DC: Authors.

Network for Public Education. (2014, March 2). NPE calls for congressional hearings. Retrieved from www.networkforpubliceducation.org/2014/03/npe-calls-for-congressional-hearings-full-text/

The New Teacher Project (TNTP). (2012). *The irreplaceables: Understanding the real retention crisis in America's public schools*. Brooklyn, NY: Author. Retrieved from tntp.org/assets/documents/TNTP_Irreplaceables_2012.pdf

Nieto, S. (Ed.). (2005). *Why we teach*. New York, NY: Teachers College Press.

No Child Left Behind (NCLB) Act of 2001, 20 U.S.C.A. § 6301 et seq. (West 2003).

Oakes, J., & Rogers, J. (2006) *Learning power: Organizing for education and justice*. New York, NY: Teachers College Press.

Palmer, P. J. (1998). *The courage to teach: Exploring the inner landscape of a teacher's life*. San Francisco, CA: Jossey-Bass.

Reynolds, L. (2014). *Imagine it better: Visions of what school might be*. Portsmouth, NH: Heinemann.

Riggs, L. (2013, October 18). Why do teachers quit? And why do they stay? *The Atlantic*. Retrieved from www.theatlantic.com/education/archive/2013/10/why-do-teachers-quit/280699/

Roesel, D., & Rampersad, A. (Eds.). (2013). *Poetry for young people: Langston Hughes*. (B. Andrews, Illustrator). New York, NY: Sterling Children's Books.

Rothwell, J. (2012). *Housing costs, zoning, and access to high-scoring schools*. Washington, DC: Metropolitan Policy Program at Brookings.

Roy, A. (2003). *War talk*. Cambridge, MA: South End Press.

Ryan, W. (1971). *Blaming the victim*. New York, NY: Pantheon Books.

S. 844–112th Congress: Race to the Top Act of 2011. (2011). Retrieved from www.govtrack.us/congress/bills/112/s844

Schaenen, I. (2014). *Speaking of fourth grade: What listening to kids really tells us about school in America*. New York, NY: The New Press.

Shaw, G. B. (2001). *Man and superman*. New York, NY: Penguin. (Original work published 1903)

Shirley, D. (2009). *Mindful teacher*. New York, NY: Teachers College Press.

Stanford Center on Poverty and Inequality. (2014). *State of the union: The poverty and inequality report, 2014*. Stanford, CA: Stanford University.

Strauss, V. (2014, March 23). The Answer Sheet: Kindergarten teacher: My job is now about tests and data, not children—I quit. *Washingtonpost.com*. Retrieved from www.washingtonpost.com/blogs/answer-sheet/wp/2014/03/23/kindergarten-teacher-my-job-is-now-about-tests-and-data-not-children-i-quit/

Taylor, P., & Cohn, D. (2012). *A milestone en route to a majority/minority nation*. Washington, DC: Pew Research Center. Retrieved from www.pewsocialtrends.org/2012/11/07/a-milestone-en-route-to-a-majority-minority-nation/?src=rss_main

Thoreau, H. D., & Bode, C. (1980). *The selected journals of Henry David Thoreau*. New York, NY: New American Library.

University of Florida. (2014, March 12). Stressful experiences have big, immediate effects on children's health. *University of Florida News*. Retrieved from news.ufl.edu/2014/03/12/kid-stress/

U.S. Census Bureau. (2010). *Back to school: 2010–2011*. Report No. CB10-FF.14. Washington, DC: U.S. Government Printing Office.

U.S. Census Bureau. (2014, March 27). State and county quickfacts. [Data derived from population estimates, American Community Survey, census of population, and housing, state and county housing unit estimates, county business patterns, nonemployer statistics, economic census, Survey of Business Owners, building permits.] Retrieved from quickfacts.census.gov/qfd/states/00000.html

U.S. Department of Education Office of Civil Rights. (2014). *Issue brief #1: Data snapshot: School discipline.* Washington, DC: Author.

Vygotsky, L. (1978). *Mind in society: The development of higher psychological processes.* Cambridge, MA: Harvard University Press. (Original work published 1935)

Weidt, M. (1997). *Revolutionary poet: A story about Phillis Wheatley.* Minneapolis, MN: Carolrhoda Books Lerner Publishing Group.

Wheelock, A. (1990). *Locked in/locked out: Tracking and placement practices in Boston Public Schools: A report.* Boston, MA: Massachusetts Advocacy Center.

Yosso, T. J. (2005). Whose culture has capital? A critical race theory discussion of community cultural wealth. *Race, Ethnicity, and Education, 8*(1), 69–91.

About the Contributors

Sonia Nieto is professor emerita of language, literacy, and culture at the University of Massachusetts, Amherst. A teacher at elementary and middle school levels for several years, and a teacher educator for over 30, she has written extensively on diversity and teacher education. Her books include *Affirming Diversity, The Light in Their Eyes,* and *What Keeps Teachers Going?,* and *Finding Joy in Teaching Students of Diverse Backgrounds,* as well as edited books *Puerto Rican Students in U.S. Schools, Why We Teach,* and *Dear Paulo: Letters from Those Who Dare Teach.* She has received many awards for her scholarly work, advocacy, teaching, and activism, including four honorary doctorates.

Berta Rosa Berriz, *Ed.D.,* was born in La Habana, Cuba, and entered 3rd grade in Philadelphia, where "becoming an American" meant surrendering ties to family culture. Professionally, this biography has driven Berriz to achieve in fields related to educational equity: as a bilingual teacher with National Board Certification (2006), national faculty at Lesley University, and a published writer, dancer, and storyteller. She earned her doctorate from Harvard Graduate School of Education (2005) for her study of the cultural identity of second-generation Puerto Rican and Dominican students, and teachers' assessments of students' academic performance. Berriz was named a Massachusetts Teacher Scholar (1992), researching the folktales of the Spanish- and English-speaking Caribbean. In partnership with Beth Handman, Berriz was awarded a Lucretia Crocker Fellowship— TEAMSTREAM (1990)—for integrating bilingual students with special needs with advanced-work students using a pedagogy that employed team teaching, thematic education, cooperative learning, and integrated cultural arts. Berriz concluded her career in Boston Public Schools as a founding co-lead teacher at the Boston Teachers' Union School (2008–2013), an innovative, teacher-run, K–8 pilot public school in Jamaica Plain, Massachusetts.

Jennifer Burgos-Carnes has always had a passion for working with children. Ever since she was a child she knew that she would one day have the privilege of working with young children in a classroom of her very own. She has a bachelor's degree in elementary education and a master's degree in divergent learning. She was awarded the Early Career Educator of Color Leadership Award in 2011 from the National Council of Teachers of English. She will begin her fifth year of teaching at an elementary school in South Carolina in the fall.

Vanessa Burgos-Kelly has enjoyed empowering 4th- and 5th-grade students since 2008. She has a bachelor of arts degree with a major in elementary education and recently obtained a masters of education degree in educational administration from the University of South Carolina. She has presented at the Latino Children's Literature Conference and National Reading Teacher Conference. Aside from teaching, she loves gardening, listening to live music, and being entertained by her husband and son.

Mary Cowhey currently teaches Title 1 math and is a math coach at Jackson Street School in Northampton, Massachusetts, where she also has taught 1st and 2nd grade since 1997. She is the author of *Black Ants and Buddhists: Thinking Critically and Teaching Differently in the Primary Grades*, winner of the 2008 National Association for Multicultural Education Phillip C. Chinn Multicultural Book Award and the 2007 *Skipping Stones* magazine Multicultural Book Award. She was a community organizer for 14 years before becoming a teacher. She has received numerous awards for her teaching and activism, including the Milken National Educator Award, the Anti-Defamation League World of Difference Award, a National League of Women Voters Award, a University of Massachusetts Distinguished Alumni Award, the Massachusetts Agricultural Science Excellence Award, and the Massachusetts Public Health Association Frontline Award. Her essays and articles have been published in numerous books, journals, and magazines about teaching. She is a co-founder of Familias con Poder/Families with Power, a grassroots organizing effort among low-income families of color that uses a popular education approach to cultivate grassroots leadership among parents/guardians and youth and to help children succeed.

Eileen Blanco Dougherty is currently a special education kindergarten teacher in the New York City public school system. Her current position allows her to work with both children who do and do not have identified special needs, as well as with their families, within the classroom setting. She has previously worked as a special education itinerant teacher throughout New York City, as well as an early childhood educator in a therapeutic day school for children with neurodevelopmental delays, including autism spectrum disorders. Her practice focuses on the development of authentic inclusion of all children in early childhood education, as well as multiculturalism and collaboration with families. She received her master's degree in early childhood special education from Teachers College, Columbia University.

Mary Ginley grew up the oldest of seven children. She graduated from St. Joseph's High School in Pittsfield, Massachusetts, in 1965; from the College of Our Lady of the Elms in Chicopee, Massachusetts, with a BA in English in 1970; and in 1989 from Westfield State College, where she received her M.Ed. Mary taught in parochial schools for 5 years and, later, in elementary schools in the inner-city and suburbs in both Massachusetts and southwest Florida. Mary was named Massachusetts Teacher of the Year in 1998 and became a National Board Certified Teacher in 1999. As an adjunct professor at the University of Massachusetts, Springfield College, and Bay Path College in Longmeadow, she conducted workshops throughout Massachusetts on the teaching of reading, writing, and math, as well as on building classroom community and multicultural education. In June of 2011, Mary retired after 42 years of teaching. In October of 2013, she was diagnosed with Stage 3 esophageal cancer (she didn't know what it was or how to spell it at the time) and after undergoing treatment at the MD Anderson Cancer Center in Houston, Texas, is cancer free. She lives in southwest Florida with her husband, Jerry, and has a daughter, a son, a stepson, and five incredibly beautiful, amazing grandchildren.

Chuck Greanoff teaches U.S. history and psychology at his alma mater and that of his parents—Lakewood (Ohio) High School (LHS). He holds a BA in history from Ohio Wesleyan, an MS from the University of Wisconsin–Lacrosse, and a PhD in psychology from Kent State University. He also holds an MS in education from Ursuline College, where he earned his teaching certificate. Before joining LHS in 2006 he was a practicing psychologist. He is the adviser for the LHS Model United Nations Club and previously served as the president of the Lakewood Alumni Foundation and on multiple school climate/levy committees. Chuck is a regular contributor on educational issues to the *Lakewood Observer*, a local open-source newspaper where he has an ongoing series on the Common Core. He resides in his hometown, and is a strong supporter of all LHS co-curricular programs, including music and athletic programs.

Criselda J. Guerra was born in Delmita, Texas. She is the daughter of Benito Juarez, also from Delmita, and Laurentina Ramos from Salineno, Texas in Starr County. She attended San Isidro ISD and graduated Salutatorian in 1968 and she began her college experience at Texas A&I at Kingsville for two years. She completed her college education with a cum laude at The University of Texas Pan-American in Edinburg, Texas in 1974. Criselda married Dario Guerra in 1968 and they became the proud parents of five wonderful sons: Dario IV, Javier Benito, Rene Ricardo, Erik Lee, and Stephen Buck. She is also the grandmother of Derrick, Zachary, Lauren Rene, Dean Austin, Branden Rene and Mia Ann Guerra. Starting her teaching career in Alton, Texas, she then moved to San Isidro, Texas, where she continues to teach. She taught Jr. High Science for 32 Years. Shortly after retiring, she was re-hired and is presently teaching Art, Geology, and Anatomy and Physiology.

Jesse Hagopian teaches history and is a co-advisor of the Black Student Union at Garfield High School, the site of the historic boycott of the MAP test in 2013. Jesse is an associate editor of *Rethinking Schools* magazine, is a founding member of Social Equality Educators (SEE), and is the editor of *More Than a Score: The New Uprising Against High-Stakes Testing.*

Mary Jade Haney is a National Board Certified Teacher (Middle Childhood Generalist). She also earned a masters of education in curriculum and instruction with a focus on arts integration. Mary Jade has been an educator for 18 years in the public school system. Her greatest joy is inspiring children to work hard and creatively develop a voice in order to challenge inequities in their educational spaces while always working toward excellence. She enjoys working with students, families, and community members at Horrell Hill Elementary School in Richland County School District One, where "We believe Success for All!" She likes to think of herself as an artist who teaches and she believes all children have the potential to succeed in life and make positive contributions to make our world a more productive place. Her favorite quote is from Dr. Maya Angelou; she encourages young people to study themselves with these words: "Young men and women, study yourself. See who you really want to be in this world and as soon as you see it, say it, put it out into the universe. YOU MUST say it and then go about the business of becoming it." Mary Jade says she will always be a teacher no matter where life takes her.

Sharim Hannegan-Martinez is a fourth-year English and Raza studies teacher at Castlemont High School in East Oakland. She was also a teacher apprentice in the East Oakland Step to College program, where she trained under master pedagogues Jeff Duncan-Andrade and Patrick Camangian for 2 years. Here, Sharim began researching effective teaching practices for combating trauma in the context of urban public schools and classrooms. She earned a bachelor's degree in Raza Studies from San Francisco State University and a teaching credential and master's degree in urban education and social justice from the University of San Francisco. Her research, which was heavily influenced by her experiences as a Latina growing up on the San Diego/Tijuana border, focuses primarily on the role of loving relationships in helping young people cope with, navigate, and heal from traumatic stressors inside of a classroom.

Matthew Hicks is from Martinez, Georgia, and graduated from the University of Georgia with a BA in English and M.Ed. in English education. Matt and his wife, Abby, have a son, Greyson, and younger daughter, Sydney. He has served his community for 12 years as an English teacher, cross country coach, and soccer coach at Cedar Shoals High School in Athens, Georgia. Outside of the classroom he has focused much of his time on supporting the postsecondary plans of his immigrant students through teaching a voluntary enrichment course for undocumented students, participating in immigration and education panels around the state, and volunteering his time and efforts with local immigration advocacy organizations. He is the previous winner of the Kenneth S. Goodman "In Defense of Good Teaching" Award and the Clarke County School District's Foundation of Excellence's Joan Humphries Teacher of Excellence Award.

John Levasseur is a graduate of the Stockbridge School of Agriculture and the University of Massachusetts in Amherst. He currently teaches chemistry and English language learner science classes in Springfield, Massachusetts. He began his teaching career while traveling in Tanzania; he has also taught internationally in Shenzhen, China. Mr. Levasseur loves to "talk shop" with his colleagues, battle weeds in his lawn and garden, and find new restaurants with curious cuisine.

Jorge López is a National Board Certified social studies teacher and activist at Roosevelt High School in the community of Boyle Heights in Los Angeles. He has been teaching since 2002, after graduating from UCLA's Teacher Education Program. In 2009 he earned a second master's degree from UCLA's Principal Leadership Institute. He has taught courses in ethnic and cultural studies that address youth, empowerment, culture, critical media literacy, and social justice. Currently the advisor for a student activist Art Club and Taking Action youth organization, Jorge is a member of a progressive teacher and student collective, Politics and Pedagogy. He recently co-authored the book *Critical Media Pedagogy: Teaching for Achievement in City Schools* (Morrell, Dueñas, Garcia, and López, 2013)., which documents the teaching, educational philosophy, and social justice work of Jorge and other teachers. Jorge has presented and collaborated with educators in various national and international conferences and schools. He continues to take on leadership roles and has developed multiple partnerships with community organizations and spaces. Jorge has served as a member of his school's Restorative Justice Task Force and LAUSD's Progressive Discipline and Safety Committee, working to eliminate the school-to-prison pipeline and create caring school-learning environments. Jorge is pursuing a PhD in teaching, learning, and culture at Claremont Graduate University.

Gregory Michie is currently in Act III of his career as an educator. From 1990–1999 he taught 7th- and 8th-graders in Chicago's Back of the Yards neighborhood. He then spent a decade as an education professor and teacher educator, preparing new teachers for work in Chicago schools. In 2012 he came full circle, returning to classroom teaching in the same school and community where he taught in the 1990s. He has published numerous essays and articles about teaching in city schools, and is the author of three books, all published by Teachers College Press: *We Don't Need Another Hero: Struggle, Hope, and Possibility in the Age of High-Stakes Schooling* (2012), *Holler If You Hear Me: The Education of a Teacher and His Students*, 2nd edition (2009), and *See You When We Get There: Teaching for Change in Urban Schools* (2005).

As a Spanish teacher at Parkway Northwest High School for Peace and Social Justice, **Christina Puntel** and her students work together to develop a global perspective, an awareness of the reality of our interconnectedness. She began teaching learning support at Sheppard School in Philadelphia in 1998. Her practice as a teacher in the public schools has been strengthened through her involvement in Philadelphia Teachers' Learning Cooperative and the Philadelphia Writing Project. She values collaboration and mindfulness, teaching in ways that celebrate her students' strengths. She lives in Philadelphia with her husband and three children.

Heather Brooke Robertson has taught pre-K–8 English as a second language, English, bilingual science, history, technology, and Spanish in Milwaukee, Madison, and Lake Geneva, Wisconsin Public Schools, and in the Glendale

Unified School District, California. She was also a bilingual and literacy instructional resource teacher (coach) and a teacher leader in Madison's Professional Development Department. She earned her master's degree in educational leadership and policy from California State University, Northridge. Passionate about learning, she is a member of MIT and the University of Wisconsin–Madison's Playful Learning Board because gaming motivates and engages students in learning. She's also interested in and implements mindfulness practices that get her and her students' bodies and minds ready for learning. Heather has found that students engage when they are interested in the topic or can relate to characters, so through her book company, Books del Sur, she imports books written by Latin American authors that are humorous and authentic. She teaches in Wisconsin, but lives in the northern suburbs of Chicago with her husband, three kids, and a dog. They love traveling, scuba diving, playing in the lakes, and playing games in their yard or at the kitchen table.

María Rosario currently teaches at Dr. Jorge Prieto Academy in Chicago. She was a part of the opening of this neighborhood public school 5 years ago, something rare and to be celebrated considering the climate of education today. The families and staff are what make this school a community center; the school belongs to the students and the neighborhood. They strive to make connections and to offer opportunities in and outside of the classroom for the transmittance of the lives of the students from home to school to community. During these past 2 decades, María has had the great privilege of teaching students in grades ranging from 2nd to 8th. Having only ever been an inner-city public school teacher, she has worked with students primarily of Hispanic and African American descent. No matter the location of the building, the classroom is a second home for her and teaching has been the vehicle for a life filled with new discoveries and learning. Being a role model for her own child, her nieces and nephews, and so many other people's children has been the greatest responsibility and has yielded the greatest joy in her life.

Michael Silverstone is a veteran of the Amherst, Massachusetts, public schools, where he was a 2nd-grade teacher for 15 years. He is now a Montessori-trained teacher working with children ages 6 through 9 in the Boston area. He is the author of a number of nonfiction books for young people, including *Rigoberta Menchu: Defending Human Rights in Guatemala* (Feminist Press: City University of New York, 1998) and *Latino Legends: Hispanics in Major League Baseball* (Red Brick Learning, 2003). With Debbie Zacarian, he has co-written *Partnerships Work! Advancing Educational Equity, Access and Engagement with Students, Families and Communities* (Corwin Press, 2015).

Nina Tepper is a consultant teacher of reading and writing who has taught in a variety of educational settings in Massachusetts since 1974. After more than 30 years in predominately inner-city public schools, she retired in 2014. Throughout her career, Nina has been a classroom teacher in both mainstream and bilingual classrooms in all grades K–12. She mentored many new and aspiring teachers, worked as a schoolwide literacy coach, and provided teacher professional development within her school districts as a Western Massachusetts Writing Project consultant and adjunct professor. In both the schools and community, Nina is passionate about literacy and the power it has to transform people's lives. She combines her interest in writing and commitment to peace and justice as coordinator of the Veterans for Peace, Voices of Peace Poetry Contest. She lives on Cape Cod with her husband in their beautiful home overlooking the salt marshes of Nantucket Sound, where they enjoy gardening and share a commitment to work on issues of social justice, veterans' rights, the environment, and peace. Their three daughters and grandchildren inspire a commitment to work for the future.

The desire to become a teacher began when **Missy M. Urbaniak** was 9 years old. Her 4th-grade teacher read books aloud to the class often and challenged Missy to be creative. It was the first time she realized just how much she loved the classroom, and she has spent the majority of her time in classrooms ever since. After earning her teacher's certificate, Missy spent a year as a long-term substitute teacher serving in Iraq with the National Guard. Following that, she taught 5th and 6th grade for 4 years in her hometown before taking her dream job teaching in a one-room country school. Missy has now taught in country schools in western South Dakota for 6 years. She follows in the footsteps of two of her great-grandmothers who also taught in one-room schoolhouses. Missy appreciates the unique setting of her classroom and enjoys the challenge of teaching children in a rural, sometimes isolated, setting. She and her husband, Joe, enjoy raising their sons on a cattle ranch that has been in his family for five generations.

Shortly after graduating from a state school in Wisconsin, **Amanda VandeHei** secured her first teaching position in the Clark County School District in Las Vegas, Nevada. Never having visited Las Vegas, Amanda packed her red Saturn and her father's mini-van, and together with her stepmother the three of them completed the cross-country trek. In the 11 years since that

trip Amanda has taught 1st, 2nd, 4th, and 5th grades. Although the elementary classroom will always be considered home for Amanda, and a place she
knows she will someday return to, she is currently an assistant professor of
elementary literacy at Nevada State College.

Pamelyn A. Williams is a 1st-grade teacher at an elementary school in New
York, and has taught for 11 years in the Harlem and South Bronx communi-
ties. She serves many roles, including United Federation of Teachers Chapter
Leader, co-chair of the School Leadership Team, and CookShop Coordinator,
and she also serves on other school committees. She is a member of Kappa
Delta Pi and the New York State Reading Association. Pamelyn is a fellow with the Literacy Teachers Initiative, a 2012 collaboration between the
Institute for Urban and Minority Education (IUME) at Teacher's College,
Columbia University, and Community School District 5 Manhattan/New
York City Department of Education. As a fellow, she has researched ways
to inspire literacy through poetry, adapt packaged curriculum with multicultural literature, and improve literacy through reciprocal teaching with
her students. Pamelyn has presented her research at Teachers College at
Columbia University and the 2013 New York State Reading Association
conference. She values education and believes that children need access to
quality, rigorous academic programs that foster social development and
character education. Pamelyn provides students with a nurturing and stimulating environment in which they can take risks and develop the necessary
skills to be successful in the world.

Index